Innovation Ecosystems and the Role of Communication

This book analyzes the role of communication in creating the value of innovation ecosystems from the perspective of the international network of technology parks and areas of innovation. It explores the relations and interactions between different stakeholders (administration, universities, business, innovation agencies), highlighting the important role of communication within successful innovation ecosystems.

The role of communication is explained using different levels of communication approach. The authors present communication as a complex process, involving all the ecosystem stakeholders who are as well motivated and involved in different roles, norms, business models, environments, organizations, cultures, etc. The book proposes novel and interdisciplinary research (management, social communication and journalism, political science and administration) focused on the potential of communication in order to design the paradigm and indicate practical implications. The authors take into consideration modern IT tools, which provide the ground for redefining the connections between stakeholders, as well as sustainable development and ESG values, which change the perspective and priorities of the ecosystem.

Innovation Ecosystems and the Role of Communication is written for scholars and researchers in the fields of innovation studies, management science, and communication studies.

Dominika Narożna is a university professor employed at the Department of Journalism of the Faculty of Political Science and Journalism at Adam Mickiewicz University in Poznan. She is a member of the Board of the Adam Mickiewicz University Foundation in Poznan and serves as the manager for public relations at the Poznan Science and Technology Park, which is part of the Foundation. She has created and is the head of the "Audiovisual Production" program (second degree studies) at UAM. From 2004 to 2010, she collaborated with TVP S.A. and then served as the spokesperson for UAM until 2017. She also headed the Press Office of the university. She is the author of numerous publications on journalism and media relations. She is a trainer and advisor in the fields of image creation and information policy. She is passionate about music (composing her own pieces and singing).

Justyna Adamska is Deputy Director at Poznan Science and Technology Park, where she has been working since 2004. With a background in management, consultancy, and specialized knowledge in innovation, communication, sustainable development (ESG), EU projects, and business support center development, she plays a key role in driving strategic initiatives within the organization. Drawing on her doctoral degree in economics from the Poznan University of Economics and Business and over 20 years of experience, she has cultivated strong connections between entrepreneurs and academia, fostering collaboration and innovation. As a Certified Innovation Coach, she guides individuals and organizations toward innovative solutions, leveraging her deep understanding of marketing tools, business strategies, and cutting-edge methodologies. Furthermore, her contributions to scholarly publications on innovation and business support centers reflect her commitment to advancing knowledge and driving business growth.

Routledge Studies in Innovation, Organizations and Technology

RIOT!

Business Models and Digital Technology Platforms
Implementation and Complexities for Digital Business
Krzysztof Bartczak

Artificial Intelligence, Co-Creation and Creativity
The New Frontier for Innovation
Edited by Francisco Tigre Moura

Knowledge Management, Leadership and Innovation in Digital Transformation
Navigating the Future of Organizations
Asha Thomas

Collaborating for Museum Innovation
Technological, Cultural, and Organisational Innovation in Spanish Museums
Chuan Li

The Economics and Regulation of Digitalisation
The Case of Türkiye
Edited by Muzaffer Eroğlu, Matthias Finger and Emin Köksal

Blockchain, Metaverse, and Digital Payments
A Global Digital Consumer Perspective
Edited by Aijaz A. Shaikh, Galimkair Mutanov and Heikki Karjaluoto

Innovation Ecosystems and the Role of Communication
Insights from European Science, Technology Parks and Areas of Innovation
Dominika Narożna and Justyna Adamska

For more information about this series, please visit: www.routledge.com/Routledge-Studies-in-Innovation-Organizations-and-Technology/book-series/RIOT

Innovation Ecosystems and the Role of Communication

Insights from European Science, Technology Parks and Areas of Innovation

Dominika Narożna and Justyna Adamska

Routledge
Taylor & Francis Group
LONDON AND NEW YORK

First published 2025
by Routledge
4 Park Square, Milton Park, Abingdon, Oxon OX14 4RN

and by Routledge
605 Third Avenue, New York, NY 10158

Routledge is an imprint of the Taylor & Francis Group, an informa business

British Library Cataloguing-in-Publication Data
A catalogue record for this book is available from the British Library

ISBN: 978-1-032-69778-9 (hbk)
ISBN: 978-1-032-69779-6 (pbk)
ISBN: 978-1-032-69780-2 (ebk)

DOI: 10.4324/9781032697802

Typeset in Sabon
by Apex CoVantage, LLC

To our beloved and forbearing families.
Especially Daria and Staś.

Contents

Figures

Tables

Acknowledgments

As we reflect on the journey of crafting this comprehensive analysis of communication within innovation ecosystems, we recognize that such an endeavor does not come to fruition in isolation. The insights and contributions gathered in this book are the result of the collective knowledge, expertise, and support of numerous individuals and organizations whose invaluable assistance and encouragement have been fundamental. We extend our deepest appreciation to these contributors, whose expertise and insights have been instrumental in shaping the analytical narratives and empirical assessments presented herein. Their involvement has ensured that the exploration of communication within innovation ecosystems is both thorough and reflective of diverse perspectives, thus enriching the scholarly discourse on this critical subject matter.

We would like to express our deepest gratitude to Ebba Lund, Chief Executive Officer of the International Association of Science Parks and Areas of Innovation (IASP). Her invaluable support played a pivotal role in the successful mobilization of the IASP members for our survey questionnaire. The commitment to driving growth, internationalization, and effectiveness within the global network of science parks and areas of innovation has significantly contributed to the enrichment of our research. The data collection, carried out through an online survey system sent to recipients via email, was instrumental in providing us with critical insights that have shaped the findings of our study. This process not only facilitated a broader engagement among stakeholders across different geographies but also enhanced the robustness of our analysis by integrating diverse perspectives from science, business, and public administration. We are profoundly thankful for the opportunity to collaborate with an organization that is at the forefront of fostering innovation ecosystems globally. Our work has greatly benefited from the shared knowledge and experiences of the IASP community, under the leadership of Ebba Lund. Special thanks are owed to several key individuals whose expert insights have significantly enriched our understanding and discussion of innovation ecosystems in this book. We extend our heartfelt thanks to our colleagues, with whom we have had the privilege of collaborating over many years. We are deeply appreciative of their enduring partnership and the substantial impact their expertise has had on this project. We are particularly grateful to Agnieszka Pałys, Director of the

Legal and Organizational Division at Wroclaw Technology Park. Her expertise and perspectives during our interviews shed crucial light on the operational dynamics and strategic communications within technology parks. Similarly, our discussions with Monika Machowska, Deputy Director of the Technology Park Division at Kraków Technology Park, provided invaluable insights into the crucial roles of collaboration, communication, and knowledge transfer in fostering successful innovation ecosystems. We also extend our gratitude to David Pitschmann, responsible for Projects and International Cooperation at Lakeside Science and Technology Park. His contributions during our expert interviews highlighted the significance of international partnerships and cooperative strategies in the global innovation landscape. These interviews, focusing on the importance of collaboration, communication, and knowledge transfer, have been instrumental in illustrating key components that drive success in innovation environments. We are especially grateful to the Communication Team of the Poznan Science and Technology Park for their assistance. We truly appreciate their dedication and skill in bringing the nuances of our research to the forefront through precise and thoughtful editing.

Very special thanks are also due to Professor Marian Gorynia, a distinguished Polish economist and former Rector of the Poznan University of Economics and Business from 2008 to 2016. Professor Gorynia's contributions were indispensable in the initial stages of our project, particularly in helping to build and refine our proposal. His deep knowledge of economic theory and his extensive experience in the academic community provided critical insights that greatly enhanced the scope and depth of our research framework. We are immensely grateful for his guidance and expertise, which helped shape the direction and execution of our work on innovation ecosystems.

Last but not least, we extend our deepest gratitude to our esteemed leader, Professor Hieronim Maciejewski – a distinguished chemist and professor at Adam Mickiewicz University and the Director of the Poznan Science and Technology Park. He has been honored for his contributions to invention and the protection of industrial property, as well as for fostering innovation in Poland. We are particularly thankful for his unwavering support and for providing us with the opportunities to develop and thrive in our fields. His visionary leadership and commitment to advancing scientific and technological progress have been a great inspiration and a significant factor in the success of our endeavors.

Finally, we would like to express our sincerest gratitude to our families, particularly our parents, Piotr and Adam, and our children, Daria and Stas. Their unwavering support and patience through the extensive hours and the demands of this project have been nothing short of extraordinary. Their understanding and encouragement have provided us with the strength and peace of mind necessary to pursue and complete this work.

Introduction

Innovation ecosystems lead the way in technological advancement and socioeconomic development in the 21st century. These dynamic networks comprised of stakeholders ranging from business environment institutions, universities, and startups to corporations and government entities collaborate to promote innovation, support new ventures, and facilitate the commercialization of new technologies. However, the functioning and success of such ecosystems are closely tied to effective communication strategies, stakeholder engagement, and resilience to unpredictable challenges, such as economic fluctuations and global pandemics.

The significance of studying innovation ecosystems lies in their potential to address some of the most pressing global challenges, including climate change, sustainable development, and the digital transformation of economies. However, despite their importance, the dynamics of how these ecosystems adapt, evolve, and respond to external shocks remain insufficiently explored. This knowledge gap has underscored the need to understand the mechanisms that enable innovation ecosystems to maintain their productivity and innovative capacity in the face of turbulence and change.

Studying innovation ecosystems is not solely the task of academics but a practical necessity for decision-makers, innovation hubs, entrepreneurs, and society as a whole. As the world becomes increasingly interconnected and reliant on technological solutions, the ability of innovation ecosystems to sustain their activities and contribute to economic growth and social prosperity becomes crucial. Moreover, the COVID-19 pandemic has highlighted the importance of the resilience of these ecosystems, emphasizing the need for adaptable, flexible, and robust frameworks that can withstand global crises.

The main goal of this book is to understand the multifaceted role of communication in innovation ecosystems. The study aims to uncover the communication mechanisms that underpin the success and functionality of these ecosystems. By analyzing current communication trends, the study seeks to assess how these trends facilitate or hinder ecosystem development. Additionally, the study addresses various communication challenges faced by entities operating within these ecosystems, encompassing interpersonal and

DOI: 10.4324/9781032697802-1

interorganizational levels, and aims to identify barriers to effective communication. Furthermore, the existence and effectiveness of defined communication strategies or plans in these ecosystems have been evaluated, focusing on specific goals that such strategies aim to achieve, such as fostering collaboration, securing funding, or promoting actions and achievements.

The authors aim to present information regarding the optimization of communication processes within innovation ecosystems, thereby increasing their overall productivity and innovative capabilities. These studies seek to unravel the complexity of innovation ecosystems, focusing on the roles of various stakeholders, the criticality of effective communication, and the building of resilience. By analyzing these elements, the book aims to contribute to a deeper understanding of how innovation ecosystems can be nurtured and sustained, offering insights into fostering innovation-friendly environments and growth. In this way, the research fills a gap in current academic and practical knowledge, providing the basis for developing strategies that enhance the ability of innovation ecosystems to cope with the challenges of the contemporary world. The significance of this research lies in its potential to inform the development of more resilient, dynamic, and integrative innovation ecosystems capable of driving future technological breakthroughs and addressing complex societal issues. Furthermore, this publication takes into account the impact of trends such as the development of artificial intelligence and sustainable development on the dynamics of innovation ecosystems.

The main thesis put forward by the authors asserts that effective communication is one of the key factors for the successful functioning of innovation ecosystems. It underscores the importance of communication pathways in supporting collaboration, knowledge exchange, and ultimately the development of innovation ecosystems across different industries and regions. This assertion formed the basis of the research endeavor examining dynamics within innovation ecosystems, particularly focusing on the role of communication processes among various stakeholders. Building upon this thesis, the authors formulated hypotheses closely related to the research topic. The first partial hypothesis posits that in innovation ecosystems, the quality and frequency of communication activities have a direct impact on stakeholder engagement and collaboration. It suggests that more effective and frequent communication within the ecosystem will lead to a higher level of engagement and collaboration among stakeholders. The second conjecture is based on the statement that the transparency and availability of communication channels in innovation ecosystems significantly influence the speed of innovation diffusion. This means that more transparent and accessible communication methods facilitate faster dissemination and adoption of innovations throughout the ecosystem. The last, third partial hypothesis suggests that the diversity of communication methods (digital platforms, face-to-face interactions, formal and informal channels) in innovation ecosystems enhances the resilience and adaptability of these systems. It suggests that ecosystems utilizing a wider range of communication methods are better prepared to survive disruptions and adapt to changes in the external environment. These partial hypotheses develop the main thesis, focusing on specific aspects of communication in innovation ecosystems, such as engagement, innovation diffusion, and system resilience. They suggest that effective communication not only is crucial for the successful functioning of these ecosystems but also plays a key role in fostering stakeholder collaboration, accelerating innovation processes, and building resilient innovation environments.

To confirm the thesis, the authors designed a survey questionnaire directed toward representatives of organizations affiliated with the International Association of Science Parks and Areas of Innovation (IASP) located in European countries. This geographical scope encompasses a diverse range of innovation ecosystems across Europe, including science parks, technology parks, industrial parks, innovation districts, small and medium-sized enterprises (SMEs), research accelerators, and venture capital entities. This comprehensive subject scope allows for the examination of a wide spectrum of communication dynamics and their impact on the functioning and success of innovation ecosystems within a specified temporal and territorial context. The study was conducted in the latter half of 2023, with the analysis of survey results taking place in the first half of 2024. These time frames provide a contemporary snapshot of communication practices and challenges in innovation ecosystems.

The book adopts a comprehensive methodological approach to the role of communication in innovation ecosystems, integrating both quantitative and qualitative research methods to thoroughly investigate the topic. The foundation of this methodology was the use of survey research – a technique that allowed for systematic collection and analysis of data from a defined population involved in innovation ecosystems. To conduct this study, a meticulously designed online questionnaire consisting of 24 questions, including both closed-ended and open-ended questions, was employed. The aim of this scientific project was to obtain detailed responses that would provide insight into various aspects of communication in these ecosystems, such as adopted communication mechanisms, prevailing trends, challenges encountered at different organizational levels, barriers to effective communication, and perceived challenges by entities operating within these ecosystems. Data collected from this survey were then subjected to a rigorous process of analysis, utilizing both quantitative and qualitative techniques for interpreting responses. This dual approach enabled researchers not only to numerically determine data significance but also to explore the nuances and complexities of communication practices and their impact on innovation within these ecosystems. By adopting this mixed methodological approach, the study aimed to achieve a comprehensive understanding of the role of communication in supporting successful innovation ecosystems. The chosen methodology ensured that the study was grounded in empirical data while also allowing for an in-depth exploration of respondents' perspectives and experiences, thereby providing a holistic picture of communication dynamics in innovation ecosystems.

Another research technique utilized to achieve the research goal was interviews. Employing a behavioral method, the authors conducted a series of interviews with representatives of innovation ecosystems. Additionally, as participants themselves, they employed the method of observing the mechanisms occurring within the ecosystem. The results of these explorations formed the basis for adopting the thesis and hypotheses. Furthermore, content analysis of individual source materials was employed.

These research methods and techniques facilitated the examination of the relationship between communication and innovation ecosystems, offering a structured narrative in five main segments. The theoretical background was established initially by examining various typologies of communication and traversing the rich landscape of literature on innovation ecosystems. These foundations underscored the pivotal role of stakeholders and emphasized the importance of resilience amid the unpredictable dynamics characterizing these ecosystems. Additionally, they examined how communication strategies are an integral part of ecosystem vitality, assuming that ecosystem dynamics are strongly influenced by the effectiveness and adaptive capacity of communication. Following these theoretical foundations, the narrative focused on practical dimensions, analyzing robust communication strategies designed to engage and motivate a wide range of ecosystem actors. Through in-depth analysis of communication at interpersonal, interorganizational, and interregional levels, insights were provided into how effective communication contributes to value creation and relationship strengthening. Subsequently, the publication presented empirical research results on communication mechanisms, barriers, and challenges, enriched with methodological details and exhaustive analysis of survey data, culminating in conclusions. In the final chapters, the concept of strengthening communication mechanisms in innovation ecosystems was presented, detailing the necessary conditions, obstacles to overcome, and effective methods for enhancing and maintaining communication effectiveness, followed by pragmatic solutions and recommendations for supporting the future development of highly connected innovation ecosystems. This detailed approach not only sheds light on the crucial role of communication in innovation ecosystems but also offers guidance for their continuous development and success.

The literature base utilized in this detailed exploration of communication in innovation ecosystems distinguishes itself with a comprehensive and interdisciplinary character, meticulously combining a wealth of empirical research with rich theoretical discussions from various academic disciplines. This broad array of sources includes foundational texts that establish fundamental principles of communication and innovation ecosystems, as well as cutting-edge research addressing the evolving challenges facing these complex networks in the digital era. By integrating insights from communication theory, organizational studies, sociology, psychology, management sciences, the literature provides a multidimensional understanding that reflects the nuanced interaction between communication processes and ecosystem dynamics.

At the core of this publication is the incorporation of diverse perspectives, ensuring that research findings are based on a wide spectrum of voices, including academic experts, industry practitioners, and decision-makers. Such an approach not only enriches the analysis with different viewpoints but also bridges the gap between theoretical knowledge and real-world applications. The literature review encompasses both historical and contemporary research, offering a chronological understanding of how innovation ecosystems have evolved and how communication strategies have adapted in response to new technological advancements and social changes.

In the quest for subject literature, considerable emphasis was placed on the intricacies of stakeholder roles and their interactions within ecosystems, highlighting the crucial role of communication in facilitating effective collaboration and knowledge exchange. This aspect of the literature underscored the diverse functions of communication – from coordinating actions, facilitating and aligning goals, to overcoming barriers and fostering innovation. Furthermore, it drew attention to the global reach of innovation ecosystems, encompassing research providing broad insights into global patterns and offering detailed analyses of specific regional or sectoral contexts. This dual perspective ensures that research findings both have universal applicability and can be tailored to specific situations. The analyzed sources meticulously addressed countless challenges and barriers that hinder effective communication in ecosystems, including cultural differences, technological disparities, and organizational silos. Through in-depth analysis of these obstacles, the literature not only identifies critical issues but also proposes a range of strategic solutions aimed at enhancing communication effectiveness. This includes the development of new communication concept, integration of digital tools and platforms, and implementation of best practices in stakeholder engagement.

1 Theoretical framework of communication and innovation ecosystems

Introduction

In modern society, communication patterns intersect and shape the dynamics of organizations and entities. The concept of "communication" is explored in this chapter as an interdisciplinary and multidimensional subject that engages scholars across various fields. Originating from Latin, the term embodies notions of sharing, unity, and connection. This chapter traces the evolution of "communication" from its historical roots, emphasizing its dual significance in modern contexts – transportation and interpersonal exchange. The narrative critically examines diverse definitions and theoretical frameworks within the field, distinguishing between the process-focused and semiotic schools of thought, which respectively emphasize the mechanics of message transmission and the interpretation of meanings in social contexts.

Subsequently, this chapter delves into the burgeoning field of innovation ecosystems, investigating its theoretical foundations and practical implications. Through a systematic review of definitions and interpretations, the authors explore the ecosystem concept's evolution from systems theory to its application in business contexts. Key findings highlight innovation ecosystems as networks of collaborative interactions with open boundaries, involving diverse stakeholders engaged in cooperative and competitive relationships. The chapter meticulously examines stakeholder typologies and roles, emphasizing the critical role of effective communication in fostering trust and resolving conflicts within these ecosystems. It also discusses the evolution of the ecosystem metaphor and the importance of resilience in navigating contemporary global challenges. Overall, this chapter offers insights into the complex interplay of stakeholders and communication in driving innovation and economic growth within ecosystems.

The chapter explores the field of innovation ecosystems, which has gained increasing attention and scholarly interest since its introduction in 1993. Emerging from this emergence is a multifaceted discourse that focuses on its theoretical underpinnings, conceptual clarity, and practical implications for the domain of innovation studies. The authors conducted a systematic

DOI: 10.4324/9781032697802-2

review of the existing definitions and interpretations of innovation ecosystems along with closely related constructs. The chapter begins by examining the widespread theoretical and historical origins of the ecosystem notion within the discourse of systems theory – a comprehensive framework for studying interactions and relationships. This chapter provides an ample overview of the set of stakeholders that shape the innovation ecosystem and goes into great detail about the roles of some of them. Bringing together literature, it meticulously outlines the typology, roles, and points of focus for different stakeholders, with particular attention to technology parks as facilitators of innovation ecosystems. Through an extensive analysis of public administrations, research and academic entities, innovation hubs, companies, investors, NGOs, consultancy and legal firms, networks, and others, stakeholders are categorized and typified. The chapter meticulously highlights the role and added value of each stakeholder in collaboration and knowledge exchange within these ecosystems, inquiring into literature to classify stakeholders into four categories: leaders, direct value creators, support entities, or contributors to entrepreneurial ecosystems.

In contemporary, global, and unpredictable environments, innovation ecosystems need to be resilient. This entails the capacity of a system to continually change and adapt while remaining within critical thresholds. Such adaptability is crucial for innovation ecosystems to cope with changes in technology, the fluctuations of techno-economic cycles, and the rise and fall of countries and trading blocs, as outlined in the chapter.

Communication typology

The concept of "communication" is interdisciplinary and multidimensional (Griffin, 2012). It is the subject of research for scientists from many fields. The diversity of definitions (Dance, 1970) in this area encounters numerous disputes and discussions in science. Adopting one proposal entails a series of significant terminological consequences.

The term "communication" comes from the Latin terms: the verb "communicare" – to make common, connect, or consult; the noun "communico" – "commonality, unity, and sense of connection"; and the adjective "communis" – "common, universal, general." Meanwhile, the noun "communicatio" has two meanings. The first one signifies providing information, the second – participation, sharing, interaction (Filipiak, 2003).

In modern times, languages adopted the term "communication." From the 14th century, it was understood in terms of "entering into community, maintaining relations with someone," and "sharing and communion." In the 16th century, with regard to the development of treaties and roads, the word gained the meaning of "message and transmission" (Kumaniecki, 1972). Since the 19th century, there have been two meanings of the term "communication." The first refers to moving from place to place through transportation. The second is the communication among living beings.

There are various proposals for defining the term "communication" in the literature on the subject. They indicate several regularities – planes of its specification – which include:

1 The accompaniment of communication with living organisms from birth to death.
2 The participation of at least two entities in a specific environment and social context, involving the transmission of information and the emergence of new "thought entities." This includes conveying and receiving information by participants in the communication process, as well as interpreting them and reacting appropriately.
3 The use of the same signs by communication participants, which is essential for mutual understanding.
4 The frequent interchange of roles among participants in the communication process.
5 The regularity that different relationships emerge among communication participants during the communication process, with participants engaging for specific purposes.
6 The rule stating that communication occurs spontaneously between people, hence there is no possibility of repeating, changing, or retracting the course of a given communication process.
7 The assumption that at least two individuals capable of contacting each other directly or indirectly, formally or informally, participate in the communication process.

(Bartosik-Purgat, 2019)

The diversity of communication finds its reference in the science of social communication. Within its framework, two dominant schools can be identified.

The first one, the school of the communication process, focuses on the way messages are transmitted from the sender to the receiver (the so-called communication act). The effect of the transmitted message is significant. It deals with how the sender encodes and decodes messages. The intention is the most important element constituting messages. It defines social interaction as a process in which one person addresses others and influences their behavior, state of mind, and emotions. This school is mainly associated with social sciences such as sociology or psychology.

The second one, the semiotic school, takes the mode of operation of communication as its point of interest, treating it as the production and exchange of meanings. They refer to the role of text in culture. The main emphasis is on interpreting meanings (Fiske, 2010).

The definition of what communication is can be clarified by showing what it is not (negative definition). Currently, the terms "communication" and "communicating" are incorrectly treated as synonyms. With the development of media used in communicative processes, these three terms cannot be equated. Although they all denote certain human activities, they are differentiated by two criteria: different "means and areas of human communicative activities" (Jachimowski, 2006).

M. Filipiak observes that in "communicating," there is a role reversal between the speaker and the listener, and there is physical contact between the subjects. On the other hand, "communicating" excludes this kind of contact and occurs through technical means of communication (e.g., media). Therefore, "communicating" is more related to interpersonal communication, whereas "communication" refers to "'technologically mediated communication." Additionally, J. Mikułowski Pomorski (1988) points out the differences between the concepts of "communication" and "communicating." According to him, the former concept is broader (more inclusive) than the latter. W. Pisarek (2008) also distinguishes between the concepts of "communicating" and "communicating with." The criterion for division here is the role of the message sender. In the first case, the sender dominates over the receiver (an authoritarian way of organizing social groups), while in the second case, they are part of a mutual exchange of information. He also implies that in the case of the word "communicating," the emphasis is more on "something" – the communicated content, while in reference to the term "communicating with" it is on "someone" – the subjects of a specific relationship, contact, or agreement.

From the above, it can be inferred that communication involves the exchange of information. This exchange occurs both during communicating – using technical means of expression, and during communicating with – through physical contact between the sender and the receiver. This process also takes place through (and with the involvement of) media.

Among the types of social communication, the following are distinguished:

1 Verbal communication – conducted using language.
2 Non-verbal communication – carried out through gestures, symbols, and other forms of expression.
3 Intentional communication – performed intentionally.
4 Unintentional communication – undertaken unintentionally.
5 Centralized communication – occurring through a coordinator who holds a central position in the group, thereby controlling the communication process in the group.
6 Decentralized communication – carried out directly, where all group members have the opportunity to freely communicate with each other.

M. Fleischer (2022) attempted a structural and functional typology of communication. He distinguished the following types of communication:

1 Phraseological communication – transporting meanings already negotiated to further solidify them.
2 Tautological communication – where people present statements that duplicate the previous statement, albeit in a linguistically altered form.
3 Thermostatic communication – intolerant of doubt, questioning, or going beyond the premises that generate statements.

4 Diagnostic communication – where the form of the statement matters more than its content.
5 Actional communication – serving to maintain action in a given social situation in order to sustain it.
6 Autistic communication – where there is no process of negotiating meanings, but only manifesting meanings without interest in the semantics represented by the other person.
7 Euphemistic communication – aimed at saying something in a way that gives the first person a convincing opportunity to claim that what was understood by the second person was not said at all.
8 Indexical communication – where the statement does not indicate what was said, but points to something that is not contained in the statement but only uses it for this purpose.
9 Cooperative communication – where negotiating meanings takes center stage in the production of statements, created during the act of communication itself, collectively by all actors, where the statement arises from the cooperation of active and equal, non-hierarchical interlocutors in a given situation.
10 Subversive communication – where people are shown their views (which are not ours), and they get offended instead of reflecting on themselves.

It should be noted that the majority of experts in the field define the term "communication" as a process. Its purpose is to convey information and exchange views, and its character depends on the participating entities – the sender and the receiver (Shuter, 1979). It is divided into formal and informal communication. In the former, the roles of the sender and the receiver are undefined and immutable. In the latter case, the participating entities exchange roles. Entities share meanings through messages established in a specific culture. T. Goban-Klas points out (2008) that they communicate through communication means (medium) in the form of language (as a means of communication); sign systems (e.g., spoken words or facial expressions); signal carriers (e.g., air vibrations, paper, memory card); instruments allowing for replication, transmission, or reception of messages (e.g., radio station, television receiver); and institutions creating messages (e.g., press, radio, television, Internet).

Researchers of the communication process school distinguish several levels (functioning in society), which – in the form of a communication pyramid – were illustrated in the 1980s by D. McQuail (1992, 2010).

The foundation of this pyramid is intrapersonal communication understood as information processing by the human central nervous system. We are dealing here with a biological and psychological process in which the individual responds to his or her needs (e.g., sleep, desire) and self-reflects or analyzes information and knowledge reaching from the outside. Next in the pyramid is interpersonal communication, which concerns communication between individuals and includes verbal and non-verbal communication, as

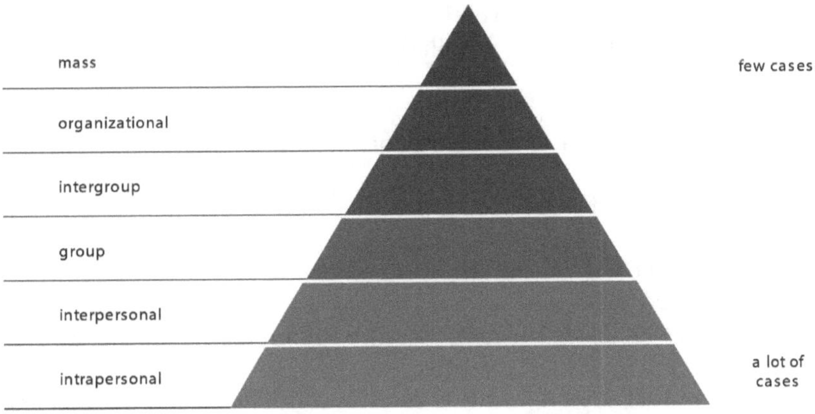

Figure 1.1 Levels of communication according to D. McQuail.

Source: Dobek-Ostrowska, B. (2004), Basics of social communication, Wrocław: Astrum, 18

well as all aspects related to the psychology of individual differences (i.e., the influence of personality, temperamental traits or level of intelligence on the way of expressing and receiving messages). It is usually direct in nature, takes place at the same time, and the entities of communication can constantly exchange roles – participants are sometimes senders, sometimes recipients. The next level in the pyramid is group communication, in which interactions take place within such cells, where the issue of direct connections, hierarchy, norms, and prohibitions begins to become clearly visible. At the next level of the ladder, intergroup communication occurs, characteristic of larger groups in which not all members have direct contact with each other, which may raise problems related to control and effective flow of information. The penultimate element of the pyramid is institutional communication, which is formalized with clearly defined authority and roles, and the highest level of communication in society is mass communication, in which crowds of people are involved, participating in the so-called public communication network, based mainly on mass media (see Figure 1.1).

Depending on the presented theoretical assumptions, experts in the field of social communication present various models of communication. It is assumed that the first of them occurred in the 4th century B.C. described by Aristotle in his work "Rhetoric" (Aristotle, 2004). He took into account: the speaker (sender), the delivered speech (message), and the listeners (recipients).

Currently, it is recognized that communication models are verbal or graphic representations that present the communication process using a diagram and thus constitute a simplification. Despite this, they have high heuristic value.

Until the present day, several hundred communication models have been developed (McQuail & Windhal, 1993). They can have the following characteristics:

1 Structural – where the elements of the communication process are presented.
2 Dynamic – where the process of communication progression is demonstrated.
3 Functional – showing the relationships between the elements of the communication process.
4 Operational – enabling the design of the communication process.

Most contemporary communication models combine all of these elements.

In the literature on the subject, the most frequently analyzed communication schemes are in the form of transmission models, the source of which is the scheme developed in 1948 by C. E. Shannon (1948; Shannon & Weaver, 1964), where the sender transmits a specific message received by the addressee (the so-called signal transmission model).

This systemic communication model, emerging from the mathematical theory of communication, did not introduce a distinction between information and communication. It also does not address the meaning (so-called sense) of the message. It mainly deals with the flow of synchronous information, requiring simultaneous readiness from both the sender and the receiver (they are available at the same time and thus can establish a communication protocol). The source of information initiates the process by creating a message, which is transformed into a signal by the transmitter and reaches the

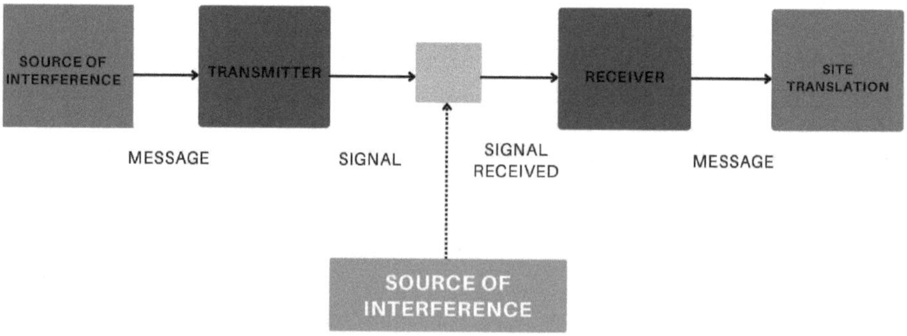

Figure 1.2 Shannon's communication model published in the article entitled *A Mathematical Theory of Communication.*

Source: Schmidt, H., Communication helplessness and contemplative practices. How do contemplative practices support communication and relationships? www.mindfully.pl/artykul/bezradnosc-komunikacyjna-a-praktyki-kontemplacyjne-jak-praktyki-kontemplacyjne-wspieraja-komunikacje-i-relacje [20.01.2024]

recipient through a channel leading to the receiver, who reconstructs the message from the received signal.

C. E. Shannon's model (later known as the Shannon-Weaver model) was the first attempt to systematically reflect on the communication process and isolate the main elements involved in it. It was adapted for the analysis of interpersonal communication.

In 1960, D. K. Berlo presented the process of machine communication based on the Shannon and Weaver model. His model, called S-M-C-R, expanded on the previous one. He identified four main elements of the communication process and their components.

The first element is the sender (S for Sender), who is the source of the message and sends it to the receiver. The sender is characterized by specific communication skills, knowledge, attitude, social system, and cultural elements.

The next element is the message (M for Message), sent from the sender to the receiver. Factors influencing it include the content, nonverbal part of the message, method of message delivery, and the structure and form in which it is sent.

The third element is the channel (C for Channel), which is the medium for sending the message. In general communication, the five senses (hearing, sight, touch, smell, and taste) serve as channels for the flow of information and influence its effectiveness (while in mass communication, technical devices serve as channels).

The last element is the receiver (R for Receiver), who receives the message sent in the communication process. The receiver must possess the characteristics attributed to the sender and additionally have listening skills.

The model of the act of persuasion is also worth presenting. Formulated by the American political scientist H.D. Lasswell (1948), he brings the communication process to five elements: sender, message, channel (medium), receiver, and effect. It is encapsulated in the following research questions: "Who says?, What does he say?, Through which channel?, To whom?, With what effect?".

This model is linear and unidirectional and does not take into account the sender's motives and the context of communication. Instead, it is aimed at learning the effects of the communication process, what thoughts and behaviors it evokes in recipients. However, the meaning is not only related to the sender, because the recipients give the message a personal understanding that may overshadow the intended meaning.

In the context of the above, it is also worth mentioning the topological model created by social psychologist Kurt Lewin (1947), who introduced the concept of information flow to analyze the communication process. He recognized that depending on the situation, information flow can be uneven and incomplete. It is influenced by barriers (so-called gates) that control individuals or institutions acting as gatekeepers. These gatekeepers can both restrict the flow of information and serve a stimulatory function by transmitting specific data to other entities.

Figure 1.3 Lasswell's model of the act of persuasion.

Source: Goban-Klas, T. (2008). Media and mass communication. Theories and analyzes of the press, radio, television and the Internet, Warsaw: PWN, 57

Another example of a transmission model is the so-called feedback model. Its creator, M.L. DeFleur, introduced the concept of isomorphism – which refers to the correspondence between the message transmitted and the message received (1966). The author of this term noticed that unambiguous understanding of a given message by both sides is never complete. The verification of this state can be achieved through feedback between the sender and the receiver, assuming roles are exchanged. Hence, his model assumes two acts of communication where the sender will also be the receiver at times (and vice versa: the receiver will also be the sender at times).

In addition to transmission models, other traditional types of diagrams for illustrating the communication process can also be found in the literature. These include:

a) The expressive or ritual model (Carey, 1975) – in which the essence of communication is considered in terms of community, participation, association, and the analysis of the communication process focuses on the representation of common beliefs.
b) The publicity/attention model (Elliot, 1972) – where the purpose of communication is not transmission, but rather attracting the attention of the audience.
c) The reception model (Holub, 1984; Jensen & Rosengren, 1990; Hall, 1980) – stemming from the trend of critical theory focusing on the reception of messages – the meaning given to messages by recipients.

In addition to traditional models, social communication theorists are increasingly creating alternative schemes that reflect the current, actual state of society's functioning, where interactivity or control of communication by the recipient is becoming more important. The Internet plays a significant role in generating these ideas. An interesting typology of information flow in this area was proposed by Dutch researchers (Bordewijk & van Kaam, 1986), who indicate four patterns of communication.

These include:

1 Allocution – in which a one-way message transmitted by a strong sender is distributed to many peripheral recipients with little chance of feedback. The sender selects the topic, time, place, and target group.

2 Conversation – where individuals independently choose other entities to communicate with. It assumes equality among the participating parties and allows for multiple communication partners.
3 Consultation – the recipient of communication seeks information from the center, meaning they determine the timing, location, and topic of communication.
4 Registration – where the sender requests specific information from the recipients.

In modern society, the four communication patterns mentioned earlier often intersect and overlap. They are concurrently applied by organizations and entities, where people work and operate within these patterns.

Communication has been accompanying humans since the beginning of life. Nowadays, the ability to communicate offers individuals the chance to shape intentional and effective social relationships, while understanding communication patterns and models allows individuals to navigate formalized aspects of life, such as the workplace or institutional sphere, effectively finding their place within them.

Overview of innovation ecosystems literature

The concept of innovation ecosystems has become prevalent in various sectors, including business, academia, and government strategies. They are adopted in a variety of settings – national and regional levels, as well as in corporate visions – reinforcing their perceived relevance in current innovation narratives. These ecosystems are intricate networks in which a variety of actors, including firms, universities, and government entities, interact, fostering the creation and diffusion of new technologies. Communication patterns play a key role in these ecosystems and their dynamics, involving the interactions of entities within – and across – firms, universities, and government entities. Thus, understanding the role of communication in innovation ecosystems is important for better understanding the dynamics underlying their efficiency and effectiveness in promoting new technologies, entrepreneurship, and creativity.

The ecosystem metaphor, inspired by interactions within natural surroundings, has been utilized as an analogy for the intricate interdependencies of a multitude of firms. This metaphor was first introduced by Moore (1993, 1996) and has gained significant recognition in esteemed academic journals, such as the *Strategic Management Journal*, featuring works by Adner and Kapoor (2010), Gulati et al. (2012), Pierce (2009), and Teece (2007). Yet, as Oh et al. (2016a) stress, as an analogy to understand biological ecosystems, it tends to oversimplify the dynamics of organizations, which can limit interdisciplinary exploration and inform the policies necessary for evolving paradigms of innovation. Still, the attractiveness of the ecosystems metaphor, especially in an age of specialization, as a way of emphasizing the "richness" of the organizational relationships among firms that has been the focus by early emulators of Adner and Kapoor (2010), remains very powerful. This metaphor breathes new life into old ideas such as organizational specialization, co-evolution, and joint value creation. An innovation ecosystem is made up of three principal components: actors, resources, and governing institutions. These come together over time to form an industrious landscape. They undergo multiple activities as their relationships evolve. New fields can emerge, along with the new rules necessary to govern them. Like species, entities compete for available resources, or they may compete to replace each other – not literally, but for roles, rules, or resources.

The study conducted by Thomas and Autio (2020) sheds further light on the standout qualities of ecosystems in contrast to other configurations such as supply chains or networks. They are quick to point out that ecosystems go beyond contractual relationships, stressing the roles and common norms that enable effective collaboration among participants. The multifaceted nature of these constructs, as characterized by a vast array of perspectives in disciplines such as business and innovation studies, nicely captures the inherent complexity of ecosystems. An innovation ecosystem may thus be succinctly defined as a complex network of interdependent actors, their actions, innovations, regulatory frameworks, and interactions that may be synergistic or competitive. The innovations in question may encompass a wide array of goods and services, technologies, and other novel solutions that may be developed by single or multiple actors and that may be introduced by entities who may be collaborators or competitors. It should be underscored that the term "innovative performance" does not imply just novel inventions but also modifications and replications. The meanings of the terms "importance" and "innovative performance" may be context-dependent, a generality that does not detract from its precision or flexibility. This conceptualization is consistent with a wide array of other interpretations of innovation ecosystems and is the very understanding presented by Granstrand and Holgersson (2020). Intersectoral collaboration emerges as a fundamental facet in the operational dynamics of innovation ecosystems. As emphasized by Granstrand and Holgersson (2020), an innovation ecosystem is conceptualized as a network of interdependent actors converging their specialized yet complementary resources toward the co-creation of value. Capital accessibility, particularly for investments in research and development, is indispensable for the genesis and implementation of innovations, a notion underscored by Nambisan and Baron (2013). Furthermore, the education and skill enhancement of the workforce stand out as another cardinal component buttressing innovative endeavors. Kukk et al. (2015) accentuate that educational programs ought to be meticulously tailored to align with labor market requisites.

The authors below present a comprehensive review of select publications that have delved into the definitions of innovation ecosystems since 1993. This retrospective analysis aims to shed light on the evolving conceptualizations and nuances associated with innovation ecosystems over the years.

The authors capture one view of the intersected nature of innovation ecosystems, but each with a unique lens. Over the years, there have been numerous and profound scholarly contributions to the realm of innovation ecosystems. Moore (1993) offered one of the earliest conceptualizations of the "business ecosystem," in which businesses operate not as singular entities but as part of interconnected networks in which each is influenced by, and has influence on, the other. Von Hippel (1988) looked at the end-users and their role in the innovation process, arguing that innovation is not a "top-down" manufacturer-driven process but one in which innovating is a collaborative process that requires the unique and insightful inputs from users and their unique needs. This helps them to co-create, with manufacturers and suppliers, a diffusion channel that is not only about businesses and suppliers but also about users and the complex ways in which they interact with one another. Chesbrough (2003) introduced the concept of "open innovation," in which firms can no longer just rely on their internal R&D for innovation but must more actively pursue, integrate, and leverage external sources of innovation, thereby extending the boundaries of the ecosystem within which it innovates. Adner (2006) offered a more "wide lens" view of the subject, arguing that to understand innovation, one had to consider the entire ecosystem within which the innovation was to take place, so that not just the innovating firms, but also suppliers, distributors, competitors, and relevant government bodies. Carayannis and Campbell (2009) proposed a "Quadruple Helix" model that argued that innovation was not just academia, industry, and government, but also media and the public, themselves stakeholders, in a multiplicity of stakeholders sharing creation of value through cooperation and co-evolution.

Each author brings a unique perspective to the concept of innovation ecosystems, emphasizing different aspects such as open collaboration, platform leadership, user-driven innovation, value creation, business ecosystem dynamics, and disruptive innovation. Atkočiūnienė et al. (2021) contribute to this rich tapestry by focusing on the critical role of communication in innovation ecosystems in the realm of creative organizations. They argue that effective communication represents the lifeblood of creative organizations, as it allows the various stakeholders within the ecosystem to exchange knowledge, identify potential collaborators, and foster a culture of creativity and innovation. In Cai (2022), a model is described that integrates existing models, augmented by societal and environmental considerations, which he calls the Neo-Triple Helix model. This model argues for a more inclusive, sustainable, and broader range of innovation.

While each scholar brings unique perspectives to the table, there are evident thematic continuities. They collectively highlight the importance of collaboration, interconnectedness, and the dynamic interplay of various stakeholders in the innovation process. The emphasis on communication, as highlighted particularly by Atkočiūnienė and Siudikienė underscores the idea that innovation is as much about effective interaction and understanding as it is about novel ideas. Together, these scholars provide a

Table 1.1 Evolution of innovation ecosystem definitions: a retrospective analysis of select publications (1993–2022).

Publication year	*Author*	*Title*	*Overview*	*Key contribution*
1993	James F. Moore	"Predators and Prey: A New Ecology of Competition" published in the *Harvard Business Review*, Volume 71, Issue 3, pages 75–86.	Moore introduced the concept of "business ecosystems" in the early 1990s. His work laid a foundation for understanding organizations not as standalone entities but as part of a larger network or ecosystem, which has implications for understanding innovation ecosystems.	The author laid the foundation for understanding businesses as part of larger, interconnected systems, influencing later discussions about innovation ecosystems.
1988	Eric von Hippel	"The Sources of Innovation"	Von Hippel explored the idea of user-driven innovation, which also implies a network or ecosystem of various actors (users, manufacturers, suppliers) contributing to the innovation process.	The author introduced the concept of user-driven innovation, emphasizing the importance of understanding and leveraging user needs and insights in the innovation process.
2003	Chesbrough, Henry	"Open Innovation: The New Imperative for Creating and Profiting from Technology"	Chesbrough discussed the idea of organizations leveraging external sources of innovation, which implies an ecosystem of various actors contributing to the innovation process.	From collaborating with external entities in the innovation process, the groundwork is laid for understanding innovation ecosystems as networks of collaborating and competing entities.

(*Continued*)

Table 1.1 (Continued)

Publication year	*Author*	*Title*	*Overview*	*Key contribution*
2006	Adner, Ron	"Match Your Innovation Strategy to Your Innovation Ecosystem" published in the *Harvard Business Review*, Volume 84, Issue 4, pages 98–107	Adner introduced the concept of the "Wide Lens" perspective on innovation, emphasizing the importance of considering the entire ecosystem surrounding an innovation, including suppliers, distributors, and other stakeholders.	He highlighted the interconnectedness of various stakeholders in the innovation process and how their alignment or misalignment can impact the success of an innovation.
2009	Carayannis, Elias G., Campbell, David F. J.	"'Mode 3' and 'Quadruple Helix': Toward a 21st Century Fractal Innovation Ecosystem"	"Mode 3" allows and emphasizes the coexistence and co-evolution of different knowledge innovation paradigms: the competitiveness and superiority of a system are largely determined by its adaptive capacity to combine and integrate modes through co-evolution, co-specialization, and co-opetition stock-flow dynamics. It is a portmanteau of "cooperation" and "competition" and refers to a strategy where businesses or entities collaborate with their competitors in certain areas while still competing in others. This approach leverages the strengths of both cooperation and competition to achieve mutual benefits and drive innovation. The "quadruple helix" highlights the importance of also integrating the perspective of the media-based and culture-based public. The result is an emerging fractal ecosystem, well-configured for business and society.	The authors describe innovation ecosystems as dynamic and co-evolving communities of diverse actors. This perspective emphasizes the interconnectedness of various stakeholders and the importance of their interactions in driving innovation. The article underscores the significance of both collaboration and competition in shaping innovation ecosystems. The "Quadruple Helix" model integrates perspectives from academia, industry, government, and the public/media, highlighting the role of diverse actors in co-creating value.

(*Continued*)

Table 1.1 (Continued)

Publication year	*Author*	*Title*	*Overview*	*Key contribution*
2011	Jackson, D.J.	"What is an Innovation Ecosystem" from the National Science Foundation in Arlington, VA	D.J. Jackson's work aims to provide a comprehensive understanding of what constitutes an innovation ecosystem. The paper likely discusses the various components and actors that make up these ecosystems and how they interact to foster innovation. Jackson would offer a clear definition of what an innovation ecosystem is, emphasizing the interconnectedness of various entities and their collective role in promoting innovation.	He offered a structured approach to analyzing and understanding the various elements that constitute an innovation ecosystem and how they interact.
2014b	Gawer, A.	"Industry Platforms and Ecosystem Innovation"	Gawer's research centers on platform strategies and how companies can leverage platform leadership to shape technological innovation and industry architectures.	The author provided insights into how platform-based businesses operate within larger ecosystems, emphasizing the role of platform orchestrators in shaping these ecosystems.
2014	W. Chan Kim and Renée Mauborgne	"W. Chan Kim and Renée Mauborgne Dispel Blue Ocean Myths"	"Blue Ocean Strategy" explores how companies can create new market spaces or "blue oceans" through innovation, which has implications for understanding innovation ecosystems.	While not directly about innovation ecosystems, their work has implications for understanding how firms can innovate within and shape their broader ecosystems.

(*Continued*)

Table 1.1 (Continued)

Publication year	*Author*	*Title*	*Overview*	*Key contribution*
2018	Michael G. Jacobides, Carmelo Cennamo, Annabelle Gawer	"Toward a Theory of Ecosystems"	The authors develop a theory of ecosystem dynamics and evolution that considers how shocks, in interdependence with incumbents' responses, affect ecosystem trajectories. The authors argue that the architecture and governance of an ecosystem are shaped by the resolution of challenges related to complementor entry, power distribution, and system-level innovation. Incumbents' solutions to these challenges depend on the relative openness of the ecosystem's architecture and governance, which changes over time. The theory provides a midrange conceptualization of the dynamic interplay between system-level interdependence and strategic action, offering a comprehensive view of why and how value shifts in ecosystems.	The author delved into the dynamics of business ecosystems, exploring how value is created, distributed, and captured within them.
2015	Clayton M. Christensen, Michael Raynor, Rory McDonald	Disruptive Research, and Innovation	While the article discusses disruptive research and innovation, it also touches upon the broader context in which these concepts operate, which can be related to the idea of innovation ecosystems. The innovation ecosystem can be seen as the environment in which disruptive technologies and innovations emerge and evolve, influencing and being influenced by various actors, technologies, and market dynamics.	The article implicitly highlights the interconnectedness between disruptive innovations and the ecosystems they operate in. Disruptive innovations, by their very nature, challenge the status quo and can lead to shifts in the innovation ecosystem, influencing actors, technologies, and market dynamics.

(*Continued*)

Table 1.1 (Continued)

Publication year	*Author*	*Title*	*Overview*	*Key contribution*
2018	Kristian J. Sund, Robert J. Galavan, and Stefano Brusoni	"Cognition and Innovation: New Horizons in Managerial and Organizational Cognition"	This paper explores the cognitive aspects of innovation within organizational structures, emphasizing the thought processes of managers and organizations.	The author suggests that understanding managerial and organizational thought processes is essential for fostering innovation, highlighting cognitive mechanisms as a foundational element in the innovation ecosystem.
2020	Morais da Silva, Rodrigo Luiz, Andréa Paula Segatto, Ana Carolina Vilela de Carvalho, and Gutemberg Ribeiro	"Social Innovation Ecosystem and the Intensity Levels of Social Entrepreneur Cross-Sector Partnerships"	This paper examines the dynamics of partnerships in the realm of social innovation, particularly focusing on the intensity of these collaborations.	It emphasizes the varying intensity levels of cross-sector partnerships and how they can drive impactful social innovation, underscoring the importance of collaboration for sustainable societal change.
2021	Atkočiūnienė, Zenona Ona, and Daiva Siudikienė	"Communication Management in Promoting Knowledge and Creativity to Foster Innovation in Creative Organizations"	This study delves into the role of communication in the innovation processes of creative organizations.	It posits that effective communication is crucial for promoting knowledge exchange, creativity, and subsequently fostering innovation in creative sectors.
2022	Yuzhuo Cai	"Neo-Triple Helix Model of Innovation Ecosystems: Integrating Triple, Quadruple, and Quintuple Helix Models"	This paper offers a comprehensive expansion of the traditional Triple Helix model by incorporating societal and environmental dimensions.	It underscores the need for broader stakeholder involvement, including academia, industry, government, society, and the environment, to foster sustainable innovation.

Source: own development

comprehensive understanding of innovation ecosystems, reflecting the complexities and nuances of the modern business landscape.

The intricate web of stakeholders, collaborative ventures, and strategic imperatives that underpin these ecosystems offers a unique lens through which we can unravel the complex dynamics of value creation and capture in the modern business landscape. The lifecycle of these ecosystems unfolds in a series of phases, each presenting its own challenges and opportunities. The lifecycle of an innovation ecosystem charts a complex course, characterized by shifting priorities, evolving dynamics, and changing leadership roles. Building on a diverse body of academic research, Dedehayir and Steinert (2016) have sketched a detailed map of that course that traverses the nuances of each phase, providing a foundational reference for anyone seeking to decipher the web of forces that drive innovation ecosystems.

In its nascent phase, the ecosystem resembles an unexplored territory. The value proposition is still ambiguous, and uncertainty prevails. Only a few early adopters and participants are present, and foundational principles are yet to be established. As noted by Autio et al. (2014), "in this 'embryonic' stage, the ecosystem structure remains rudimentary." Organizations are in exploration mode, seeking potential opportunities and forging initial partnerships. Gawer and Cusumano (2002) added that this phase is characterized by fluidity in leadership dynamics as emerging ecosystems have a constantly evolving power structure.

As the ecosystem matures and enters the growth phase, its dynamics undergo noticeable shifts. The once faint value proposition begins to crystallize, attracting a larger pool of participants. Collaborative ventures become commonplace, with partners finding mutual benefit from their alliance, as observed by Iansiti and Levien (2004b). The focus in this phase transitions from value creation to value capture. Organizations are no longer merely exploring; they are actively seeking ways to commercialize their innovations, protect their intellectual property, and establish a distinct market position. This phase also witnesses the rise of dominant players, entities that wield significant influence over the ecosystem's direction.

During the growth phase, the ecosystem demonstrates the crystallization of its value proposition. The value of participation becomes increasingly evident, leading to a surge in collaboration, as theorized by Iansiti and Levien (2004b). The strategic emphasis shifts to value capture, with organizations aiming to monetize their innovations, safeguard their intellectual property, and establish a sustainable competitive position, as reinforced by Parker et al. (2016). Dominant organizations emerge, consistent with the "keystone" notion advanced by Iansiti and Levien (2004b).

Approaching maturity, an ecosystem is characterized by a stable value proposition (Adner, 2017), a dense network of interdependent participants, and well-defined, albeit flexible, boundaries (Adner, 2017). Innovation during this phase is incremental, normal, path-dependent, and complementary within entrenched, smooth, and self-reinforcing architectures of technologies and routines (Teece, 2007). As new network participants join the ecosystem, the focus shifts to richly interconnecting and collaborating with the community, rather than opportunistic exchange in a market (Adner, 2017). It is important to note that the boundaries of an ecosystem are not fixed; they can be flexible, allowing those involved to move away from the notion of a static entity with predetermined lines separating insiders from outsiders. Instead, a developmental view of the ecosystem can be adopted, which is more aligned with the reality of ecosystems. This concept aligns with Fleming's (2001) idea of recombinant innovation, which emphasizes the importance of integrating and reconfiguring existing knowledge components in order to drive technological advancement. It highlights the dynamic and evolving nature of ecosystems. These boundaries, representing the ecosystem's core competencies and value drivers, better illustrate how the nature of innovation transforms (Teece, 2007).

As the network of participants becomes denser, the focus shifts from radical to incremental innovations that capitalize on and leverage the existing knowledge infrastructure. The aim of such innovations is to enhance and refine an existing value proposition, enabling the ecosystem to continuously provide something of value to customers. In mature ecosystems, organizations concentrate on maximizing their strategic, operational, and value potential. These changes are viewed as methods to approach the optimal way of extracting the rents associated with their business model, as articulated by Chesbrough (2006).

At this stage, many innovations are less about commercializing a specific idea or innovation, but more about inventing the ecosystem to monetize it. Thus, they increasingly revolve around market design, where participant loyalty becomes a critical component of competitive strategy. Loyalty within ecosystems is a prized asset because the more loyal a participant is to the core, the more trust we have in their commitment over the long term. Trust serves as the linchpin of commitment. Without trust, participants may not commit to the core of an ecosystem as enthusiastically as they might otherwise, as noted by Adner (2017).

In the evolving landscape of leadership within organizational ecosystems, a paradigm is emerging where traditional hierarchical power structures play an increasingly significant role in governing collective entities, such as interfirm networks and global value chains. As suggested by Kapoor and Lee (2013), power imbalances within these ecosystems profoundly affect their operational rules and governance. The stability of such ecosystems is called into question, serving as platforms for firms or consortia to converge, thereby amplifying lock-in effects in a rapidly changing global environment (see Adner & Kapoor, 2010). Indeed, disruptions such as rapid technological obsolescence, shifts in consumer preferences, or macroeconomic disturbances can quickly expose inadequately negotiated business models, leading to the collapse of their value proposition and triggering a phase of disruptive reinvention (Adner & Kapoor, 2010; Christensen et al., 2015).

Predicting the trajectories of such reinventions is challenging, but it is likely that the leadership dynamics within these ecosystems will undergo transformation. A new generation of leaders may emerge to navigate the ecosystem's path in an era of uncertainty and innovative vision (Adner, 2017). Indeed, these pivotal leaders, referred to as keystones, may accelerate the cycle of value creation and innovation, potentially undermining or overthrowing the very innovations that initiated the ecosystem (Adner & Kapoor, 2010). These keystones represent factions engaged in an ongoing endeavor to construct new power dynamics, recognizing that their success is intricately linked to the collective's success. Therefore, the sustainability of an ecosystem hinges on achieving equilibrium, a discipline uniquely provided by the keystone leader within the context of their broader coalition (Adner & Kapoor, 2010).

The lifecycle of an innovation ecosystem serves as a testament to the dynamism and adaptability inherent in modern business landscapes. It underscores the importance of continuous innovation, strategic foresight, and effective partnerships, from the nascent stages of the ecosystem to its maturation into a critical mass phase. This lifecycle offers valuable insights for companies, governments, and academics grappling with the ever-changing opportunities and challenges present in today's business environment. By understanding and leveraging the dynamics of innovation ecosystems, stakeholders can better navigate the complexities of the contemporary business landscape and drive sustainable growth and development.

Key stakeholders and their roles within the innovation ecosystems

Innovation ecosystems are dynamic and multifaceted networks comprising various stakeholders who collectively contribute to the creation, diffusion, and utilization of new knowledge and innovations. These stakeholders play diverse roles that are integral to the functioning and evolution of innovation ecosystems. This comprehensive exploration delves into the types, roles, and significance of these key stakeholders within innovation ecosystems, with a particular emphasis on the role of technology parks in facilitating and enhancing these ecosystems. Drawing from the academic literature, this analysis provides insights into how stakeholders drive innovation, foster collaboration, and contribute to the growth and sustainability of innovation ecosystems. The authors conducted a systematic literature review unveiling diverse roles within innovation ecosystems. The review leads to the discovery of the range of stakeholders and their roles within innovation ecosystems, in addition to a synthesis of the findings. The authors then present the data in an easy-to-reference, comprehensive list of stakeholders and the roles they play within innovation ecosystems.

Innovation ecosystems are dynamic and multifaceted networks, comprising various stakeholders who collectively contribute to the creation, diffusion, and utilization of new knowledge and innovations. These stakeholders play diverse roles that are integral to the functioning and evolution of innovation ecosystems. This comprehensive exploration delves into the types, roles, and significance of these key stakeholders within innovation ecosystems, with a particular emphasis on the role of technology parks in facilitating and enhancing these ecosystems. Drawing from the academic literature, this analysis provides insights into how stakeholders drive innovation, foster collaboration, and contribute to the growth and sustainability of innovation ecosystems. The authors conducted a systematic literature review unveiling diverse roles within innovation ecosystems. The review leads to the discovery of the range of stakeholders and their roles within innovation ecosystems, as well as a synthesis of the findings. The authors then present the data in an easy-to-reference, comprehensive list of stakeholders and the roles they play within innovation ecosystems.

These innovation ecosystem stakeholders comprise a dynamic network in which innovation is nurtured, developed, and brought to market, driving economic growth and societal progress. Each stakeholder group supports and shapes the innovation process in distinct ways, contributing different strengths, perspectives, and types of value to the innovation ecosystem. Their unique roles and interdependencies are the key to unlocking the full potential of these ecosystems, creating a culture of continual innovation and mutual, collective growth. As the business landscape continues to evolve, the importance of robust innovation ecosystems – and the organizations that understand how to foster and invest in them – will only grow.

These roles were grouped thematically into leadership, direct value creation, value creation support, and entrepreneurial ecosystem roles (Dedehayir et al., 2018). Examples drawn from the literature were combined with the activities and significance of each role to provide a complete understanding of what each contributes to the innovation ecosystem. As Adner and Kapoor (2010) note, they are technology leaders who shape the technological interdependence that mediates the performance of firms in new technology generations, and without whom the innovation system is less effective. The leader can initiate development of the ecosystem, ensuring cooperation from key organizations and providing complementary products and services. Literature references such as Clarysse et al. (2014) support the overall conclusion, emphasizing the role of universities and research organizations in generating knowledge and inventions that can be used by the direct value-creating actors. This is the role typically represented by an actor who has taken hold of leadership and has the benefit of greater influence in the ecosystem due to market share, technological advantage, or strategic positioning as a market shaper.

Dominant among direct value creation roles are entities such as entrepreneurs, startups, and innovative firms, which serve as an interface for the conversion of embryonic ideas and technological developments into commercially applicable products and services (Tsujimoto et al., 2018). These actors function as a critical intermediary in the innovation ecosystem, tasked with the transition of knowledge from genesis to practical business application (Gibbons et al., 1994).

Table 1.2 Comprehensive overview of stakeholders in innovation ecosystems.

Group	*Stakeholders*	*Contribution to innovation ecosystems*
Public institutions	Government and regulatory bodies	Regional or national administrations play a pivotal role in shaping the innovation landscape through policies, regulations, and incentives that encourage innovation. Additionally, organizations responsible for establishing industry standards and regulations can have a significant impact on innovation.
	Economic development agencies	Organizations focused on promoting economic growth and innovation within specific geographic areas are crucial drivers of innovation within those regions. Additionally, organizations that provide grants and support for research, innovation, and social impact initiatives play a vital role in fostering innovation and advancing societal progress.
Academic and research institutions:	Government research and development agencies	Public organizations responsible for conducting research in various fields, often with a focus on scientific and technological advancements, serve as fundamental pillars of innovation ecosystems.
	Universities and research organizations	They contribute to innovation through research, technology transfer, and talent development, playing a crucial role in driving scientific and technological advancements forward within innovation ecosystems.
	Research and development (R&D) centers	Independent research organizations and centers play a crucial role in driving innovation forward by conducting cutting-edge research and collaborating with other stakeholders within innovation ecosystems.
	Educational institutions	Schools, colleges, and vocational training centers play a vital role in innovation ecosystems by providing education and skills development to future innovators.
Innovation hubs	Technology parks, incubators, accelerators	These physical and virtual platforms serve as facilitators for collaboration, knowledge exchange, and the provision of resources to innovators.
	Co-working spaces	Creative and dynamic spaces where small firms, freelancers, and startups can interact, collaborate, and co-create.

(*Continued*)

Table 1.2 (Continued)

Group	*Stakeholders*	*Contribution to innovation ecosystems*
	Innovation districts	Designated urban areas with a strong mix of knowledge institutions, companies, and startups focused on innovation, often without a specific sectoral focus.
Companies	Startups and entrepreneurs	These stakeholders are at the forefront of innovation, bringing fresh ideas and disruptive technologies to the ecosystem.
	Established corporations	Large companies participate as stakeholders by engaging in open innovation, collaborating with startups, and tapping into external sources of innovation.
	Suppliers and service providers	Companies that provide essential services, materials, and technologies play a crucial role in supporting innovation efforts within the ecosystem.
Investors and funding institutions	Venture capitalists, angel investors, government grant agencies, and corporate venture arms	They provide the financial resources necessary to support innovation, including funding and mentorship.
	Crowdsourcing and crowdfunding platforms	Online platforms enable individuals and organizations to collectively fund and source innovative projects and ideas.
	Social and environmental impact investors	Investors and funds dedicated to supporting innovations that have a positive social or environmental impact play a crucial role in driving forward socially responsible innovation.
Non-Governmental Organizations (NGOs) and Civil Society		These organizations champion social and environmental causes and leverage innovation for positive societal impact, playing a vital role in driving social and environmental progress.
Consultants and advisors	Experts	Experts in various fields play a crucial role in innovation ecosystems by offering guidance, mentorship, and strategic advice to startups and innovators, contributing to their growth and success.
	Mentorship and advisory networks	Programs and individuals who offer guidance, advice, and mentorship to budding entrepreneurs and innovators play a vital role in nurturing talent and fostering innovation within ecosystems.
Legal and intellectual property professionals	Lawyers, patent agents, and intellectual property experts	They assist in protecting and commercializing innovations.

(*Continued*)

Table 1.2 (Continued)

Group	*Stakeholders*	*Contribution to innovation ecosystems*
Networks	Associations and industry groups	Organizations that bring together businesses within specific industries to foster collaboration and innovation.
	Networking organizations and meetup groups	Local and online communities that facilitate networking, knowledge exchange, and collaboration among innovators.
	Clusters	Clusters concentrate on geographic proximity and specialization, featuring geographically concentrated structures with a specific industry focus. They involve companies within a particular industry or region, emphasizing cooperative interactions among members. Clusters may also have formal governance structures or leadership within their narrower focus.
Others	Media and marketing agencies	These stakeholders play a role in promoting and disseminating information about innovative products and services, thereby contributing to their visibility and adoption within the ecosystem.
	Market Research Firms	Organizations that provide data and insights play a crucial role in helping innovators understand market trends and consumer preferences, thereby aiding in the development and refinement of innovative products and services.
	Artificial intelligence and technology providers	Companies specializing in providing advanced technologies, including AI, play a pivotal role in enhancing innovation processes by offering cutting-edge tools and solutions that facilitate automation, data analysis, and decision-making, thereby accelerating the development and implementation of innovative ideas and solutions.
	Customers and end users	The ultimate beneficiaries of innovation are the end-users, whose needs and preferences serve as the driving force behind the development of new products and services. Their feedback, adoption, and satisfaction with innovative solutions determine the success and impact of innovation within the ecosystem.

Source: own development

Innovation ecosystems are characterized by the early and sustained presence of startups and entrepreneurs, entities that introduce new ideas, disruptive technologies, and an entrepreneurial spirit into the ecosystem. These stakeholders often emerge from academic research or prior industry experience, with the goal of transforming unique and potentially circuitous innovative concepts into commercially viable businesses (Rothaermel et al., 2007). Startups play a crucial role in testing, pushing, experimenting, and challenging the edge, that is, the status quo, which they do most successfully in environments featuring access to resources, mentorship, and potentially compatible partners (Shane & Venkataraman, 2000; Eisenhardt & Schoonhoven, 1990), which may serve to transform innovations into significant breakthroughs as well as initiate an innovation ripple effect throughout the community at large.

Direct value creation roles also include the supplier, who delivers critical component offerings, ranging from materials to technologies to services, which are essential to the continued operation of the ecosystem. The user is another direct value creation role that is crucial to the ecosystem. Feedback from and the participation in the ecosystem by the user are critical and key to the iterative evolution of the ecosystem.

The foundation of every innovation ecosystem is comprised of knowledge creators and diffusers, primarily comprising universities, research institutions, and think tanks (Smith et al., 2016). These stakeholders are the wellspring of innovation, engaging in research, development, and the dissemination of new ideas, technologies, and practices. They generate the intellectual foundation upon which the ecosystem thrives. Their research outputs, patents, and publications not only drive innovation within the ecosystem but also attract talent, investors, and collaborators. By fostering an environment of continuous learning and knowledge sharing, knowledge creators and diffusers contribute significantly to the ecosystem's vitality.

The supporting actor roles, most critical for actors in value creation, include investors, venture capitalists, and support services comprising technology parks, incubators, and accelerators. These entities play vital roles in providing the essential financial resources, mentorship, and support services necessary to nurture innovation (Kapoor & Lee, 2013).

Kapoor and Lee (2013) also cite the roles of regulators and policymakers in creating the regulatory framework and the policies that can foster, or stifle, innovation. The role of industry associations and technology standards bodies is also discussed by Kapoor and Lee, which is crucial for the assimilation and compatibility of new technologies within the ecosystem.

Central to different innovation ecosystems are facilitators such as technology parks – entities that facilitate interactions, collaborations, and transactions among stakeholders. In the case of technology parks, they are important stakeholders, often operating as physical or virtual spaces designed for collaboration, knowledge exchange, and innovation. As catalysts for startups, technology parks play a critical role in providing access to resources, mentorship, and networking opportunities. Empirical studies affirm that technology parks play a significant role in the success of an innovation ecosystem, as these entities attract talent, create knowledge flows, and foster an environment for entrepreneurial ventures (Adamska, 2013; Audretsch & Belitski, 2017; Albahari et al., 2019; Bellavista & Sanz, 2017; Chan & Lau, 2018; Scott, 2016).

Technology parks also often function as intermediaries, providing a link between startups and key stakeholders such as investors, corporations, and research institutions, solidifying their role as central nodes in the ecosystem (Etzkowitz & Klofsten, 2005). Offering a spectrum of shared labs, business development support, and a variety of networking events, technology parks are an essential part of the vibrancy of the ecosystem.

Collaboration is a mandate in any innovation ecosystem, with small and medium enterprises (SMEs) benefiting significantly; SMEs are able to leverage the larger network to gain access to resources, knowledge, and the market (Doe et al., 2018). Innovation hubs, in the same vein, are critical in that they provide the infrastructure, resources, and communication to coordinate and share the flow of information (Lavgan, 2016). By networking stakeholders and providing collaborative spaces, technology parks make the ecosystem more efficient, whether in terms of the physical space through co-working hubs or virtual space using online communities.

These facilitators go beyond providing physical space to also facilitate collaborations, define strategy, and create an environment conducive to innovation (Pisano & Verganti, 2008). They can supercharge stakeholder engagement, from startups and SMEs to larger firms, through networking, state-of-the-art infrastructure, and access to R&D facilities.

A cornerstone of innovation ecosystems is collaborations and partnerships; SMEs rely on these relationships to provide access to larger networks that offer resources, expertise, and a direct line to the market (Doe et al., 2018). Innovation hubs demonstrate that regional economic success is as much about social and political capital as it is about talent; they are able to drive local economic growth and competitiveness by working to garner local businesses, government, and the community around events, incubators, and a number of knowledge-sharing initiatives.

The focus on establishing vibrant innovation communities is seen in the varied approach, in which a range of expertise from a multitude of fields often occupies the same space in an ecosystem, mentorship is willingly provided, and business expertise is volunteered and often shared with resident companies. Regent often aligns with the work of the technology parks by openly advocating policies, funding, and programs that help grow the innovation ecosystem.

Corporations are also increasingly recognizing the value of innovation ecosystems and are actively engaging as stakeholders. They bring extensive resources, market reach, and industry expertise. Corporations are interested not only in internal R&D but also in tapping into external sources of innovation through open innovation strategies (Chesbrough, 2003). By collaborating with startups, research institutions, and smaller firms, corporations can access novel technologies, expand their product portfolios, and remain competitive in rapidly evolving markets (West & Bogers, 2014). Their involvement as stakeholders bridges the gap between established industry players and emerging innovators.

Innovation ecosystems are often geographically concentrated in clusters or regions known for their specialized expertise. These clusters become stakeholders themselves, creating a unique environment that fosters innovation. Silicon Valley in California, the Boston-Cambridge area in Massachusetts, and the Research Triangle Park in North Carolina are renowned examples of such innovation hubs (Porter, 1998). Clusters benefit from the co-location of diverse stakeholders, including universities, research institutions, startups, and established companies. They provide an ecosystem within an ecosystem, facilitating knowledge spillovers, talent retention, and collaboration (Saxenian, 1994).

Stakeholders in innovation ecosystems are not limited to the business and academic sectors. NGOs and civil society organizations also play a role, particularly in addressing societal challenges through innovation. These stakeholders advocate for social and environmental causes, leveraging innovation to create solutions (Kaplinsky et al., 2019). Their involvement ensures that innovation ecosystems consider broader ethical and sustainable dimensions, aligning innovation efforts with societal needs and values.

In conclusion, stakeholders within innovation ecosystems are diverse and multifaceted, each contributing a unique perspective and set of resources. Their roles are interdependent, creating a collaborative environment that drives innovation, economic growth, and societal progress. The active participation of stakeholders, including investors, startups, corporations, clusters, and technology parks, amplifies the ecosystem's impact and ensures its resilience in the face of ever-evolving challenges and opportunities.

Technology parks, in particular, act as catalysts, facilitators, and enablers, amplifying the impact of various stakeholder roles and enhancing the ecosystem's capacity to drive innovation, foster collaboration, and contribute to economic and societal progress. In essence, technology parks seamlessly intertwine with multiple roles within the innovation ecosystem. They are not just passive infrastructural entities but active participants that drive innovation, collaboration, and technological advancement. Their presence amplifies the efficacy of the ecosystem, making them indispensable in the contemporary innovation landscape.

While all these actors are integral to the functioning of innovation ecosystems, their relative activity and influence can vary based on the specific context, region, industry, and the stage of development of the ecosystem. However, the literature consistently underscores the importance of collaboration, interaction, and co-evolution among these actors in fostering a vibrant and dynamic innovation ecosystem.

Building resilience in unpredictable times as the main approach of innovation ecosystems

The concept of resilience in innovation ecosystems is informed by natural resilience, defined as "the capacity of ecosystems to absorb disturbance and reorganize while undergoing change so as to still retain essentially the same function, structure, identity, and feedbacks" (Walker et al., 2004). Like their natural counterparts, innovation ecosystems are subject to a broad range of perturbations and require a framework that enables them to absorb and adapt to change. The principles of natural resilience articulated in the work of van Oppen et al. (2015), Drever et al. (2006), and Power et al. (1988) provide a valuable lens for elucidating the resilience of innovation ecosystems.

Van Oppen et al. (2015) explore the idea of assisted evolution in coral reefs, calling for interventions that enable ecosystems to "evolve-select" in ways that boost their resilience to environmental stress. This is no different from the need for purposive strategies in innovation ecosystems that build their adaptive capacities and establish mechanisms for rapid recovery from crises. The application of assisted evolution in corals might also be viewed as the strategic deployment of resources and capabilities into innovation ecosystems to harden these systems to economic and technological disruption.

Drever et al. (2006) investigate how natural disturbances can enhance ecological resilience in forests by inducing "communities with high diversity, high hierarchy, or spatial heterogeneity among its members." For innovation ecosystems, it is this very diversity – of talents, disciplinary orientations, and stakeholder interests – that allows them to function as shock absorbers during times of rapid change, offering the prospect of alternative pathways forward (Holling, 1973).

Power et al. (1988) consider the multi-scalar influences of biotic and abiotic processes in shaping the structure and function of river and stream communities, providing a model with which to understand how physical conditions and biotic interactions can give rise to resilient systems. This dual emphasis is directly applicable to innovation ecosystems, for which the "hardware" (Doyle, 2006; Pouder & St. John, 1996) of physical infrastructure and the "software" of collaborative networks give rise to the capacity of these systems to bend, recover, and ultimately retain their core identity.

From this perspective, resilience is enhanced by three key principles that directly apply to resilience in innovation ecosystems: diversity and redundancy, connectivity, and feedback mechanisms. These principles provide redundancy in the system's shared awareness and amplify an ecosystem's responses to a variety of ideas and contributors, allowing the system to be more robust and less vulnerable to potential disruptions (Alireza Khorakian & Majid Shami Zanjani, 2020, as cited in Teece, 2018). In the context of resilient entrepreneurial ecosystems, Kim et al. (2018) ascertain that connectivity – in terms of the rapid sharing of information – is important because its parallel in nature is the efficient distribution of resources that makes more of a system's components available for use by other components. In adaptive and transformative systems, feedback mechanisms ensure that complex interactions among players occur, allowing learning and evolutionary processes to accelerate in a given system (Konietzko et al., 2020). Drawing a parallel between this and what is required for such mechanisms to lead to adaptability and transformative capabilities, Markard et al. (2012a) suggest that these requirements are flexibility and a responsiveness to fit, action, and learning, even as the system experiments to discover fit and sustain itself. In short, these principles of resilience point us to a culture of exploratory and experimental learning, rather than complacency and control, as the best way to navigate the uncertainties of technological and market landscapes (Teece, 2018). Furthermore, as Teece (2018) points out, systems with resilience capacity are those capable of transforming themselves in response to major shocks and disturbances. Given the amount of change that innovation ecosystems are undergoing, they have ample opportunity to use this capacity to truly transform them, in marked contrast to the "building back" that many systems use to emerge from crises. These studies can therefore provide us with a rich perspective on how we can enhance our understanding of the dynamics of resilience in innovation ecosystems, and how global innovation ecosystems not only are resilient – they use crises as opportunities for growth and renewal.

Innovation ecosystems are central to economic and technological development, serving as dynamic nexuses among stakeholders, technologies, and socioeconomic processes. The resilience of these ecosystems is paramount in the volatility of the contemporary global landscape characterized by swift technological shifts, fluctuating economic conditions, and ongoing socio-political uncertainties. Resilience is not merely indicative of survival, but rather about flourishing in the face of disruption, adapting to change, and continuous innovation. This resilience is rooted in the complexity and adaptive capacity of complex adaptive systems and collaborative networks, navigating the entropic risks and complex socio-political realities, particularly in urban mega projects. The literature recommends that contemporary governance fully grapple with the uncertainties navigated by socio-ecological and urban systems embroiled within socio-technical transitions and paths and distributed across social networks and digital platforms (Anderies et al., 2010; Markard et al., 2012b; Meerow & Newell, 2015).

Anderies et al. (2010) called for a politics of social-ecological resilience to govern sustainable socio-technical transitions that emphasize the questions of socio-technical environment and the management of uncertainties over policy processes and power relations, and the agenda of relevant socio-political constituencies over time. Meerow and Newell (2015) called for a resilience approach combining both top-down and bottom-up coordination of urban governance and planning to leverage design and creativity within communities and stakeholder networks, creating systems of relationships and sustained urban areas in times of radical socio-technical transformation and reconfiguration. They argued that this planning would involve the development of a different understanding of governance that builds off lessons from adaptive governance distributed across time and space, focusing on bottom-up and network-level collaboration, innovation, and problem-solving necessary to make room for design creativity under conditions of urban crises or more persistent forms of uncertainty.

These contributions to scholarship suggest that the key priority of effective governance should be the creation of resilient innovation ecosystems in which to leverage wise creativity in socio-political and integrated socio-ecological co-production contexts as pathways through economic and socio-political uncertainties, ensuring sustained growth and innovation in tumultuous times.

"Shaping Cooperation in a Fragmenting World," a World Economic Forum (2024) report, offers a timely analysis of the geopolitical backdrop of the 21st century and its implications for global cooperation. Resilience in a fragmenting world demands flexible frameworks capable of adapting as the geopolitical landscape changes and complex global challenges continue to mount. Without them, global stability and cooperation among nations, organizations, and other stakeholders are not possible. As the report notes, flexible frameworks are vital in a fragmented world for several reasons.

First, they provide the agility to respond dynamically to crises and challenges that emerge suddenly. With geopolitical tensions, environmental crises, and technological disruptions that can alter the global equilibrium from one day to the next, flexible mechanisms allow the international community to respond and react rapidly. This is necessary not only with the crises of the moment but with anticipation – catching threats in their incipient state.

Secondly, flexible frameworks enable inclusive cooperation. By incorporating diverse perspectives and expertise, they ensure that solutions are exhaustive and take into account the needs and aspirations of all. This is particularly essential in addressing global challenges such as climate change that have impacts and responsibilities unevenly distributed around the globe. Flexible frameworks are able to incorporate different models of cooperative behavior, from bilateral and multilateral accords to innovative public-private partnerships, to deal with the problem from a variety of angles simultaneously.

In addition, flexible frameworks also support the principle of subsidiarity – decisions are made at the most appropriate level. This tends to maximize the effectiveness of global governance protocol by empowering local and regional actors who understand better than anyone the specific challenges they face. It can also foster innovation by encouraging the formulation of solutions that are specifically tailored to succeed in their particular environment.

With regard to global security, the report highlights the need to establish new ad hoc, functional bodies specific to the issue to manage challenges as they emerge that include relevant stakeholders. These functional bodies serve as a model of flexible frameworks that allow them to penetrate the complexity of international relations and security concerns and move past them, focusing on real-world deliverables by eschewing the broader geopolitical tensions that could limit their application. There is no shortage of need for these flexible frameworks.

Climate action can likewise benefit from the application of substantive protocols. The report argues that climate-forward lending policies and the implementation of climate technology diffusion can help improve trust in global climate governance. For this reason, the formation of adaptive frameworks that formalize a life cycle model for assessing changing technological innovation and financial flows, which can be directed where they are most needed at any given time, could greatly benefit global climate governance.

In summary, the report emphasizes that flexible frameworks that promote resilience are essential for achieving global cooperation in the 21st century. By offering agility, inclusiveness, and embracing local approaches, these frameworks enable engagement with the complexity of the modern world, thereby fostering resilience and cooperation amid fragmentation.

Amidst the pandemic, the International Association of Science Parks and Areas of Innovation convened discussions with international experts and practitioners. The document titled "The Resilience of Innovation Ecosystems" (2022) provides a thorough analysis of the resilience demonstrated by startups, innovation ecosystems, and science parks, especially in response to the challenges presented by the COVID-19 pandemic. The examination covers a wide range of aspects, including open innovation strategies and the significant contributions of science parks and innovation districts. The document includes case studies that illustrate the themes, providing a practical perspective on the adaptive strategies and resilience demonstrated by these entities.

The case study on Telefonica's Open Innovation Strategy examines the company's strategic approach to open innovation. It highlights the importance of large organizations incorporating the perspectives of startups and creating frameworks that facilitate successful collaboration. The document also explains how the pandemic has disrupted the startup ecosystem. It provides examples of startups adapting strategies, identifying new customer segments, and innovating during crises.

Tech Parks Arizona's response to the pandemic demonstrates an increase in startup involvement within their program. They have diversified their initiatives into sectors such as agri-tech and biosciences, highlighting the versatility and adaptability of innovation districts during crises. MedTech Zone, during national lockdowns and natural disasters, demonstrates the resilience of startups within the zone. The sustained production of essential medical supplies highlights their agility and robustness.

The IASP dialogues covered not only how science parks and innovation hubs sustained their communities, large and small companies, and entrepreneurs during the pandemic, but also the ways they approached this unique period in history with adaptability and collaboration. Together, we are inventing the future, addressing how the unprecedented circumstances of the pandemic have pushed the professional landscape to an irrevocable inflection point that will be seen as the signature of our age across all industries.

This creative destruction of innovation as a topic has never been more salient, as it moves from being part of the discourse around competitive advantage and proactive climate change mitigation to an existential choice for the future of humanity and the biosphere. The glaring lesson of the pandemic is that the overwhelming problems facing humanity are global and tangled, requiring the broadest and fastest embrace of innovation as a global strategy, not the province of any regime.

In sectors as varied as food, pharmaceuticals, electronics, and raw materials, global value chains are characterized by fragility, with serious implications for sustainable development for both our planet and its human and non-human residents. The pandemic has illuminated our under-preparedness for crisis and underscored that we must transform our systems of innovation and associated paradigms in which we educate our professionals. Incremental moves are not enough. A responsibility has been set for our generation to respond to planetary constraints and milestones, not to our risk tolerance, our means of innovation, or our investment readiness.

This means peri-industrializing our societies, maintaining them within planetary boundaries, but also socially sustainable, metropolitan, global, multi-racial, and bottom-up: The world economy is in the decisive decade, again. The planet is impressed by our actions, but time for global sustainability across all sectors, value chains, urban infrastructures, and currents of consumption beckons. Such success could leave as a bequest from our generation a world much improved from the one we inherited.

In energy, the imperative is to perpetrate an irrevocable shift of our energy systems to their renewable, digital, and electronified terminus, and to achieve a storage and a digital intelligence dividend, including leveraging profound behavior shifts. Policy and technology are necessary but not sufficient. At the same time, we have an extraordinary opportunity to reimagine and finally transform our mobility systems and cities to those without fossils, incorporating new vehicles, modes, and business models incentivizing the optimization of logistics for goods and people. These must contribute positively to both human health and its extended metabolisms, requiring unprecedented collaboration among engineering, process engineering, and urban planning.

Our food systems are currently unsustainable, unhealthy, and un-resilient and need to be reconsidered if they are to be regenerative to both our human health and the environment. This will require iterations of innovation and research in new types of food, methods of making it, and business models and incentives that shape our desires and physical purchases, cultural preferences, and meal times, all at the same time.

As for health, while our innovative technologies come online with the capacity to save lives at an unprecedented level, we should be equally committed to their spread through new risk management models generally and inclusive and truly productive health systems. Just as the COVID-19 pandemic has shown the idiocy of our past global value chains, it also demonstrates the radical transformation that is needed to our global innovation policy to permit this.

Innovation ecosystems demonstrate resilience in various scenarios, as exemplified by their ability to adapt during the COVID-19 pandemic. Many ecosystems quickly pivoted their operations to produce essential goods and services necessary for pandemic mitigation. During this critical period, the scientific community focused on vaccine development, demonstrating the adaptive capacity of researchers. Governments also played a crucial role by enacting policy modifications and providing substantial financial backing to enhance the ecosystem's resilience. Innovation ecosystems possess inherent strength and flexibility, as evidenced by their adaptive responses to unforeseen challenges and ability to pivot toward addressing emergent societal needs.

Developing resilience within innovation ecosystems requires a delicate balancing act – with a stable base and flexible operations. You must also be able to focus on the present while keeping an eye on what lies ahead. Strategies contributing to greater resilience include investing in education and skills, implementing policies that encourage risk-taking and entrepreneurial behavior, as well as nurturing an innovation-centered culture. This multifaceted approach toward building resilience requires systems that value diversity, connectivity, and adaptability on one hand, and openness and shared learning on the other. It is these capabilities that allow such systems to adjust and evolve amidst uncertainty. The resilience of these ecosystems becomes not just an essential precondition for their own success, but also central to societal advancement as a whole in a rapidly changing global landscape (Hosseini et al., 2021). A central theory is to build resilient human capital and the capacity for communication and collaboration among stakeholders. The complex systems engineering of decision-making that underpins these systems – "brain networks and interactions," as it were – is therefore analogous to blood circulating life through an organism. More than just providing a platform for information exchange and sharing of resources, these interconnections also foster a support culture that can quickly adapt to changes and challenges. The injection of digital tools and technology plays a core role in such an endeavor, serving as platforms for the rich collaboration needed throughout innovation ecosystems; they also provide information sources and decision-making abilities required to cope with various complex uncertainties that arise in present-day circumstances (Brown & Mason, 2017).

The definition of resilience within innovation ecosystems is realized through several strategic underpinnings. One is that broad-based diversification across projects, technologies, and collaborations ensures that specific outside impacts are spread evenly among many nodes in an ecosystem – thereby limiting their effects. Great flexibility and adaptability are the foundation of resilience for ecosystems, allowing them to respond quickly in the face of any shock. This aspect of resilience can be found in scholarly studies about how ecosystem resilience strategies originated (Oh et al., 2016a).

Similarly, fostering an environment that encourages continual learning and innovation on all fronts for decades to come is crucial. It also requires recognizing and paying attention not only to academic, business, and government organisms but also to their roots. It is in such organisms, in fact, that the integrated collaboration among many stakeholder perspectives and resources takes place, which is crucial to making these dynamic systems resilient – as has been spotlighted by studies identifying effective resilience strategies within business ecosystems (Thomas & Autio, 2020; Tsujimoto et al., 2018a).

The interaction between communication and the dynamics of innovation ecosystems

Effective communication is crucial for holding together the various elements of an innovation ecosystem. Behavioral logics within innovation ecosystems are intricately linked to communication, as effective communication plays a fundamental role in the functioning and evolution of these ecosystems. The following points elucidate the interconnectedness between behavioral logics and communication within innovation ecosystems, drawing from relevant academic literature.

Scholarly discourse emphasizes the key role of co-creation and collaborative endeavors within the milieu of innovation ecosystems, as evidenced by seminal works such as those by Adner and Kapoor (2010) and Lusch et al. (2010). The establishment of efficacious conduits for communication is deemed indispensable for the exchange of knowledge, ideas, and perspicacity among the heterogeneous constituents of these ecosystems (Powell et al., 1996). It is posited that lucid and unfettered communication practices are conducive to the enhancement of collaborative ventures and are instrumental in the joint creation of value within the ecosystemic collective (Hargadon & Sutton, 1997).

The construct of trust emerges as a salient aspect of the embedded networks characteristic of innovation ecosystems (Burt, 1992). The edification of trust is contingent upon communication processes that bolster transparency and dependability (Morgan & Hunt, 1994). It is through steadfast and transparent communication that the edifice of trust relationships is constructed and sustained, underpinning the efficacy of collaborative interactions and the dissemination of knowledge within the ecosystem (Dyer & Singh, 1998).

The imperative of adept network management is underscored in the context of orchestrating the multifarious activities of ecosystem participants (Gulati, 1995). Central firms or coordinating bodies are reliant on strategic communication modalities to guarantee the seamless functioning of the ecosystem (Gulati et al., 2012). Communication in this context involves various tasks such as sharing information, aligning objectives, and fostering engagement among participants (Zineldin, 2004).

The importance of meeting consumer demands is emphasized in innovation ecosystems (Normann & Ramirez, 1993). Interacting with customers and end-users is essential for gaining insights, preferences, and evaluative feedback (Grönroos, 2000). Such communication channels are instrumental for ecosystem actors to tailor their value propositions in alignment with market requisites, thereby engendering value (Prahalad & Ramaswamy, 2004).

Innovation ecosystems thrive on the exchange of knowledge and ideas (Iansiti & Levien, 2004a; Powell et al., 1996). Scholarly symposia, digital fora, and other platforms facilitate the propagation of innovative tenets and industry best practices (Wuchty et al., 2007). These fora serve as crucibles for researchers, entrepreneurs, and ecosystem affiliates to disseminate their scholarly findings and solicit peer feedback (Hansen, 1999).

Conflicts often arise within innovation ecosystems due to divergent interests and stakeholder heterogeneity (Eisenhardt, 1989). It is posited that efficacious communication is an indispensable instrument for the constructive resolution of such discordances (De Dreu & Weingart, 2003). The facilitation of open dialogue is essential for articulating concerns, negotiating resolutions, and preserving a consonant ecosystem ambiance (Lewicki et al., 2003).

The behavioral logics of innovation ecosystems are characterized by their adaptive and evolutionary propensities (Basole, 2009). Communication channels convey information regarding changes within the ecosystem, emerging technologies, and market trends (Cohen & Levinthal, 1990). This communication infrastructure supports the collective ability of ecosystem participants to adapt to new conditions and take advantage of emerging opportunities (Geroski et al., 1997).

Central to the functioning and evolution of innovation ecosystems is effective communication, which is the lifeblood of behavioral logics within these ecosystems. Remarkably, in nearly all articles, our academic sources find that effective communication is paramount for innovation ecosystems to be participatory and healthy.

The establishment of platforms for knowledge co-creation among the heterogeneous collection of innovation ecosystem co-creators (Adner & Kapoor, 2010; Lusch et al., 2010) is essential. Without these platforms, the full benefits of collaborations enabled by an ecosystem cannot be reached. These platforms are effective only when ecosystem affiliates can communicate candidly and openly with one another because transparency is essential to building and maintaining a successful relationship in which value is co-created (Powell et al., 1996).

The formation of trust is a central part of the embedded networks that characterize innovation ecosystems (Burt, 1992). Trust formation, of course, is also dependent on the communication processes that make it possible for those in the relationship to be transparent and reliable over time (Morgan & Hunt, 1994). Through ongoing communication, trust-based relationships are built and continue to support members to collaborate and for knowledge to flow among them (Dyer & Singh, 1998).

The need for network orchestration is critical for orchestrating the many different activities of ecosystem participants (Gulati, 1995). This orchestration must occur within ecosystems, through strategic communication aimed at making clear the purposes of the network, sharing information, and engaging network members (Gulati et al., 2012; Zineldin, 2004).

Customer intimacy is also important (Normann & Ramirez, 1993). Customer and end-user interactions are necessary so that the ecosystem-awareness of the members is bolstered, making them better positioned to gain insights, preferences, and evaluative feedback (Grönroos, 2000), which can then be used to modify and adapt their respective value propositions to meet market requirements and thus create value (Prahalad & Ramaswamy, 2004). The importance of knowledge and idea flows in innovation ecosystems (Iansiti & Levien, 2004a; Powell et al., 1996) cannot be overstated. Academic conferences, digital forums, and other platforms facilitate the diffusion of innovative ideas and industry best practices (Wuchty et al., 2007). These avenues enable researchers, entrepreneurs, and other members of the innovation ecosystem to share their latest findings and receive feedback from their peers (Hansen, 1999). Conflict is inevitable in innovation ecosystems due to divergent interests and the heterogeneous nature of stakeholders (Eisenhardt, 1989). Effective communication is critical for resolving such conflicts successfully (De Dreu & Weingart, 2003). Through open communication, involved parties can express their concerns and negotiate mutually acceptable solutions, thereby preserving the ecosystem's harmony (Lewicki et al., 2003). The adaptive and evolutionary nature of behavioral logics within innovation ecosystems (Basole, 2009) underscores the need for communication channels to relay changes in the ecosystem, including the emergence of new technologies and marketing trends (Cohen & Levinthal, 1990). This infrastructure enables the entire ecosystem to adapt collectively to new realities and exploit emerging opportunities (Geroski & Schröder, 1997).

The interplay between the structural components of an innovation ecosystem, such as firms, universities, government institutions, and other actors, shapes its dynamics. The diffusion of tacit knowledge, often at the heart of groundbreaking innovations (Bathelt et al., 2004), is crucially influenced by informal networks, social interactions, and serendipitous encounters. These communication channels contribute to the social capital of the ecosystem, fostering an environment where knowledge spillovers can occur, and new ideas can flourish. Communication acts as a conduit for this interplay, facilitating the negotiation of meanings, the establishment of trust, and the coordination of actions (Cunningham et al., 2016). Communication facilitates ecosystem adaptation and evolution through iterative feedback loops in response to internal and external stimuli. It enables the exchange of knowledge, strengthens collaborative efforts, and aligns objectives among diverse stakeholders (Ritala & Almpanopoulou, 2017). Communication within these ecosystems is iterative, ensuring that information is not only disseminated but also interpreted, contextualized, and applied in ways that drive innovation forward.

Examination of the interplay between communication and the dynamics of innovation ecosystems is a multifaceted and complex area that necessitates comprehensive inquiry. The domain is multifaceted and complex; communication within these ecosystems is not merely a transfer of information, but a complex and iterative process that both shapes and is shaped by the evolving dynamics of the ecosystem. As a concept, the idea of an innovation ecosystem refers to the network of actors, institutions, and processes that foster innovation in particular environments. It is a dynamic system continuously influenced by the flow of knowledge and ideas (Oh et al., 2016b). The Research Electronic Data Capture (REDCap) consortium discussed by Harris et al. (2019) is such an innovation ecosystem in which communication played a central role. It originated at Vanderbilt University and grew into an international consortium by creating a network of software platform partners. Effective communication strategies promoted knowledge sharing and collaboration across national boundaries. The authors explain how this case illustrates that communication can surmount geographical and institutional boundaries to create a collaborative environment conducive to innovation (Harris et al., 2019). In innovation ecosystems, communication is not simply the exchange of information; it is the creation of a shared language and understanding among diverse participants. This is essential, as Godfray et al. (2010) demonstrated in their study on food security, if the goal is to address global grand challenges. Successfully feeding a growing global population requires a multifaceted approach that includes diverse stakeholders. Effective communication among these stakeholders assures that different perspectives and expertise are integrated and results in more comprehensive and sustainable solutions (Godfray et al., 2010).

The communication network structure within innovation ecosystems is paramount. An understanding of these structures is required, as underscored by Strogatz (2001), who emphasized the significance of understanding the structure of complex networks. This understanding is particularly relevant to innovation ecosystems, where the flow of information through its networks, the strength of ties between different entities, and the centrality of nodes can considerably impact ecosystem performance (Costa & Paula, 2013). The performance of an ecosystem heavily relies on how well-connected its nodes are. Diagrams of communication systems, as described by Strogatz (2001), can reveal which nodes in the network preferentially lead to others through the transit of information. Clustering, periphery, and plexity are dependent upon the relationships among nodes. Importantly, well-connected nodes and strong ties in networks enhance the communication of knowledge, which is crucial to innovation (Strogatz, 2001).

Bidirectional communication shapes the dynamics of innovation ecosystems not only by transmitting information from more developed to less developed entities but also by enabling feedback loops where learning is mutual. Given that maintaining innovation over time demands effective communication, reciprocal communication fosters a culture of continuous learning and adaptation.

We argue that the digital transformation has amplified the significance of – yet also complicated – the communication of innovation within innovation ecosystems. This is because digital platforms have become essential assets within innovation ecosystems for enabling communication, collaboration, and knowledge exchange among diverse stakeholders.

These platforms offer functionalities that are distinct from traditional forms of communication, enabling more efficient, scalable, and dynamic communication within innovation ecosystems. Real-time collaboration within innovation ecosystems is essential as the exchange of ideas facilitates the innovation process. Furthermore, digital platforms democratize the management of innovations by providing an equitable platform for various participants, including small enterprises, individuals, and researchers, regardless of their position, size, or resource constraints. Resources, information, and networks are more accessible with the aid of digital platforms.

In a data-intensive environment, these platforms rapidly integrate data streams from a host of sources, synthesizing them to provide valuable insights by identifying complex patterns that inform decision-making for innovation. Additionally, digital platforms provide the infrastructure for scaling operations within innovation ecosystems, enabling the management and automation of processes within stakeholder networks, which are often highly complex, thus facilitating sustainable growth.

Therefore, digital platforms serve as more than just communication tools; they act as catalysts for community building. As described by Iansiti and Lakhani (2014), these platforms facilitate the sharing of knowledge, best practices, and experiences among participants in the ecosystem, fostering a collaborative spirit within the community. These virtual communities and networks, fostered and sustained by the digital platforms that underpin innovation ecosystems, have enabled new ways of collaborating and communicating, resulting in a more inclusive and diverse innovation landscape that transcends national borders (Yoo et al., 2010).

However, this digital transformation also brings challenges that are not insurmountable. One of the most significant challenges is ensuring the effective management and leveraging of digital communication. Examples include information overload and the need for new competencies to effectively respond to digital communication for innovation within these ecosystems. The digital platforms and communication tools provide an efficient and scalable means of delivering knowledge, facilitating real-time collaboration and feedback essential in an innovation process that continually accelerates and iterates the design of new ideas and technologies. Such competitive advantages are most significant for actors who effectively leverage the distributed knowledge and capabilities across an innovation ecosystem, as well as those who can efficiently coordinate the global networks of actors involved in complex products and services (Baldwin & Clark, 2000).

The persistent challenge of the digital divide in the innovation process and the equitable distribution of innovation benefits must not be overlooked.

Unless innovation ecosystems bridge this gap to ensure that the benefits of innovation are assessed by a broad cross-section of society, the full spectrum of social needs and opportunities for innovation will remain unrealized for all societal actors.

Despite the substantial challenges in managing digital communication platforms and processes, the potential to accelerate the rate and value of innovation is incomparably larger. These challenges of digital transformation and technologies can only be overcome through the ongoing process of assembling innovation ecosystems.

Strategies for communication play a crucial role in the development and growth of innovation ecosystems as they gain traction. A review conducted by Al-Fuqaha et al. (2015) on the Internet of Things (IoT) highlights the critical importance of communication in the enabling technologies, protocols, and applications that form the foundation of the IoT. The IoT presents numerous challenges, including the complexity of technology integration and the necessity of establishing communication protocols to ensure interoperability among different devices. Understanding these communication challenges is essential for both the development and practical implementation of IoT solutions.

Achieving adequate communication requires collaboration among researchers, developers, and industry stakeholders, which necessitates extensive research and development efforts focused on the IoT itself. This includes efforts to describe protocols, mechanisms, and interactions comprehensively. By addressing these communication challenges, innovation ecosystems can effectively support the advancement and implementation of IoT technologies.

Additionally, these challenges stem from the communication processes occurring among the embedded systems within the IoT, the gateway connecting these systems, and the Internet, which involve tens of billions of devices speaking simultaneously. Various protocols and technologies enable such communications, each distinguished by factors such as the implementing node and the security protocol in place. Determining when these systems can communicate and prioritizing data flows on the network further complicate the establishment of communication within the IoT. Consequently, this represents one of the most significant research, development, and implementation challenges of the IoT.

Moreover, it is crucial to communicate open problems in this field to researchers, particularly those in remote geographical areas. This highlights the principal communication challenges in both the development and practical application of IoT technologies. Firstly, understanding the real-time constraints for communication quality is essential, as the volume of information being transmitted often exceeds the capacity for real-time communication. Additionally, there is a need for a robust communication system capable of efficiently processing these configurations, given the complexity involved in coordinating these communications.

Communication lies at the heart of yet another significant challenge: how to automate systems within the IoT to enable self-building capabilities. Such systems require a high degree of adaptability to adjust their coordination needs quickly and in response to environmental conditions. Consequently, communication within the IoT poses an intractable problem, characterized by chaos and irregularity, driving extensive research and development efforts in this field (Al-Fuqaha et al., 2015).

Similarly, the digital transformation and proliferation of digital technology have posed similar challenges in managing and leveraging communications in other fields of complex systems, such as scientific research. The advent of digital technology has enabled observational and experimental knowledge to be digitized and analyzed rapidly, leading to the creation of new scientific knowledge that was previously unattainable. However, the importance of this digital information cannot be overstated in the research process, as it forms the basis for analysis and communication of new observational or experimental data worldwide (Ball, 2010; Bound, 2012; Breen, 2006).

This process of analysis and data creation involves a more subtle and complex form of communication, where knowledge is transmitted globally to enable the planning and implementation of new research endeavors. Unlike the IoT, this communication process often follows a linear structure, involving different actors and roles in the communication chain, depending on the type of research data being transmitted (Antunes & Figueira, 2009).

Communication across disciplines is often celebrated as a means of overcoming the rhetorical and conceptual barriers that divide academic communities. Cummings and Kiesler's (2005) research explores the ways in which communication strategies and technologies can mitigate the division between scientific disciplines. By creating common languages and facilitating shared understanding, digital platforms can enable researchers from different fields to communicate so seamlessly that the division becomes a meaningful site of collaboration and community. The researchers found that this form of communication enabled researchers to leap over the gaps between fields and to collaborate on research that was not only university but innovative (Cummings & Kiesler, 2005). Cummings and Kiesler's (2005) research on cross-disciplinary collaboration in scientific research, which led to the development of models and frameworks, such as best practice documentation of cross-disciplinary collaborative models and guidelines, that have served as the foundation of digital platforms and tools created for cross-disciplinary collaboration, such as new project and network models, common language and concept sets and digital infrastructures, and collaborative science models for value co-production and innovation. The models and frameworks model, for example, includes documentation of the necessity of cross-disciplinary work and best practices for both establishing common languages and methodologies and for technologies that support seamless communication and data sharing, regardless of the locale of the researchers or the discipline; the models gave birth to such digital collaboration tools as online workspaces, project management tools, and research and data and findings sharing platforms. The research resulted in the development of training and workshops, for instance, which are offered in such areas as translational science, where between-discipline communication is the difference between the bench and the patient. These training initiatives will provide training to enable researchers to encode concepts so that they can be understood across different labs and fields, to decode concepts from other labs and fields, and to use simulation and other advanced methods so that knowledge from one field can enhance understanding in another. This research has also resulted in the development of research networks that are collaborations first, which are establishing best practices, such as the current creation and demonstration of communities where researchers are developing the community culture of the new national model clinical and translational science communities, where the model is that researchers will be sharing resources, ideas, and best practices, as well as training materials and subjects across phyla. The research has also manifested itself in higher education curricula at various levels, including early student engagement, such as in high school and earlier, with new organizational science curricula. In these programs, students are trained in ancillary skills such as encoding and decoding the thoughts and experiments that make up the sciences in question. In addition, this research is being incorporated into advanced graduate training and seminar degree programs. For instance, an NIH-funded program for T-32 programs trains postgraduates in molecular science, such as genomics, proteomics, and molecular imaging, so that they might learn one other's languages and share one another's subjects and laboratories (Cummings & Kiesler, 2005).

Furthermore, this research has led to the establishment of research networks that prioritize collaboration, such as the creation of communities where researchers develop the community culture of new national model clinical and translational science communities. Here, researchers share resources, ideas, and best practices, as well as training materials and subjects across disciplines.

In conclusion, communication emerges as a vital cornerstone in shaping the behavioral logics that underpin innovation ecosystems. The scholarly literature elucidates the critical roles that communication plays in nurturing shared goals, fostering trust and respect, exchanging and interpreting diverse forms of knowledge and expertise, mediating differences, resolving conflicts, and coordinating adaptive responses within these complex and dynamic structures. The adept execution of communication strategies is essential to harnessing the potential of diverse ecosystem participants, enabling them to align their actions and intentions in manners that accelerate innovation and value co-creation.

Bibliography

Adamska, J. (2013). Impact of technology parks on the competitiveness of regions. *Science and Innovation*, 94–97.

Adner, R. (2006). Match your innovation strategy to your innovation ecosystem. *Harvard Business Review*, *84*(4), 98–107.

Adner, R. (2017). Ecosystem as structure: An actionable construct for strategy. *Journal of Management*, *43*(1), 39–58.

Adner, R., & Kapoor, R. (2010). Value creation in innovation ecosystems: How the structure of technological interdependence affects firm performance in new technology generations. *Strategic Management Journal*, *31*(3), 306–333.

Albahari, A., Catalano, G., & Landoni, P. (2019). The influence of science and technology park characteristics on firms' innovation results. *Papers in Regional Science*, *98*(2), 1247–1264.

Al-Fuqaha, A., Guizani, M., Mohammadi, M., Aledhari, M., & Ayyash, M. (2015). Internet of things: A survey on enabling technologies, protocols, and applications. *IEEE Communications Surveys & Tutorials*, *17*(4), 2347–2376.

Anderies, J. M., Ryan, P., & Walker, B. H. (2010). The politics of social-ecological resilience and sustainable socio-technical transitions. *Ecology and Society*, *15*(1), 9.

Antunes, P., & Figueira, C. (2009). Knowledge communication in research: A framework for understanding the transmission of research data. *International Journal of Information Management*, *29*(3), 210–218.

Aristotle. (2004). *Rhetoric*. PWN.

Atkočiūnienė, Z. O., & Siudikienė, D. (2021). Communication management in promoting knowledge and creativity in fostering innovations in the creative organizations. *Creativity Studies*, *14*(2), 549–576.

Audretsch, D. B., & Belitski, M. (2017). Entrepreneurial ecosystems in cities: Establishing the framework conditions. *Journal of Technology Transfer*, *42*(5), 1030–1051.

Autio, E., Kenney, M., Mustar, P., Siegel, D. S., & Wright, M. (2014). Entrepreneurial innovation: The importance of context. *Research Policy*, *43*(7), 1097–1108.

Baldwin, C. Y. (2012). Organization design for business ecosystems. *Journal of Organization Design*, *1*(1), 20–23.

Baldwin, C. Y., & Clark, K. B. (2000). *Design rules: The power of modularity*. MIT Press.

Ball, R. (2010). Data handling and analysis in research: A new approach. *Data Science Journal*, *8*, 1–10.

Bartosik-Purgat, M. (2019). *New media in the marketing communication of enterprises on the international market*. PWN.

Basole, R. C. (2009). Visualization of interfirm relations in a converging mobile ecosystem. *Journal of Information Technology*, *24*(2), 144–159.

Bathelt, H., Malmberg, A., & Maskell, P. (2004). Clusters and knowledge: Local buzz, global pipelines and the process of knowledge creation. *Progress in Human Geography*, *28*(1), 31–56.

Bellavista, J., & Sanz, L. (2017). Success variables in science and technology parks. *Journal of Business Research*, *70*, 289–298.

Berlo, D. K. (1960). *Process of communication: Introduction to theory and practice*. Holt, Rinehart and Winston.

Bordewijk, J. L., & van Kaam, B. (1986). *Towards a new classification of tele-information services* (pp. 16–21). InterMedia.

Bound, J. (2012). The dynamics of data sharing and data reuse in scientific research. *Information Systems Journal*, *22*(3), 235–246.

Breen, M. (2006). Data and information sharing in the digital age: Implications for research and practice. *Journal of Information Science*, *32*(4), 301–311.

Bresnahan, T. F., Gambardella, A., & Saxenian, A. (2001). "Old economy" inputs for "new economy" outcomes: Cluster formation in the new Silicon Valleys. *Industrial and Corporate Change*, *10*(4), 835–860.
Brown, R., & Mason, C. (2017). The resilience of entrepreneurial ecosystems. *Journal of Business Venturing Insights*, *8*(11), 99–104.
Burt, R. S. (1992). *Structural holes: The social structure of competition*. Harvard University Press.
Cai, Y. (2022). Neo-triple helix model of innovation ecosystems: Integrating triple, quadruple, and quintuple helix models. *Triple Helix Journal*, *9*(1), 76–106.
Carayannis, E. G., & Campbell, D. F. J. (2009). 'Mode 3' and 'quadruple helix': Toward a 21st century fractal innovation ecosystem. *International Journal of Technology Management*, *46*(3/4), 201–234.
Carey, J. (1975). A cultural approach to communication. *Communication*, *2*, 1–22.
Chan, K. F., & Lau, T. (2018). Science and technology parks: Future challenges. *Technological Forecasting and Social Change*, *123*, 275–286.
Chesbrough, H. W. (2003). *Open innovation: The new imperative for creating and profiting from technology*. Harvard Business Press.
Chesbrough, H. W. (2006). *Open business models: How to thrive in the new innovation landscape*. Harvard Business School Press.
Christensen, C. M., Raynor, M. E., & McDonald, R. (2015). What is disruptive innovation? *Harvard Business Review*, *93*(12), 44–53.
Clarysse, B., Wright, M., Bruneel, J., & Mahajan, A. (2014). Creating value in ecosystems: Crossing the chasm between knowledge and business ecosystems. *Research Policy*, *43*(7), 1164–1176.
Cohen, W. M., & Levinthal, D. A. (1990). Absorptive capacity: A new perspective on learning and innovation. *Administrative Science Quarterly*, *35*(1), 128–152.
Costa, R. L., & Paula, D. R. (2013). The structure of innovation ecosystems. *Technological Forecasting and Social Change*, *80*(7), 1251–1260.
Cummings, J. N., & Kiesler, S. (2005). Collaborative research across disciplinary and organizational boundaries. *Social Studies of Science*, *35*(5), 703–722.
Cunningham, P., Dolan, B., Kelly, K., & Young, G. (2016). Trust, commitment and cooperation in business relationships: The role of communication. *Industrial Marketing Management*, *58*, 1–13.
Damschroder, L. J., Aron, D. C., Keith, R. E., Kirsh, S. R., Alexander, J. A., & Lowery, J. C. (2009). Fostering implementation of health services research findings into practice: A consolidated framework for advancing implementation science. *Implementation Science*, *4*, 50.
Dance, F. E. X. (1970). The "concept" of communication. *Journal of Communication*, *20*, 201–210.
Dedehayir, O., Mäkinen, S. J., & Ortt, R. J. (2018). Roles during innovation ecosystem genesis: A literature review. *Technological Forecasting and Social Change*, *136*, 18–29.
Dedehayir, O., & Steinert, M. (2016). The hype cycle model: A review and future directions. *Technological Forecasting and Social Change*, *108*, 28–41.
De Dreu, C. K. W., & Weingart, L. R. (2003). Task versus relationship conflict, team performance, and team member satisfaction: A meta-analysis. *Journal of Applied Psychology*, *88*(4), 741–749.
DeFleur, M. L. (1966). *Theories of mass communication* (5th ed.). David McKay.
Dhanaraj, C., & Parkhe, A. (2006). Orchestrating innovation networks. *Academy of Management Review*, *31*(3), 659–669.
Doe, J., Smith, A., & Johnson, M. (2018). Innovation ecosystems and SME collaboration: Leveraging networks for resource access and market reach. *Journal of Business Innovation*, *10*(4), 245–267.
Doyle, P. (2006). *Value-based marketing: Marketing strategies for corporate growth and shareholder value*. John Wiley & Sons.

Drever, C. R., Peterson, G., Messier, C., Bergeron, Y., & Flannigan, M. (2006). Can forest management based on natural disturbances maintain ecological resilience? *Canadian Journal of Forest Research*, *36*(9), 2285–2299.
Dyer, J. H., & Singh, H. (1998). The relational view: Cooperative strategy and sources of interorganizational competitive advantage. *Academy of Management Review*, *23*(4), 660–679.
Eisenhardt, K. M. (1989). Building theories from case study research. *Academy of Management Review*, *14*(4), 532–550.
Eisenhardt, K. M., & Martin, J. A. (2000). Dynamic capabilities: What are they? *Strategic Management Journal*, *21*(10–11), 1105–1121.
Eisenhardt, K. M., & Schoonhoven, C. B. (1990). Organizational growth: Linking founding team, strategy, environment, and growth among U.S. semiconductor ventures, 1978–1988. *Administrative Science Quarterly*, *35*(3), 504–529.
Elliot, P. (1972). *The making of a television series – A case study in the production of culture*. Constable.
Etzkowitz, H., & Klofsten, M. (2005). The innovating region: Toward a theory of knowledge-based regional development. *R&D Management*, *35*(3), 243–255.
Fauconnier, G. (1975). *Mass media and society*. Leuven University Press.
Filipiak, M. (2003). *Homo communicans: Introduction to the theory of mass communication*. Maria Curie-Skłodowska Publishing House.
Fiske, J. (2010). *Introduction to communication studies* (3rd ed.). Routledge.
Fleischer, M. (2022). *Typology of communication*. Primum Verbum.
Fleming, L. (2001). Recombinant uncertainty in technological search. *Management Science*, *47*(1), 117–132.
Fleming, L., & Waguespack, D. M. (2007). Brokerage, boundary spanning, and leadership in open innovation communities. *Organization Science*, *18*(2), 165–180.
Gawer, A. (2014a). Bridging differing perspectives on technological platforms: Toward an integrative framework. *Research Policy*, *43*(7), 1239–1249.
Gawer, A. (2014b). Industry platforms and ecosystem innovation. *Journal of Product Innovation Management*, *31*(3), 417–433.
Gawer, A., & Cusumano, M. A. (2002). *Platform leadership: How Intel, Microsoft, and Cisco drive industry innovation*. Harvard Business School Press.
Gawer, A., & Cusumano, M. A. (2014). Industry platforms and ecosystem innovation. *Journal of Product Innovation Management*, *31*(3), 417–433.
Geroski, P. A., Machin, S., & Van Reenen, J. (1997). The profitability of innovating firms. *RAND Journal of Economics*, *28*(2), 198–211.
Geroski, P. A., & Schröder, M. (1997). The profits of innovating firms. *International Journal of Industrial Organization*, *15*(3), 271–294.
Gibbons, M., Limoges, C., Nowotny, H., Schwartzman, S., Scott, P., & Trow, M. (1994). *The new production of knowledge: The dynamics of science and research in contemporary societies*. Sage Publications.
Gleick, J. (1987). *Chaos: Making a new science*. Viking Press.
Goban-Klas, T. (2008). *Media and mass communication: Theories and analyzes of the press, radio, television and the Internet*. PWN.
Gobble, M. M. (2014). Charting the innovation ecosystem. *Research-Technology Management*, *57*(4), 55–57.
Godfray, H. C. J., Beddington, J. R., Crute, I. R., Haddad, L., Lawrence, D., Muir, J. F., Pretty, J., Robinson, S., Thomas, S. M., & Toulmin, C. (2010). Food security: The challenge of feeding 9 billion people. *Science*, *327*(5967), 812–818.
Godin, B. (2015). *Innovation contested: The idea of innovation over the centuries*. Routledge.
Gomez-Uranga, M., Miguel, J. C., & Zabala-Iturriagagoitia, J. M. (2014). Epigenetic economic dynamics: The evolution of big internet business ecosystems, evidence for patents. *Technovation*, *34*(3), 177–189.

Granstrand, O. (1984). The evolution of the video cassette recorder industry and the main frame computer industry in Japan. *CIM Working Paper*. Chalmers University of Technology.

Granstrand, O. (1993). The evolution of Nordic mobile telephony. *Working Paper*. Department of Industrial Management of Economics. Chalmers University of Technology.

Granstrand, O. (2000). *Corporate innovation systems: A comparative study of multi-technology corporations in Japan, Sweden, and the USA*. Dynacom Series. Chalmers University of Technology.

Granstrand, O. (2018). *Evolving properties of intellectual capitalism: Patents and innovations for growth and welfare*. Edward Elgar Publishing.

Granstrand, O., & Holgersson, M. (2020). Innovation ecosystems: A conceptual review and a new definition. *Technovation*, 90–91.

Grant, R. M. (2016). *Contemporary strategy analysis: Text and cases edition*. John Wiley & Sons.

Griffin, E. A. (2012). *A first look at communication theory* (2nd ed.). McGraw-Hill Book Company.

Grindley, P. (1995). *Standards, strategy, and policy*. Oxford University Press.

Grönroos, C. (2000). *Service management and marketing: A customer relationship management approach* (2nd ed.). John Wiley & Sons.

Guerrero, M., Urbano, D., Fayolle, A., Klofsten, M., & Mian, S. (2016). Entrepreneurial universities: Emerging models in the new social and economic landscape. *Small Business Economics*, *47*(3), 551–563.

Gulati, R. (1995). Social structure and alliance formation patterns: A longitudinal analysis. *Administrative Science Quarterly*, *40*(4), 619–652.

Gulati, R., Wohlgezogen, F., & Zhelyazkov, P. (2012). The two facets of collaboration: Cooperation and coordination in strategic alliances. *Academy of Management Annals*, *6*(1), 531–583.

Hall, S. (1980). Coding and encoding in the television discourse. In S. Hall (Ed.), *Culture, media, language*. Hutchinson. Retrieved August 27, 2023, from https://ia600209.us.archive.org/12/items/ktoub2/02CHallEncodingDecoding.pdf

Hannah, D. P., & Eisenhardt, K. M. (2018). How firms navigate cooperation and competition in nascent ecosystems. *Strategic Management Journal*, *39*(12), 3163–3192.

Hansen, M. T. (1999). The search-transfer problem: The role of weak ties in sharing knowledge across organization subunits. *Administrative Science Quarterly*, *44*(1), 82–111.

Hargadon, A., & Sutton, R. I. (1997). Technology brokering and innovation in a product development firm. *Administrative Science Quarterly*, *42*(4), 716–749.

Harris, P. A., Taylor, R., Minor, B. L., Elliott, V., Fernandez, M., O'Neal, L., McLeod, L., Delacqua, G., Delacqua, F., Kirby, J., & Duda, S. N. (2019). The REDCap consortium: Building an international community of software platform partners. *Journal of Biomedical Informatics*, *95*, 103208.

Holgersson, M., Granstrand, O., & Bogers, M. (2018). The evolution of intellectual property strategy in innovation ecosystems: Uncovering complementary and substitute appropriability regimes. *Long Range Planning*, *51*(2), 303–319.

Holling, C. S. (1973). Resilience and stability of ecological systems. *Annual Review of Ecology and Systematics*, *4*, 1–23.

Holub, R. (1984). *Reception theory*. Methuen.

Hosseini, S., Barker, K., & Ramirez-Marquez, J. E. (2021). Comprehensive framework of influential factors on innovation ecosystem resilience: Using meta-synthesis and structural equation modeling. *International Journal of Engineering*, *34*(2), 331–345.

Hughes, T. P. (1994). Beyond the economics of technology. In O. Granstrand (Ed.), *Economics of technology: Seeking strategies for research and teaching in a developing field* (pp. 425–437). North-Holland.

Hwang, V. W., & Horowitt, G. (2012). *The rainforest: The secret to building the next silicon valley*. Regenwald.
Iansiti, M., & Lakhani, K. R. (2014). Digital ubiquity: How connections, sensors, and data are revolutionizing business. *Harvard Business Review*, *92*(11), 90–99.
Iansiti, M., & Levien, R. (2004a). *The keystone advantage: What the new dynamics of business ecosystems mean for strategy, innovation, and sustainability*. Harvard Business School Press.
Iansiti, M., & Levien, R. (2004b). Strategy as ecology. *Harvard Business Review*, *82*(3), 68–81.
International Association of Science Parks and Areas of Innovation. (2022). *The resilience of innovation ecosystems*. www.iasp.ws/ref.aspx?id=32388&action=show
Jachimowski, M. (2006). *Regions of periodical media communication: Press and political science study on the democratization of media communication*. Publishing House of the University of Silesia.
Jackson, D. J. (2011). *What is an innovation ecosystem*. National Science Foundation.
Jacobides, M. G., Cennamo, C., & Gawer, A. (2018). Towards a theory of ecosystems. *Strategic Management Journal*, *39*(8), 2255–2276.
Jensen, K. B., & Rosengren, K. E. (1990). Five traditions in search of the audience. *European Journal of Communication*, *5*(2/3), 207–232.
Kaplinsky, R., Terheggen, A., & Tijaja, J. (2019). The role of business models in promoting inclusive innovation. *Journal of Cleaner Production*, *220*, 121–133.
Kapoor, R., & Lee, J. M. (2013). Coordinating and competing in ecosystems: How organizational forms shape new technology investments. *Strategic Management Journal*, *34*(3), 274–296.
Katz, R., & Tushman, M. L. (1992). Realizing the potential of the corporate venture. *Harvard Business Review*, *70*(3), 90–101.
Khorakian, A., & Zanjani, M. S. (2020). Comprehensive framework of influential factors on innovation ecosystem resilience: Using meta-synthesis and structural equation modeling. *International Journal of Engineering*, *33*(12), 235–248.
Kim, P. H., Wennberg, K., & Croidieu, G. (2018). The resilience of entrepreneurial ecosystems. *Journal of Business Venturing Insights*, *9*, 99–104.
Kim, W. C., & Mauborgne, R. (2014). Dispel blue ocean myths. *Harvard Business Review*, *92*(5), 64–68.
Koen, P., Ajamian, G., Burkart, R., Clamen, A., Davidson, J., D'Amore, R., Elkins, C., Herald, K., Incorvia, M., Johnson, A., Karol, R., Seibert, R., Slavejkov, A., & Wagner, K. (2001). Providing clarity and a common language to the "fuzzy front end". *Research-Technology Management*, *44*(2), 46–55.
Konietzko, J., Bocken, N., & Hultink, E. J. (2020). Circular ecosystem innovation: An initial set of principles. *Journal of Cleaner Production*, *253*, 119942.
Kshetri, N. (2014). Developing successful entrepreneurial ecosystems: Lessons from a comparison of an Asian tiger and a Baltic tiger. *Baltic Journal of Management*, *9*(3), 330–356.
Kukk, P., Moors, E. H. M., & Hekkert, M. P. (2015). The complexities in system building strategies. *Technological Forecasting and Social Change*, *98*, 176–188.
Kumaniecki, K. (1972). *Polish-Latin dictionary*. PWN.
Kumar, P., Dass, M., & Kumar, S. (2015). From competitive advantage to nodal advantage: Ecosystem structure and the new five forces that affect prosperity. *Business Horizons*, *58*(4), 469–481.
Lasswell, H. (1948). The structure and function of communication in society. In L. Bryson (Ed.), *The communication of ideas*. Harper.
Lavgan, R. (2016). The role of innovation hubs in coordinating and sharing information flows. *International Journal of Innovation Management*, *20*(3), 123–145.
Letaifa, S. B. (2014). The uneasy transition from supply chains to ecosystems: The value-creation/value-capture dilemma. *Management Decision*, *52*(2), 278–295.

Leten, B., Vanhaverbeke, W., Roijakkers, N., Clerix, A., & Van Helleputte, J. (2013). IP models to orchestrate innovation ecosystems: IMEC, a public research institute in nano-electronics. *California Management Review*, *55*(4), 51–64.

Lewicki, R. J., Saunders, D. M., & Barry, B. (2003). *Negotiation*. McGraw-Hill/Irwin.

Lewin, K. (1947). Channels of group life. *Human Relations*, *1*, 143–153.

Li, J. F., & Garnsey, E. (2013). Building joint value: Ecosystem support for global health innovations. In J. E. Oxley, B. Silverman, & R. Adner (Eds.), *Advances in strategic management* (Vol. 30. Collaboration and Competition in Business Ecosystems, pp. 69–96). Emerald Group Publishing Limited.

Li, J. F., & Garnsey, E. (2014). Policy-driven ecosystems for new vaccine development. *Technovation*, *34*(12), 762–772.

Li, Y. R. (2009). The technological roadmap of Cisco's business ecosystem. *Technovation*, *29*(5), 379–386.

Lindgren, R., Eriksson, O., & Lyytinen, K. (2015). Managing identity tensions during mobile ecosystem evolution. *Journal of Information Technology*, *30*(3), 229–244.

Link, A. N., & Scott, J. T. (2016). Identifying factors affecting the activities of technology parks. In *Innovation, entrepreneurship, and technological change*. Oxford University Press.

Lusch, R., Vargo, S. L., & Tanniru, M. (2010). Service, value networks and learning. *Journal of the Academy of Marketing Science*, *38*(1), 19–31.

MacGregor, N., & Madsen, T. L. (2013). Recovery following disruption to an ecosystem: The effects of the internet bust on community evolution. *Journal of Leadership & Organizational Studies*, *20*(4), 465–478.

Maia, C., & Claro, J. (2013). The role of a proof of concept center in a university ecosystem: An exploratory study. *Journal of Technology Transfer*, *38*(5), 641–650.

Mäkinen, S. J., & Dedehayir, O. (2013). Business ecosystems evolution – An ecosystem clockspeed perspective. In J. E. Oxley, B. Silverman, & R. Adner (Eds.), *Advances in strategic management* (Vol. 30. Collaboration and Competition in Business Ecosystems, pp. 99–125). Emerald Group Publishing Limited.

Mäkinen, S. J., Kanniainen, J., & Peltola, I. (2014). Investigating adoption of free beta applications in a platform-based business ecosystem. *Journal of Product Innovation Management*, *31*(3), 451–465.

Maracine, V., & Scarlat, E. (2008). Dynamic knowledge and healthcare knowledge ecosystems. *Proceedings of the 9th European conference on knowledge management* (pp. 459–470). Academic Conferences International Limited.

Markard, J., Raven, R., & Truffer, B. (2012a). Sustainability transitions: An emerging field of research and its prospects. *Research Policy*, *41*(6), 955–967.

Markard, J., Raven, R., & Truffer, B. (2012b). *A multi-level perspective on innovation ecosystems for path-breaking innovation*. Research Policy.

Markham, S. K., Ward, S. J., Aiman-Smith, L., & Kingon, A. I. (2010). The valley of death as context for role theory in product innovation. *Journal of Product Innovation Management*, *27*, 402–417.

McQuail, D. (1992). *Media performance: Mass communication and the public interest*. Sage Publications.

McQuail, D. (2010). *McQuail's mass communication theory* (6th ed.). Sage Publications.

McQuail, D., & Windahl, S. (1993). *Communication models* (2nd ed.). Longman.

Meerow, S., & Newell, J. P. (2015). Resilience and complexity: A bibliometric review and prospects for industrial ecology. *Journal of Industrial Ecology*, *19*(2), 236–251.

Mikułowski Pomorski, J. (1988). *Information and communication: Concepts, mutual relations*. Wydawnictwo Ossolineum.

Moore, J. F. (1993, May–June). Predators and prey: A new ecology of competition. *Harvard Business Review*, pp. 75–86.

Moore, J. F. (1996). *The death of competition: Leadership & strategy in the age of business ecosystems*. Harper Paperbacks.

Morais da Silva, R. L., Segatto, A. P., de Carvalho, A. C. V., & Ribeiro, G. (2020). Social innovation ecosystem and the intensity levels of social entrepreneur cross-sector partnerships. *REGEPE Entrepreneurship and Small Business Journal*, *9*(4), 617–640.
Morgan, R. M., & Hunt, S. D. (1994). The commitment-trust theory of relationship marketing. *Journal of Marketing*, *58*(3), 20–38.
Nambisan, S., & Baron, R. A. (2013). Entrepreneurship in innovation ecosystems: Entrepreneurs' self-regulatory processes and their implications for new venture success. *Entrepreneurship Theory and Practice*, *37*(5), 1071–1097.
Normann, R., & Ramirez, R. (1993). From value chain to value constellation: Designing interactive strategy. *Harvard Business Review*, *71*(4), 65–77.
Oh, D.-S., Phillips, F., Park, S., & Lee, E. (2016a). Innovation ecosystems: A critical examination. *Technovation*, *54*, 1–6.
Oh, D.-S., Phillips, F., Park, S., & Lee, E. (2016b). A multi-level perspective on innovation ecosystems for path-breaking innovation. *Technological Forecasting and Social Change*, *136*, 215–226.
Overholm, H. (2015). Collectively created opportunities in emerging ecosystems: The case of solar service ventures. *Technovation*, *39–40*, 14–25.
Parker, G. G., Van Alstyne, M. W., & Choudary, S. P. (2016). *Platform revolution: How networked markets are transforming the economy – and how to make them work for you*. W. W. Norton & Company.
Pierce, R. (2009). Evaluating information: Validity, reliability, accuracy and triangulation. In R. Pierce (Ed.), *Research methods in politics* (pp. 79–99). Sage Publications.
Pisano, G. P. (2015). You need an innovation strategy. *Harvard Business Review*, *93*(6), 44–54.
Pisano, G. P., & Verganti, R. (2008). Which kind of collaboration is right for you? *Harvard Business Review*, *86*(12), 78–86.
Pisarek, W. (2008). *Introduction to the science of communication*. Wydawnictwo Akademickie i Professionalne.
Porter, M. E. (1998). Clusters and the new economics of competition. *Harvard Business Review*, *76*(6), 77–90.
Porter, M. E., & Kramer, M. R. (2011). Creating shared value. *Harvard Business Review*, *89*(1/2), 62–77.
Pouder, R., & St. John, C. H. (1996). Hot spots and blind spots: Geographical clusters of firms and innovation. *Academy of Management Review*, *21*(4), 1192–1225.
Powell, W. W., Koput, K. W., & Smith-Doerr, L. (1996). Interorganizational collaboration and the locus of innovation: Networks of learning in biotechnology. *Administrative Science Quarterly*, *41*(1), 116–145.
Power, M. E., Tilman, D., Estes, J. A., Menge, B. A., Bond, W. J., Mills, L. S., Daily, G., Castilla, J. C., Lubchenco, J., & Paine, R. T. (1988). Challenges in the quest for keystones. *BioScience*, *46*(8), 609–620.
Prahalad, C. K., & Ramaswamy, V. (2004). Co-creating unique value with customers. *Strategy & Leadership*, *32*(3), 4–9.
Ritala, P., & Almpanopoulou, A. (2017). In defense of "eco" in innovation ecosystem. *Technovation*, *60–61*, 39–42. https://doi.org/10.1016/j.technovation.2016.11.003
Rong, K., Hu, G., Lin, Y., Shi, Y., & Guo, L. (2015). Understanding business ecosystems using a 6C framework in Internet-of-Things-based sectors. *International Journal of Production Economics*, *159*, 41–55. https://doi.org/10.1016/j.ijpe.2014.09.003.
Rosenkopf, L., & Tushman, M. L. (1998). The coevolution of community networks and technology: Lessons from the flight simulation industry. *Industrial and Corporate Change*, *7*(2), 311–346.
Rothaermel, F. T., Agung, S. D., & Jiang, L. (2007). University entrepreneurship: A taxonomy of the literature. *Industrial and Corporate Change*, *16*(4), 691–791.
Saxenian, A. (1994). *Regional advantage: Culture and competition in silicon valley and route 128*. Harvard University Press.

Scott, W. R. (2016). *Institutions and organizations: Ideas, interests, and identities* (4th ed.). Sage Publications.
Shane, S., & Venkataraman, S. (2000). The promise of entrepreneurship as a field of research. *Academy of Management Review, 25*(1), 217–226.
Shannon, C. E. (1948). A mathematical theory of communication. Part 1. *The Bell System Technical Journal, 27*, 379–423.
Shannon, C. E., & Weaver, W. (1964). *A mathematical theory of communication* (10th ed.). University of Illinois Press.
Shuter, R. (1979). *Understanding misunderstandings: Exploring interpersonal communication.* HarperCollins Publishers.
Smith, A., Brown, J., & Jones, R. (2016). Building innovation ecosystems: The role of universities and research institutions. *Journal of Innovation Management, 10*(2), 123–145.
Strogatz, S. H. (2001). Exploring complex networks. *Nature, 410*(6825), 268–276.
Sund, K. J., Galavan, R. J., & Brusoni, S. (Eds.). (2018). *Cognition and innovation: New horizons in managerial and organizational cognition.* Emerald Publishing Limited.
Teece, D. J. (2007). Explicating dynamic capabilities: The nature and microfoundations of (sustainable) enterprise performance. *Strategic Management Journal, 28*(13), 1319–1350.
Teece, D. J. (2018). Approaches for resilience and antifragility in collaborative business ecosystems. *Technological Forecasting and Social Change, 151.*
Thomas, L. D. W., & Autio, E. (2020). Innovation ecosystems. *SSRN Electronic Journal.* https://papers.ssrn.com/sol3/papers.cfm?abstract_id=3476925
Tsujimoto, M., Kajikawa, Y., Tomita, J., & Matsumoto, Y. (2018a). A multi-level perspective on innovation ecosystems for path-breaking innovation. *Technological Forecasting and Social Change, 136*, 49–58.
Tsujimoto, M., Kajikawa, Y., Tomita, J., & Matsumoto, Y. (2018b). Unpacking the innovation ecosystem construct: Evolution, gaps, and trends. *Technological Forecasting and Social Change, 136*, 30–48.
Uzzi, B. (1997). Social structure and competition in interfirm networks: The paradox of embeddedness. *Administrative Science Quarterly, 42*(1), 35–67.
van Oppen, M. J. H., Oliver, J. K., Putnam, H. M., & Gates, R. D. (2015). Building coral reef resilience through assisted evolution. *Proceedings of the National Academy of Sciences, 112*(8), 2307–2313.
Vargo, S. L., & Lusch, R. F. (2016). Institutions and axioms: An extension and update of service-dominant logic. *Journal of the Academy of Marketing Science, 44*(1), 5–23.
von Hippel, E. (1988). *The sources of innovation.* Oxford University Press.
Walker, B., Holling, C. S., Carpenter, S. R., & Kinzig, A. (2004). Resilience, adaptability and transformability in social–ecological systems. *Ecology and Society, 9*(2), 5.
Wasserman, S., & Faust, K. (1994). *Social network analysis: Methods and applications* (Vol. 8). Cambridge University Press.
West, J., & Bogers, M. (2014). Leveraging external sources of innovation: A review of research on open innovation. *Journal of Product Innovation Management, 31*(4), 814–831.
West, J., & Wood, D. (2013). Evolving an open ecosystem: The rise and fall of the Symbian platform. In J. E. Oxley, B. Silverman, & R. Adner (Eds.), *Advances in strategic management* (Vol. 30. Collaboration and Competition in Business Ecosystems, pp. 27–67). Emerald Group Publishing Limited.
Wilkinson, M. D., Dumontier, M., Aalbersberg, I. J., Appleton, G., Axton, M., Baak, A., & Mons, B. (2016). The FAIR Guiding Principles for scientific data management and stewardship. *Scientific Data, 3*, 160018.
World Economic Forum. (2024). *Shaping cooperation in a fragmenting world report.* www.weforum.org/publications/shaping-cooperation-in-a-fragmenting-world/

Wuchty, S., Jones, B. F., & Uzzi, B. (2007). The increasing dominance of teams in production of knowledge. *Science*, *316*(5827), 1036–1039.
Yoo, Y., Henfridsson, O., & Lyytinen, K. (2010). The new organizing logic of digital innovation: An agenda for information systems research. *Information Systems Research*, *21*(4), 724–735.
Zahra, S. A., & Nambisan, S. (2012). Entrepreneurship and strategic thinking in business ecosystems. *Business Horizons*, *55*(3), 219–229.
Zineldin, M. (2004). Co-opetition: The organisation of the future. *Marketing Intelligence & Planning*, *22*(7), 780–789.

2 Strong communication in reaching and motivating all actors of innovation ecosystems

Introduction

This chapter delves into the key role of communication within organizational settings, emphasizing its significance not just as a mere conduit for information, but as a fundamental component that permeates all aspects of the innovation ecosystem. Through an interdisciplinary approach that weaves together theories from social communication, management, psychology, cognitive science, and sociology, this section provides a comprehensive analysis of the complex nature of communication. It posits communication as a multifaceted process integral to the exchange of data, motivation of personnel, building of relationships, and establishment of emotional connections within organizations.

Communication is portrayed as an essential element across various operational levels of an organization, critically influencing management processes and organizational dynamics. The chapter highlights the challenges and barriers that can hinder effective communication, with a particular focus on interpersonal interactions. By exploring different stages and dimensions of interpersonal communication, and various forms that communication can take within and between entities, the text provides a detailed insight into the mechanisms that underpin organizational discourse.

A significant portion of the chapter is dedicated to examining influential factors that affect the quality and effectiveness of communication. These include individual attributes, organizational cultures, technological interfaces, and physical and psychological environments in which communication occurs. By analyzing these factors, the chapter offers valuable perspectives on how they shape the dynamics of communication and, by extension, affect the overall efficacy of organizational operations.

In addition to internal communication mechanisms, this chapter also provides a nuanced examination of communication styles, including the ground-breaking concept of "neuronal synchronization" between speaker and listener. This concept illustrates how physiological processes can enhance or impede the transmission of messages, thus affecting mutual understanding and collaborative efforts. The complexities of communication networks are

DOI: 10.4324/9781032697802-3

discussed, detailing the roles of various communication media in facilitating the flow of information between sender and receiver(s).

As the narrative progresses, it shifts focus toward external communication strategies. It covers crucial topics such as organizational identity, image, and reputation management, alongside strategic communication planning. The chapter discusses how communication gaps can arise and the methodologies to bridge these gaps, including effective networking and the strategic use of social media. These discussions are critical for organizations looking to enhance their external visibility and interaction with broader stakeholder groups.

Lastly, the chapter sets the stage for understanding communication as a cornerstone of functionality within innovative organizations. It frames communication not only as a foundational element of organizational operations but also as a dynamic and strategic tool that can significantly enhance interactions within and across the boundaries of the innovation ecosystem. Through this lens, the chapter aims to equip readers with a deeper understanding of the strategic applications of communication. This includes fostering innovation, resolving problems, and enhancing collaboration among diverse stakeholders, ultimately contributing to the organization's competitive edge and adaptive capacity in the ever-evolving business landscape.

Communication as a key value in relationships approach

For some, communication constitutes the exchange of information, while for others, it is understood more broadly as a significant element of interpersonal relationships, something that builds and constitutes such relationships. From the perspective of language theory, "communication is a plane of acquiring knowledge, acquiring skills, and transmitting information to other people" (Eysenck & Keane, 2000, pp. 363–364). M.A. Hogg and G.M. Vaughan (2005, p. 576) describe communication as the transmission of information with specific meanings from one person to another.

Certainly, communication is a process "in which participants create and share information with each other in order to achieve mutual understanding" (Rogers & Kincaid, 1982, p. 16). It occurs at various levels. As mentioned in the first chapter, D. McQuail identified five levels of communication (McQuail, 2010), including:

a) Intrapersonal communication – it is a biological and psychological process where information is processed within the individual (Cunningham, 1992, pp. 1–2). The sender and the receiver are the same entity, and the dialogue with oneself arises based on one's own feelings and beliefs (Gesell, 2007, pp. 5–6). It influences other types of communication while being influenced by them.
b) Interpersonal communication – a psychological process through which an individual communicates and receives information during direct contact

with other people (face-to-face conversations). It involves the exchange of verbal and non-verbal symbols for collaboration. J. Stewart's definition describes interpersonal communication as "the type, quality, or kind of contact that occurs when individuals speak or listen in a manner that maximizes what is personal" (Stewart, 2002, p. 25). This process is continuous because the sender constantly conveys a specific message through body posture, gestures, facial expressions, and words, and the receiver interprets it.

c) Group (organizational) communication – refers to the process of exchanging information among group members (interactions occur between three or more people). It is geared toward task accomplishment and involves overcoming barriers related to obligations, socio-emotional needs, and environmental factors. In this case, the communication process serves as the primary tool to deal with these issues and constitutes a general model of group decision-making.
d) Institutional communication – a formalized process in which specific roles are assigned to senders and receivers, and authority and control over the latter are clearly defined.
e) Mass communication – conducted through the media (traditional and new). It is the broadest communication process utilizing complex technology (Jasnowitz) – it enables the dissemination of messages to large groups of people (Chaffee & Metzger, 2001), regardless of distance or time.

In the 21st century, all levels of communication occur within the innovation ecosystem. Employees make decisions based on internal dialogue (intrapersonal communication). Employees communicate directly with each other in the workplace (interpersonal communication). Employers use communication as a tool to accomplish tasks with employees (organizational communication) and formalize processes through communication (institutional communication). They also utilize media to reach both internal and external environments (mass communication) using modern technologies. This is done through both linguistic and non-linguistic communication.[1]

Communication fulfills several important functions in the human resource management process in organizations, including within the innovation ecosystem. These functions include (Listwan, 2004, p. 289):

a) informational – providing necessary information for decision-making and task coordination;
b) instructional – issuing commands and explaining who, when, and what actions need to be taken to achieve specified goals;
c) control – exercising control and evaluating the work performed, as well as providing feedback on the evaluation results;
d) motivational – strengthening engagement in organizational tasks, goal achievement, involving management actions aimed at motivation;

e) integrative – integrating individual units into one organizational whole, it is a process of socialization and professional assimilation;
f) emotional (expressive) – expressing opinions and feelings such as dissatisfaction, concerns, frustrations, and a "safety valve" in interpersonal relationships.

Among the key aspects of communication in the innovation ecosystem, the establishment of collaboration between various entities such as businesses, universities, research institutes, startups, and investors stands out. This facilitates the transfer of knowledge and know-how among different participants, making scientific and technological achievements accessible and utilized by various parties, thus accelerating the innovation process. It also serves as a method for problem-solving through problem identification, information exchange, and attempts at discussion to find solutions. Through communication, participants in the innovation ecosystem can also develop networks and build business and academic relationships. Communication also plays an important role in promoting innovative products, technologies, and services, making them available in the market. Informing potential customers, business partners, and investors about innovative solutions enables the commercialization of research and development outcomes (Pałys, 2023).

Communication is a means of conveying information that is hindered by so-called "communication barriers" (Lunenburg, 2010, pp. 1–11). These are disruptions that occur between the sender and receiver in this process (Pearce et al., 1984, pp. 518, 526). Generally, most typical communication misunderstandings are related to the incorrect interpretation of verbal code by an individual, stemming from physical (e.g., hearing difficulties, slips of the tongue) or semiotic reasons (e.g., linguistic deficiencies in expressions). German communication researcher H. Reimann distinguishes three types of disturbances (Reimann, 1974, p. 99), misunderstandings concerning: the substance of the sign – its material use as a carrier of specific content; the potential of the sign – its interpretational possibilities; and the value of the sign – the concreteness of its meanings.

From an operational standpoint, communication barriers can be categorized into groups (cf. Pachori, 2023a, pp. 29–30):

a) Individual communication barriers – comprising errors and disturbances caused by incorrect interpretation of verbal and non-verbal codes, stemming from biological, personality, or intellectual conditions, or arising from discrepancies in communicative goals and attitudes.
b) Social communication barriers – arising from cultural and environmental differences among partners, membership in open or elitist social environments, social control establishing formalized communication rules, technicization, institutionalization, and commercialization of information.

c) Technical communication barriers – related to the kinesthetic specificity of partners and the physical environment (e.g., noise and other physical limitations of the environment and communication partners, malfunctioning of the information channel relay, inadequately selected relay – information channel).

From a holistic perspective within the innovation ecosystem, the main communication barriers include:

a) Language barrier: Lack of proficiency in English as a business language hinders international communication among participants.
b) Diverse action perspectives and understanding of reality: Various entities in the innovation ecosystem (businesses, universities, research institutes, startups) have their own goals, language, and organizational culture, making communication between them challenging.
c) Lack of trust: Unfamiliarity among innovation ecosystem participants limits openness in collaboration, impacting communication processes.
d) Competition and conflicts of interest: Competition among different entities in the innovation ecosystem can lead to antagonisms, affecting communication between conflicting actors.
e) Lack of engagement and participation: Inactive participation in the innovation ecosystem reduces the intensity of communication, weakening information flow.
f) Information overload: Even rationally justified, uncontrolled quantitative and qualitative flow of messages can lead to negative consequences and increase uncertainty among communication process partners.

In management theory, motivation is recognized as one of the fundamental functions of management. It is crucial for organizations (Burton, 2012, p. 6). Motivation involves optimizing employees' behaviors through appropriately selected tools – sets of material (financial) and non-material (non-financial) means that, by satisfying employees' needs, influence their engagement in work. The emphasis on utilizing these tools has evolved over the past few decades (Hackman, 1977, pp. 129–130) in relation to internal and external conditions and views on motivation.[2] Currently, in business environment institutions, a situational and flexible approach to motivating participants in the innovation ecosystem is dominant. It involves individually treating employees, which depends on internal conditions (e.g., individual needs, values, and aspirations) and external conditions (e.g., rewards, penalties, and social incentives). In addition to reward systems, professional development, and delegating responsibility, communication, including feedback, is considered among the motivational techniques that managers can use to stimulate their employees to achieve better results. It often depends on the leader to motivate them (so-called leadership motivation). Regular communication with employees, providing them with feedback on their work, and acknowledging their achievements can significantly influence their engagement based on the adopted motivation system in the organization. In the context of significant importance, the issue of "feedback" becomes relevant, which is the recipient's reaction to the message after its decoding. It tells us whether the message was heard/seen and understood. It involves the reciprocal impact of the effect of a specific phenomenon on its cause. It is a process in which the communicative action of the sender turns into the communicative reaction of the recipient. It can be direct or indirect, immediate or delayed, and positive (enhancing actions) or negative (weakening actions). From a management perspective, feedback represents the process of evaluating and analyzing the effects of actions. When applied, we receive feedback, which is essential for professional development (Stone & Heen, 2015, p. 348). It is a mechanism that enables continuous improvement and adaptation based on external or internal feedback (Chandler & Grealish, 2019). It provides employees with data on how others perceive their behaviors and actions (e.g., as part of their annual assessment). It is also a significant element of team management (Coyle, 2023, p. 384), allowing managers to track progress, identify problematic areas requiring improvement, and encourage employee self-development (Scott, 2019, p. 336).

Communication, as the process of transmitting information and achieving mutual understanding among individuals (Keyton, 2011), is a significant element of social interaction (Lunenburg, 2010). It constitutes a fundamental life skill that largely determines professional fulfillment and happiness in relationships with others (McKay et al., 2019). In a world where boundaries between cultures and geography blur due to technological advancement, the ability to effectively communicate and build business relationships becomes a key factor in success (Lewis et al., 2003). Interaction, both in direct form and through digital media, plays a central role in the development and maintenance of these relationships.

Interpersonal communication

Interpersonal communication is an essential element in entrepreneurship and management. It is directly linked to the fundamental functions of management, namely planning, organizing, motivating, and controlling. It is a psychological process through which individuals transmit and receive information during interactions with other people. The process of interpersonal communication consists of several stages on the part of the sender and receiver. Initially, the sender formulates thoughts about what they want to convey. Accompanying these thoughts are intentions (conscious and unconscious) and emotions (positive and negative). The former are the reasons why we want to communicate something to someone. The motives for sending a message may include:

a) satisfying the sender's needs (physiological, emotional, intellectual);
b) meeting the recipient's needs;

c) acquainting the recipient with the sender's views and emotions;
d) relieving tension and thereby releasing oneself from negative emotions;
e) jointly solving a task between the sender and receiver.

(Bough & Condrill, 1998, p. 111)

Due to the emotions expressed, the communication process is characterized by high dynamics. External stimuli can influence the variability of reactions between the sender and the receiver. Hence, it is a variable process.

In the second stage, encoding takes place. Thoughts are transformed into a specific form within which they are to be communicated. Communication can be verbal or non-verbal (Pachori, 2023b, pp. 25–26). To increase the effectiveness of communication, it is important to select a code that is accessible and understandable to both the sender and the receiver. Encoding of the message depends on the sender's knowledge (a set of credible data about the surrounding world) and experience (the ability to use knowledge). Then, the message is ready to be sent through selected communication channels (verbal, non-verbal, written) and media (e.g., email, telephone, video chat, etc.). In the next part, the receiver receives the encoded message, which they filter – they select certain elements of the data. This is done due to the multitude of signals being transmitted or due to the receiver's level of concentration. The receiver then attempts to decode and interpret the message. The received codes provide a basis for reconstructing the message received from the sender, after which the receiver – according to their knowledge and skills – processes the filtered message into their own symbols and assigns them meaning. They interpret the information (articulate intentions) and relate it to their own experiences, giving it meaning.

The above process exemplifies a type of one-way communication, involving the transmission of a message from the sender to the receiver without obtaining feedback (e.g., a newsletter sent from an employer to an employee). We also distinguish two-way communication (Harrison & Williams, 2020, pp. 310–318), in which both parties are active participants in the communication process, exchanging information, opinions, and feelings, as well as actively listening and reacting to each other's messages. This is an interactive process that requires engagement from both participants. Two-way communication is more precise because the sender can determine whether the message has been understood by the receiver and can provide additional information if necessary. Moreover, this form of communication fosters the development of relationships between the sender and the receiver. In this scheme, the sender can become the receiver, and the receiver can become the sender. The latter awaits feedback. This form of communication allows for asking questions, expressing opinions, and interpreting the interlocutor's behavior, providing a basis for understanding the intentions of the other party.

From the perspective of interpersonal communication, it is essential, for the purposes of this publication, to adopt five axioms presented in the literature (Watzlawick et al., 1967, p. 284). The first assumes that every behavior carries communicative significance (including avoiding agreement). The second underscores the dual nature of the message. It consists not only of its content (information) but also of its relational aspect (the sender's attitude toward the receiver). The next axiom views the message in two ways: as a response to the partner's message, reinforcing the partner's previous behavior, or as a stimulus for the partner's subsequent specific behavior (the circular nature of communication). Both sides mutually influence each other through interaction, hence the cause and effect of partners' behaviors cannot be rigidly determined. The following axiom delineates communication into verbal and nonverbal components. Both are crucial for a complete and accurate communication process. The final axiom distinguishes between complementary interactions (one partner yields to the other, who initiates the action) and symmetrical interactions (partners are somewhat on equal footing).

Characteristics of interpersonal communication, as a complex and multidimensional phenomenon, were outlined by O. Hargie et al. (2004, pp. 13–22), identifying five features. The first asserts that communication is transactional, possessing a dynamic and variable nature. The sender formulating the message influences the receiver, who in turn affects the sender through their feedback reaction. The second of the scientists' mentioned features speaks to the inevitability of communication. In social situations, people, aware of their presence, interact with each other almost automatically. The third feature emphasizes the purposefulness of communication, as the individuals participating in it have a goal of interaction in mind, aiming to achieve a desired outcome. Another feature is the multi-channel nature of communication. Information is most often delivered on multiple levels – the substantive content of the message and the relationship between the interaction participants. The final feature underscores the irreversibility of communication, where spoken words and expressed gestures cannot be retracted. However, the direction of communication itself can change, depending on the actions and intentions of its participants. Interpersonal communication in this sense is a two-way and multifaceted process (Narula, 2006, p. 410). This means that at least two people participate in it, engaging in a dynamic and evolving sequence of communication events, mutually influencing each other and collectively shaping the stable outcome of the interaction.

It is worth emphasizing that during interpersonal communication, the following dimensions are realized:

a) Informational dimension – conveying messages – particular importance is attached to it by four rules of cooperation by H.P. Grice (1980, pp. 91–114), namely the rules of quantity, relevance, quality, and manner. Conveying information related to the conversation topic and providing it in the appropriate quantity, considering relevant and truthful information using specific channels and tools, are important for the full realization of the informational dimension of communication.

b) Emotional-energetic dimension – the sender's attitude toward the receiver – analogies to linguistic expressive and impressive functions according to R. Jakobson (1989, pp. 77–124) can be found here.
c) Participation – joint participation in something – enables the transition from message to contact. Based on the jointly shared knowledge about common actions, communication process participants engage in shared activities. They are focused not so much on themselves but on the subject of communication (Clark, 1996, p. 432).
d) Relational dimension – concerns the relationship between the sender and the receiver – P. Watzlawick et al. (1967, p. 304) – as already mentioned – believe that there are two types of relationships between individuals: symmetrical (characterized by equality and mutual reflection of behaviors between the sender and the receiver) and complementary (complementing one partner's behavior with the behaviors of the other, where one person occupies a higher position and the other a subordinate, lower position). Both types of relationships are determined by the social context and the roles played.

The aforementioned four dimensions of communication can influence the development of communication process participants, provided that: all of them occur simultaneously in the process of interpersonal communication and appear in the correct proportions, depending on the situation, the individuals involved in communication, and the communicative goal they pursue (Frydrychowicz, 2005, p. 97).

It is worth emphasizing that individual determinants of communication behaviors can be divided into factors of biological, socio-professional, and psychological nature. The first are associated, for instance, with the division of employees into women and men (often stereotypical). Female gender is often associated by employers with traits such as empathy, expressiveness, and emotionality. On the other hand, in the perception of men – employees, traits like rationality, tendency toward dominance, or the desire to control the course of conversation prevail (Wood, 2009, p. 372). Also, the criterion of age plays a role in communication processes in the context of interlocutors' behaviors. Older individuals are expected to exhibit greater caution in word choice, distance, and rationality. Younger people, however, are expected to be more open, spontaneous, and at the same time, are anticipated to display greater impulsivity (which is often justified) in communication actions (Rosengren, 2006, p. 72). These factors also include health status (poor health condition hampers the communication process) and attractiveness (people tend to attribute positive traits to attractive individuals, which facilitate the achievement of their intended goal). Social-professional factors include marital status or economic status, which (due to their level) can either hinder or facilitate communication due to the sense of confidence or uncertainty, for example. This catalog also includes education and profession. Individuals with higher education or specific professions (e.g., academic teacher) are expected to have better communication skills. Psychological factors include abilities – including competencies (Olson, 2002, p. 173; Spitzberg et al., 1994, pp. 83–202) and experience, intelligence, personality, need system, motivation, and espoused values.

Effective interpersonal communication is a process that should culminate in finding meaning for its participants (Bolton, 1986, p. 324). Ch. Duhigg (2024, pp. 19–21) distinguished three different speeches in interpersonal communication. The first serves decision-making and focuses on "what is really going on?" The next one focuses on emotions, with the predominant question being "how do we feel?" The third one has a social dimension, aimed at discovering "who we are?" All three of these orientations are closely related. Misunderstandings occur when people engage in different types of conversations. Because "effective communication requires recognizing the type of communication we are dealing with, and then mutual adaptation" (ibid., p. 23). Therefore, in interpersonal communication, it is valuable to apply clarifying conversations, conducted based on four principles contained in the following imperatives:

a) Pay attention to the type of conversation.
b) Talk about your goals and ask others what they aim for.
c) Ask other people about their feelings and share your own.
d) Check whether identities are important for this conversation.

The purpose of clarifying conversation is to understand what is happening in others' minds and share with them what is happening in ours. It enables mutual adjustment of interlocutors by showing all participants that our intention is to understand the other side and build mutual bonds. In this aspect, it should be assumed that in the process of interpersonal communication, there is a transition from interaction to communication and to contact. This means that communication process participants first interact with each other, then – while being in interaction – communicate and sometimes establish contact between each other. Thus, interaction, communication, and contact can be recognized as stages of the interpersonal communication process (ibid., p. 36).

Research by scientists (Müller et al., 2018, pp. 198–210; Richardson et al., 2007, pp. 407–413) indicates that to communicate with someone, one must build a bond (Ackermann & Bargh, 2010; online; Mogan et al., 2017, pp. 13–20). Communication serves this purpose. Already in 1995, E. and A. Aron took on the task of verifying whether there is a technique for building bonds (creating closeness) among individuals who do not know each other. They established that the fact of having the same views or experiences does not determine the building of relationships.[3] However, the rule that undoubtedly helped in their establishment boiled down to asking a series of questions within the communication process. Questions served as a method of opening up to the interlocutor (Aron et al., 1997, pp. 363–367). They were dubbed the "Fast Friends Procedure." However, this procedure only worked when experiment participants asked each other questions alternately. This reciprocity allowed the interlocutors to adapt to the highs and lows of the other party. Scientists proved that emotional bond arises through asking deep questions and reciprocating vulnerability to hurt (so-called "emotional contagion"). They noticed that people become susceptible to this when we show sensitive areas in conversation and expose ourselves to judgment (which creates a sense of intimacy in us). The conclusion of the research boiled down to the observation that asking deep questions about feelings, experiences, values, and beliefs increases vulnerability to hurt, thus emotionally infecting, resulting in building a bond. In the context of the significant importance, the element of human emotional intelligence takes on empathy as the ability to recognize and empathize with the emotions of others, the ability to put oneself in the shoes of that person, and to look at the situation from their point of view.

In the realm of interpersonal communication, the quality and effectiveness of human interaction are influenced by several factors: active listening (such as the ability to focus on the speaker, understand their point of view, and respond to their messages in a way that demonstrates interest and empathy); verbal expression (expressing one's thoughts, feelings, and needs using words in a clear, understandable, and respectful manner to other participants in the conversation); nonverbal communication (gestures, facial expressions, body posture, and tone of voice convey a wealth of information about our intentions and emotions); emotional intelligence (understanding one's own emotions and the ability to recognize and manage the emotions of others to build healthy relationships).

Active listening is a technique involving attentive and conscious reception of what the speaker is saying. This includes not only understanding the meaning of verbal communication but also paying attention to nonverbal aspects. Its purpose is to holistically understand the sender's message, which facilitates building relationships between communication partners. It also helps to mitigate the risk of being misled by the speaker. This is significant, as researchers (DePaulo et al., 1996, pp. 979–995) have suggested that individuals lie on average once or twice a day, implying that daily encounters with falsehoods are probable during interactions with others. Conversely et al. (2004, pp. 48–59), based on their research, found that each person in the communication process plays the role of both deceived and deceiving. Therefore, active listening also serves as a barrier against (conscious or unconscious) attempts by the sender to mislead the recipient.

Effective interpersonal communication relies on a solid foundation of verbal communication between the speakers. Friedemann Schulz von Thun (2003), in his book "The Art of Talking: Analysis of Disturbances," presented four basic pillars supporting the communication process and its proper understanding, developed from a research project and termed "basic principles of the Hamburg concept of better communication." The first of these pillars entails simplicity in formulating statements (sentences should be short and factual). The next pillar is structured composition in constructing text according to the accepted grammar rules of the language, as well as conciseness referring to succinctness in expressing thoughts. Additional stimulation, or appropriate stylistic means, constitutes the final pillar of information delivery (ibid., 10–11). Verbal expression also entails choosing such verbal attire that will not cause cognitive dissonance in the recipient. It should therefore be based on respect for the interlocutor.

People communicate non-verbally through facial expressions, tone of voice, gestures, body posture and movements, touch, and gaze. Effective interpersonal communication entails the ability to decode the nonverbal communication of the speaker. When interpreting someone's behavior, individuals can largely "put it into words" and then "they become a verbal phenomenon" (Knapp, 1979, p. 3). Nonverbal communication carries attitudes, informs about experienced emotions, and indicates the type of experiences, both individual and culturally grounded. It provides the opportunity to directly control not only the entire communication process but also the environment in which communication takes place (Hickson & Stacks, 1985, p. 15).

The initiator of research into emotional intelligence was H. Gardner (1989, p. 529), who included in it: intrapersonal intelligence, involving skills related to understanding and regulating one's own emotions (self-relationships), and interpersonal intelligence, which relies on the ability to understand and manage interpersonal relationships (relationships with others). Meanwhile, D.R. Caruso and P. Salovey included the following components in emotional intelligence: recognizing and becoming aware of one's own and others' emotions, using emotions in thinking and actions, understanding emotions, and managing emotions (Caruso & Salovey, 2009, pp. 8–9). An important element from the perspective of leadership in an organization is the specific phenomenon of emotional contagion in the communication process. All emotional skills are based on the fact that people can influence each other's mood. This is a natural phenomenon that occurs continuously (Śmietańska, 2017, p. 32). Thus, recognizing and consciously managing the emotions of the interlocutor based on the discovery and articulation of one's own emotions allows for increased effectiveness of communication and contributes to building positive relationships.

The process of interpersonal communication, which undergoes transformations depending on place, time, and space, requires special predispositions from its partners. Being an evolving process over time, it obliges them to continuously analyze mutual behaviors and changing sequences of statements. Increasing the effectiveness of individual acts and the entire process of communication is possible only by considering its variability, which can be the cause of many misunderstandings. Therefore, when discussing the process of interpersonal communication, special attention should be paid to errors and disturbances occurring in it. Communication barriers can be corrected, on the one hand, by properly chosen verbal and nonverbal communication forms, or on the other hand, by feedback, which enables partners in interpersonal communication to establish specific meanings of the expressions they use.

D. Halloran stated: "One should not take for granted the assumption that information necessarily reduces uncertainty. Indeed, and this is entirely clear from research, under certain circumstances, providing information can quite clearly lead to an increase in uncertainty" (Halloran, 1983, p. 160). According to him, this happens in the case of information overload, which in the 21st century can contribute to the emergence of communication noise between the sender and the receiver.[4,5] Its manifestation is redundancy, which is a kind of surplus (informational and meaningful), the assumption of which is to support the understanding process in communication but can become a barrier to it. Its variation in the form of reduplication (repetition, which draws the listener's attention to a specific part of the statement) can also contribute to disruptions in the communication act due to excessive development of the statement. The role of the sender in interpersonal communication is to choose vocabulary in such a way as to mitigate this risk.

During the process of interpersonal communication between the sender and the receiver, the phenomenon of "dissonance" may also occur. This refers to a situation in which the receiver disregards information that is inconsistent with their beliefs. Researchers (Potocki et al., 2003, p. 41) termed this phenomenon an "information gap" and identified two manifestations of it. The first is the "gap of informational hope," which occurs when the receiver receives incomplete information that does not allow them to take expected actions, while simultaneously hoping for its completion in the future from the sender. The second is the "gap of informational disagreement," when the receiver disagrees with part or all of the message and does not use it to make any decision. In this case, the effectiveness of communication may depend on the vigilance of the sender, who can retransmit the information or ask the receiver for their opinion on the content conveyed.

Mutual understanding, which is key to collaboration, can be facilitated through the aforementioned feedback. J. Stankiewicz (2006, pp. 56–57) categorized it into four types. The first is estimated feedback, which occurs when we discuss our opinion or present our position on a particular matter. The second is positively assessing feedback, which serves to maintain contact with the receiver and express our approval on a given matter. The third is negatively assessing feedback, which helps clarify any ambiguities and correct errors made by the sender. The last is non-assessing feedback, which refers to our judgments and opinions on a specific matter, showing interest in the partner's messages. This classification, supplemented by J. Ober (2013, p. 263), includes three additional types of feedback: confirming, which occurs when the receiver confirms receipt and understanding of the message from the sender; supplementary, which is the receiver's request for additional information to complement the messages; and nonverbal, which involves gestures, body movements, and facial expressions that communicate our feelings about the received messages to the sender. All of the above feedback types become helpful in moments of incomplete clarity in understanding the content of the message by the receiver.

In the context of interpersonal and group communication, it is valuable to refer to communication styles (Pecukonis, 1990, pp. 113–143) regarding the work environment. This term can be considered in two ways:

a) As a level of communication taking into account the number of people involved in the communication and the degree of closeness of contact between these individuals.
b) As a category dividing people based on how they function in the communication process.

For the purposes of this publication, the authors – considering the analysis of the innovation ecosystem in terms of communication – will primarily refer to the second understanding of this concept. From this perspective, four communication styles can be distinguished (Rancer & Avtgis, 2006, p. 321):

a) Aggressive – an aggressive person expresses what they want and what their needs are without considering the other side of the communication.
b) Assertive – an assertive person can express their opinion without offending others, while also acting in accordance with their own feelings.
c) Passive – a passive person often lacks their own opinion and yields to others, giving the impression of weakness and insecurity, and is easily manipulated.
d) Passive-aggressive – a person with this style can easily be mistaken for a passive individual because they appear quiet and submissive, but they manipulate others to achieve their goals.

It's worth emphasizing that the most effective communication style is the second one mentioned earlier. The assertive style allows for expressing one's opinion in interpersonal communication in a non-offensive manner. The communicator articulates their needs without violating ethical principles toward the interlocutor. This style is essential for conflict resolution and achieving agreement.

Communication styles can also be categorized on the basis of the criterion of focus. Using this criterion, three categories of individuals can be distinguished. The first focuses on themselves, the second on the partner, and the third on both themselves and the receiver. The first two styles represent a non-partnered form of communication, while the last one embodies a partnered communication style, which is highly essential in the contemporary world.

Intergroup communication

Interpersonal communication elements also pertain to group communication and intergroup communication within an organization. The linkage between management and communication in an organization occurs on several levels. Processes such as planning, organizing, controlling, or accounting for effective implementation require efficient communication. Managers of an organization continuously communicate with other entities or subordinate teams. H. Mintzberg noted as early as 1973 that managers spend 50–90% of their working time on conversations (Mintzberg, 1973, p. 165). He identified three types of roles played by managers that are related to the communication process. The first – interpersonal – boils down to the symbol of leadership in an organizational unit tasked with understanding all actors in that ecosystem. The second – informational – pertains to acquiring knowledge necessary for performing duties and also transmitting information to others about the functioning of the unit. The last – decisional – comes down to implementing decisions made based on acquired information and communicating to the environment about their adoption (Mintzberg, 1975, pp. 5–10). Conscious communication is the tool for effectively fulfilling these roles.

From the perspective of organizational functioning, B. Galambaud's statement (1988, p. 17) about the impossibility of equating informing with communicating seems valid (Deetz, 1995, p. 68). The former occurs when the relationship occurs between individuals and facts (aiming to equip people with relevant data). The latter requires the establishment of relationships among process participants (its goals go beyond the informational aspect). From this perspective, informing equips employees with data about what is happening in the organization, while communicating creates a sense of belonging to it, increases motivation, and builds relationships between entities (Donjean, 2006, pp. 69–70).

Thus, communication in the organization has two groups of goals related to informing and communicating. The first aims to transmit data necessary for its daily functioning, while the second is associated with shaping a sense of belonging to the organization (Rencker, 2008, p. 36). An interesting approach in this regard is presented by Donjean (2006, p. 15), for whom communication serves as a management tool supporting the implementation of organizational strategy. Its primary goal is to provide personnel with information necessary for both the smooth functioning of the organization and the proper fulfillment of duties by its members. Transmission of messages enables the accomplishment of employee tasks and collaboration. The researcher also considers the communicative aspect, aimed at generating a sense of identity with the organization (through motivating people, developing organizational culture and values, promoting cooperation, building a positive company image among staff, and increasing the level of employee integration).

The main division of communication in the organization boils down to distinguishing between internal and external communication. The former is defined as an organized process of exchanging information, knowledge, and values, often associated with the conducted business strategy. In the literature, it is increasingly treated as an independent process that influences many aspects of organizational functioning and encompasses multiple areas of impact (Clutterbuck et al., 2003; Quirke, 2008; Scholes, 1997; Smith & Mounter, 2008; Wright, 2009; Byczyk, 2022). In contemporary enterprises, it is becoming increasingly fundamental. The latter (on which the authors will focus in the next subsection) involves conveying information between the organization and entities within and outside the business environment, aimed at achieving the organization's goals. Its primary recipients are potential consumers. In the case of the B2B market (Business-to-Business), these are other economic entities, while in the case of B2C (Business-to-Consumer), they are individual customers. Its goal is to shape the organization's solid reputation and build consumer loyalty. In the context of other entities in the external environment, its task is to shape a positive image and create an atmosphere of trust in the organization or to garner support for the tasks undertaken.

Due to the nature of information flow in the organizational structure, three types of communication can be distinguished: vertical, horizontal, and diagonal (Leśniewski et al., 2023, pp. 38–43). The first is divided into upward and downward communication (Guthrie, 2021). Vertical downward communication originates at the highest level of management and then moves down the levels until it reaches the performers (starting from the top management and descending through the organizational structure to non-managerial employees). In this channel, information about the mission, goals, and rules of organization functioning is conveyed, as well as commands, orders, and prohibitions, expressing expectations from organization members, evaluating employees, informing about their performance, and providing motivational stimuli. It can be modified, filtered, or stopped at various management levels. On the other hand, vertical upward communication involves conveying information from subordinates to superiors. Usually, this communication occurs in a hierarchical manner, based on the organizational hierarchy (employees at lower levels communicate with superiors positioned at higher levels in the organizational structure). In this case, subordinates provide information, reports on completed tasks, present inquiries about filling information gaps, and seek advice on employee actions, as well as communicate problems, complaints, or present ideas and suggestions for improving work. The second type of communication – horizontal communication – takes place within the organization between employees holding equivalent positions. It often occurs informally to bypass direct supervisors in order to quickly solve a particular problem or implement actions based on mutual agreements. Its main goals are: coordinating the actions of individual departments, sharing knowledge and supplementing missing information, disseminating requested information, assisting in solving problems related to cooperation between various units, resolving problems and conflicts between employees/departments, and integrating employees. On the other hand, the diagonal (oblique) form of communication concerns units positioned at the same level in the organizational structure that are not subordinate to each other. This form most often occurs in the communication of informal groups, to which individuals not connected in the organizational and task hierarchy belong. They are bound together by bonds of friendship and personal relationships (Sypniewska, 2013, p. 86).

Taking into account the manner of message transmission, communication can take the following forms: verbal and non-verbal, oral and written, direct (messages go directly to communicating parties) and indirect (involving a mediator). In the latter case, the first type allows for more effective understanding compared to the latter, as it reduces communication noise and activates the sender and receiver more in the communication process (van Vuuren et al., 2007, pp. 116–128). This is evidenced by the latest research conducted by D. Battiston et al. (2021, pp. 575–609), which provide evidence of a positive causal relationship between the possibility of direct communication and team productivity.

Currently, there is a clear tendency to reduce the number of levels in the organizational structure while expanding it horizontally. This inclination can also be considered in terms of communication (information flow). An overly complex, hierarchical organizational structure carries many dangers, including deliberate or unintentional distortion of information by individuals at different levels, hiding negative information, transforming the meaning of information through incorrect interpretation and misunderstanding (individual perception), and information lagging in various cells. However, it should be noted that in a horizontal structure, communication behaviors can also be threatened by behaviors such as rivalry between department employees, reluctance to share knowledge due to viewing it as a competitive factor, or information overload.

In addition to the direction of information flow and organizational structure, a factor determining communication behaviors is related to the existing organizational culture in the workplace – an established set of internal cooperation norms and practices (Kocoń, 2009, p. 149). It affects the communication climate between employees. Elements arising from organizational culture, such as autonomy, recognition of achievements, development opportunities, emotional support, rights to take risks or make mistakes, and the ability to provide constructive criticism, influence the communication atmosphere (cf. Cameron & Quinn, 2011, p. 242).

Using the criterion of factors differentiating the nature of the relationship between the sender and receiver, the following forms of communication in organizations, including groups, are indicated:

a) Unidirectional and bidirectional (Harrison & Williams, 2020, pp. 310–319) – the first in organizations can be equated with informing the recipients by the sender of messages (top-down vertical), where no feedback is expected; in the second, senders aim to obtain information through feedback regarding the reception of the content they have transmitted (sender and receiver switch roles).
b) Symmetrical and asymmetrical (Grunig, 2002, pp. 93–124) – in the first, communicating individuals have similar or the same professional status (e.g., employees holding equivalent positions at work); in the second, one

side of the communication process has a privileged position (e.g., a higher position), while the other has a lower professional status and accepts the superiority of the interlocutor.

c) Formal and informal – the first is associated with the vertical flow of information and primarily concerns the performance of tasks dedicated to employees by the organization. Information transmission is governed by organizational procedures. The second is a consequence of relationships developed among organization employees based on sympathy or shared views. It develops in crisis situations or when vertical information flow is insufficient (incomplete or inaccurate) or distorted. It involves spontaneous acts of communication among employees. This second type of communication is usually faster than the first and uses unofficial channels of information flow (Stoner et al., 1999, pp. 518–519).
d) Defensive and supportive – the first refers to the recipient's behavior toward the sender's communication form, manifested in manipulation or demonstrating a sense of superiority; the second involves the recipient continuing communication with the initiating sender (Stoner & Wankel, 1994, p. 443).

All the above forms of communication occur in modern organizations. The dominance of some of them is associated with the adopted communication system. The latter boils down to establishing and implementing certain rules, procedures, and tools within the functioning of the entity in the field of communication. A well-planned system promotes, among other things: increased employee engagement and motivation, building and/or reinforcing the organizational culture in the employees' awareness, increased loyalty to the company, improved interpersonal relationships (including understanding between management and employees), and understanding employees' need for change and reducing resistance to their implementation.

Assuming that communication in the organization depends not only on the skills, level of awareness, or good intentions of the management, a communication plan should be developed. Within this plan, it is necessary to:

a) Address employees' information needs by communicating the scope and level of this demand to the managerial staff and specify their expectations regarding the content they receive.
b) Identify key areas crucial for the organization's success and, for each of them, establish communication goals and methods that evoke the desired attitudes from employees (Harrison, 2019, pp. 42–50).
c) Segment employee groups according to their information needs and tailor communication methods to them.
d) Develop a detailed program for using communication channels for each employee group.
e) Establish rules for assessing the effectiveness of communication processes and their impact on the company's functioning using objective or subjective measures (Lesly, 1998, p. 826).

The smooth progress of communication affects the state of interpersonal relationships, which in turn translates into the effectiveness of individual employees and teams, their loyalty, and attachment to the company. R. V. Lesikar (1977, pp. 336–337) identified four factors of effective communication in organizations. These are:

a) Formal communication channels – most commonly utilized by the managerial staff, where information is typically transmitted via email (alongside memos or official notes) and flows vertically from top to bottom. These channels primarily concern organizational functioning, task execution, and duties.
b) Power structure – a factor influencing the quality of communication, dependent on who holds which role in the organization and to what extent that person possesses communication knowledge and skills that they employ in their work.
c) Task specialization – the quality of communication in a specialized group in a particular field differs from other teams profiled in different areas of knowledge (e.g., differing specialized jargon).
d) Information ownership – this factor boils down to possessing knowledge about topics indirectly or directly related to the organization's functioning, which are neither widely known nor generally available. In the communication process, such information can confer an advantage to the possessor.

Communication is a crucial aspect of relationship-building in the workplace (both at a professional and social level), and its internal dimension can be used as an important tool for organizational success (Fetoshi & Shahini-Hoxhaj, 2023, pp. 70–88). It serves four primary functions: informing (providing data necessary for decision-making), motivating (increasing staff engagement and effectiveness by providing knowledge about progress in tasks), expressing feelings and fulfilling social needs (the group as a source of interpersonal contacts), and controlling (supervising members' behaviors through the flow of data about their work tasks). Each group communication fulfills at least one of these four functions (Robbins, 1998, p. 216; Rosengren, 2006, p. 45).

B. Kożusznik (2007, p. 158) distinguished three levels of communication within groups and between groups as part of members' communicative act: phatic (conducting conversations that do not reveal views, emotions, values), instrumental (directly conveying information without emotional charge aimed at eliciting specific behavior in the interlocutor), and affective (during conversation, views, emotions, and values are revealed, aimed at mutual acquaintance and understanding). Practice indicates that employees' communication in organizations most often occurs at the instrumental level. However, in the context of group communication, the phatic and emotional components become significant.

In 2010, scientists found that the degree of neural alignment (Kingsbury & Hong, 2020, pp. 651–666) between "speaker-listener" (neural synchronization), allows for determining the effectiveness of communication (Stephens et al., 2010, pp. 14425–14430). Furthermore, researchers, in order to determine how synchronization occurs, discovered a group of communication-savvy individuals, whom they termed "central node" or "main source of information" (Duhigg, 2024, p. 12). In the work environment, such a communication entity listens attentively to create a safe conversational climate. They seek to communicate with others, can express feelings, and have no problem explaining the duties and tasks assigned to employees. Managerial informational roles focus on acquiring and disseminating information through communication, while decision-making roles require managers to make rational decisions and convey them to others (Holstein-Beck, 2004, pp. 57–58). In reference to the above, while also considering the criterion of the sender's goal behind the communication, informational and persuasive communication can be distinguished. In the first, the sender does not seek to influence the attitudes or behaviors of the recipients, and the goal of communication is understanding and comprehension between the parties of the communicative act. In the second, communication serves to promote interactive relationships between the parties of the process, and its goal becomes shaping, reinforcing, and changing behaviors and attitudes in accordance with the sender's intention.

At the group level, the communication behaviors of individuals in an organization are shaped by the leadership style of their superiors and the type and nature of the communication network that connects individual units within the group. The way a leader interacts with subordinates influences the team's communication dynamics. In the classic categorization of leadership styles by K. Lewin et al. (1939, pp. 269–308), researchers distinguished three styles: autocratic, democratic, and laissez-faire. A leader preferring an autocratic style maintains a distance from employees; their communication, typically initiated by themselves, is limited to a minimum and primarily takes on a one-way and formalized character. Consequently, communication within this framework is at risk of increased barriers. A manager practicing a democratic style aims to reduce communication barriers – in this case, the communication process is two-way and symmetrical and is based on openness. Such an environment encourages subordinates to take initiative, stimulates their creativity in generating and implementing new ideas, and fosters mutual exchange of thoughts. With a laissez-faire leadership style, the flow of work-related information is formalized and sporadic (typically prompted by employees). Managers usually combine different leadership styles depending on the situational context.

The communication among group members occurs within the framework of communication networks. Generally, the literature on the subject (Potocki, 2001, pp. 36–37; Rogala, 2013, pp. 109–110) distinguishes five patterns of such networks. They differ in terms of information flow, the leader's position, and effectiveness in fulfilling various types of tasks. In the context of five-member teams, the communication network model known as the "wheel" is highlighted, in which communication flows through the first person who acts as the leader, receiving and passing on the message to the next person. This model is characterized by the highest level of centralization. A slightly lower level of centralization is found in the "Y" pattern, where two team members are close to the center of information. The next model – the "chain" – exemplifies the most even access to information by all group members, with individuals at both ends of the network having contact with only one other group member. The "circle" pattern eliminates this issue by closing the information loop. On the other hand, the "all-channel" pattern assumes that each group member has the same position in accessing information and participating in the communication process (this is the most decentralized model).

In practice, it is observed that the effectiveness of certain networks in the context of task accomplishment depends on the nature of the tasks. Highly centralized networks, where the leader coordinates the flow of information, are dedicated to routine and simple tasks. Decentralized networks, where there is the possibility of sharing information and open communication, serve the effectiveness of accomplishing non-standard and complex tasks. Bearing this in mind, managers operating within an organization should select the most optimal communication networks depending on the existing circumstances.

At this point, attention should also be drawn to the informal variation of communication networks within the organization, known as the "grapevine model" (rumors), which is organized by employees and permeates the entire organizational structure (Michelson & Mouly, 2000, pp. 57–68). It often consists of several networks without official organization sanction, which intersect with each other. They intersect at points – individuals well-informed about the organization – who belong to many unofficial networks. This pattern does not consider the placement of these individuals in the organizational structure (their position). It connects its members in every combination of directions: vertical, horizontal, and diagonal.

K. Davis (1969, p. 634) distinguished four types of gossip chains. In the first type, "single thread," the accuracy of the transmitted information is the lowest because it moves on the principle of "Chinese whispers." The second type, "gossipmonger," involves interesting information that is not directly related to work. The initiator of the communication is one person who passes it on to the other employees within this chain. The third type, "accidental," is associated with interesting yet relatively unimportant information for the organization. It is passed on to random individuals who, in turn, spread it further on the same principle. The last type within this classification, "bunch," constitutes the dominant pattern of gossip networks in the organization. The type of information being transmitted is current, related to work, and interesting to the individuals transmitting it. In this configuration, the initiator of the communication flow passes it on to selected individuals – connectors.

These connectors then transmit it to employees they trust or from whom they would like to gain benefits from the conveyed content.

The execution of tasks assigned to internal communication occurs at various levels, directions, and modes of communication. Therefore, it is important to carefully select the tools, the use of which must be tailored to the specific communication need.

Communication means (communication channels) in an organization, through which information can reach employees, can be grouped according to their purpose of use (Olsztyńska, 1999, p. 32) as follows:

- Means related to information transmission (print media – e.g., company publications and employee reports), electronic and audiovisual media – e.g., the Internet, and others such as suggestion boxes or complaint boxes;
- Means related to direct communication and interpersonal relations (formal ones, e.g., internal memos or employee conferences, and informal ones, e.g., personal communication or consultations);
- Means influencing the shaping of the company's image in the eyes of employees (e.g., visual identification system, exhibitions, competitions for employees and their families, employee clubs).

The composition of the toolkit should be dependent on the ability to use it appropriately. For the purposes of formal internal communication in an organization, a variety of tools related to new technologies are employed. The opportunities provided by these tools primarily ensure faster information transfer, the establishment of a modern organizational image, and facilitate the sharing of knowledge and experience among employees.

Interorganizational communication

A systemic approach to communication posits that interpersonal communication is more than the sum of its parts, more than the sum of the meanings of individual utterances. It conceptualizes communication as a system that possesses a certain degree of openness and limitation. It can change within certain defined boundaries and undergo development, stagnation, or regression. The complexity of the structure of this process depends on the degree of diversity of variability of elements within the system. The individual components of communication are interdependent. At the same time, each system is somewhat independent of its environment, able to independently shape its actions and determine its goals (Fisher, 1985). H. Guetzkow emphasizes that the communication system boils down to patterns of transmission and interpretation of messages among organizational units and between these units and their organizational environment (Guetzkow, 1965, p. 18). This holistic approach to communication allows for its characterization at the interorganizational level.

In the effective functioning of an organization to build competitive advantage over other entities operating in the environment, besides well-formulated strategic goals, intellectual capital, innovation, and organizational culture, communication plays a significant role in creating space for the flow of these resources. Strategic communication, in the case of integrated organizational communication, is essential for building long-term relationships between the organization and its external environment. Treating business environment institutions as actors sharing knowledge and setting trends in innovation (educational function), attempting to establish ties both among themselves and with entities from the environment, one must attribute significant (if not crucial) importance to the accompanying communication strategy.

Institutional communication (commonly referred to as corporate communication in English) involves actions aimed at generating and conveying information to individuals, groups, and communities, as well as obtaining feedback, carried out by an organization and its representatives. It can take place both internally and externally within the organization. Both the internal and external dimensions require the establishment of a communication policy, including informational aspects, by the management of the company. The first, which is a broader concept compared to the second, entails a set of actions undertaken (planned and consciously) by these entities in accordance with the strategies adopted within them. Through controlling and managing the flow of information, its task is to shape the organization's image and enhance the effectiveness of the policies implemented by these organizations. On the other hand, the information policy is limited to the communication of specific data that do not utilize persuasive elements (Dobek-Ostrowska & Wiszniowski, 2001, pp. 49–50).

External communication helps to build the company's image and differentiate it in the market from other competitive entities. Many theorists and practitioners in the field of communication marginalize the role of internal communication in favor of external communication. However, it is important to emphasize that employees can be the most important audience for the organization's efforts in shaping its actual image (Christensen & Askegaard, 2001, pp. 292–315). If they identify with the organization, they contribute to building competitive advantage through their relationships with customers (Hardaker & Fill, 2005, pp. 365–376).

Organizations are created by people and for people; therefore, the relationships formed within the cooperation between partners are primarily relationships between the employees of both organizations. The quality of these interactions, their form, and frequency significantly influence how the company is perceived by its counterparts. The way employees treat customers, the level of service, competencies, and communication skills determine whether the organization is perceived as strong or weak. Moreover, the staff is a key carrier of the company's image. Therefore, effectively conducted internal communication is a fundamental condition for the success of all communication activities of the company (Byczyk, 2022, pp. 122–123).

P. Kotler presented image as the way in which the entity wants to be identified by its audience (Kotler, 1994, p. 279). On the other hand, W. Budzyński defined it as "a complex intellectual or sensory interpretation, a way of perceiving someone or something; a product of the mind resulting from deduction based on available premises, both real and imaginary, conditioned by impressions, beliefs, ideas, and emotions" (Budzyński, 2008, p. 47). In the literature on the subject (Adamus-Matuszyńska, 2010, pp. 11–12), the concept of image is essentially understood in three meanings: as the perception of the entity shaped in people's minds (a set of cognitive schemas including stereotypes and prejudices), or as a set of meanings and symbols that make the entity recognizable (a collection of visual and non-visual signs), and also as the way people describe and relate to the entity (a collection of behavioral patterns).

A.I. Baruk (2006, pp. 32–33) distinguished four types of image:

a) Real image – portrays how society perceives the entity with which it interacts;
b) Mirror (internal) image – created within the organization by employees;
c) Desired (target) image – the image that the entity would like to evoke in its audience and how it would like to be perceived;
d) Optimal image – represents the average of all the aforementioned images.

Taking into account the above meanings and types of image, it can be assumed that it is a way of imagining someone about someone/something, which may – but does not have to – be consistent with the actual state of affairs (Narożna, 2018, pp. 106–108). Therefore, it is often said not so much about "presenting the image" but about "creating the image" of the company. Its significance depends primarily on how the organization is perceived, to a lesser extent on how it operates.

Properly creating the image of an organization allows, among other things, for:

a) increasing the quantity and value of products or services offered by the company;
b) building trust and credibility toward the company in the eyes of customers and economic entities;
c) finding investors;
d) reducing the risk of financial liquidity loss;
d) vestablishing new business relationships;
f) creating and/or consolidating a good position of the company in the environment.

Formally responsible for creating the image of the company is a dedicated organizational unit (e.g., public relations department) or a person appointed by its management. Practically, the influence on how such organizations will be perceived by others depends on every employee working in them.

Effective actions in creating the organization's image should be linked to a strategy established by the organization (Steyn, 2003, pp. 168–183). It will be important to determine the company's identity – treated in material terms as a set of characteristics that distinguish the organization from its competitors (Kocoń, 2009, pp. 143–152) – based on values (ideas guiding the entity), mission (justification for the organization's existence), and vision (the concept of the entity's functioning). It is necessary to specify image objectives, methods for measuring effects, ways to achieve them, and the time allocated for their realization. Simultaneously, opinion research regarding the perception of key stakeholders about the analyzed company should be conducted. Then, the results of the exploration should be compared with what the strategy assumes, and actions aimed at achieving the intended effects should be taken (subject to evaluation within the adopted timeframe). It is necessary to determine the budget, units responsible for this process, and the methods and tools used to achieve the goals outlined in the strategy.

The signals sent by the company to its environment contribute to the comprehensive image of the company. They should be as consistent as possible to build its credibility and reputation (Barnett et al., 2006, pp. 26–38) considered in terms of the tangible value of the organization.[6] Therefore, it is essential to integrate communication activities aimed at the customer and the market with the organization's internal aspects. The necessity of a comprehensive approach to various areas covered by communication activities arises from deficits in the organization's communication system. Deficiencies often occur when transmitted messages are characterized by inconsistency in content (temporal or formal) or contradiction. The analysis of communication deficits (so-called communication gaps) is conducted precisely in terms of the consistency of internal communication with external communication. It occurs if the organization's employees are not sufficiently informed about communication activities aimed at external actors or if these activities are mutually exclusive (Zajkowska, 2011, p. 64). Incompatibility regarding the consistency of messages, the selection of instruments, and the set goals can lead to discrepancies between employee attitudes and those of external contractors, which can negatively affect the entire organization's image. Hence, communication actions directed outside the organization must be based on an efficient internal communication process.

Lack of authenticity in image, that is, its weak connection to organizational reality, results in a missed opportunity to leverage it as a strategic asset for the entity. K. Wójcik (2021, pp. 1061–1076) identifies opportunities to mitigate this risk in:

a) Shifting away from viewing image as the primary goal (sole measure of effectiveness and efficiency) in favor of reputation.
b) Giving clear priority to shaping optimal relationships with the environment as a goal that aligns not only with contemporary PR paradigms but

also with concepts of corporate social responsibility, thereby resulting in the creation of an image that faithfully reflects organizational reality.

c) Professionalizing image management – in deliberate shaping utilizing knowledge of strategy and program development principles, their implementation and evaluation, and integrating PR services into strategic organizational management.

It is worth noting that image creation is a long-term process dependent not only on internal factors (company actions) but also on external ones (independent of the company). Hence, there is a continuous need to establish and maintain relationships with the environment to influence what others think and articulate about the company through information dissemination and actions. In the event of a crisis, it is essential to possess transmission channels necessary for conveying persuasive messages.

Over the past decades, due to rapidly changing circumstances, organizations must continually adapt to new conditions of operation. This requires flexibility and embracing the principle of "lifelong learning." A learning organization (Do & Mai, 2022, pp. 1230–1253), on one hand, has the ability to learn itself, and on the other hand, it creates space and formal conditions for individuals to think, ask questions, reflect, and learn, as well as encourages them to challenge the existing state of affairs and propose improvements (McKenna & Beech, 1997, p. 256). M. Machowska, Deputy Director of the Technology Park Department at Krakow Technology Park (Poland), emphasizes that in communication, one must be willing to change and adapt to evolving realities. It is essential to listen to the voices of other entities and respond to changing environments. Therefore, she advocates that the most crucial elements in the innovation ecosystem, concerning communication, are people and a well-functioning network of contacts.

Networking involves establishing lasting, long-term, and systematic relationships (including business relationships) with the aim of cooperation based on trust (Granovetter, 1973, pp. 1360–1380). Within this framework, actors exchange knowledge and skills. The outcome of these efforts should be the achievement of (common) goals with the support of partners who share similar interests and values, based on the principle of reciprocity (Castells, 2007, p. 532). Operational networking entails participation in various industry events, conferences, training sessions, and online networking activities (such as Goldenline or LinkedIn), as well as social activities (including local ones).

Building and expanding a network of contacts require effective communication at the interpersonal, intergroup, and organizational levels (Leonardi et al., 2013, pp. 1–19). An individual must possess communication skills to establish contacts (Sutton, 2003, p. 113). At the intergroup level, they should be able and willing to build relationships, including through the use of language. From the organizational communication perspective, as a representative of a particular entity seeking partners with similar values or business activities, one must demonstrate openness to be accepted into the network and embraced by its other members.

Informal networks (e.g., those operating within organizations) and formal networks (established among representatives of different organizations) play a significant role in exchanging thoughts and views among their participants, focusing on building and maintaining interpersonal relationships (Gibson et al., 2014, pp. 146–161). These networks can form the aforementioned networked communities, which, due to shared beliefs, constitute a strong interest group within organizations (in relation to the employer) or at the interinstitutional level (toward decision-making centers operating in their area of activity). Thus, D. Pitschmann (Pitschmann, 2023) from Lakeside Science and Technology Park GmbH (Austria) is justified in pointing out that in the communication process in the 21st century, in addition to networking, greater emphasis should also be placed on social media in communication within the innovation ecosystem, where it is not enough just to be present, but active participation is required. Over the past years, social media platforms have strengthened their position (in terms of increasing user numbers and scope of influence) and play a significant role in the communication process (Weimann et al., 2014). They connect people who, through communication processes, inform others about themselves – their thoughts and worldview. "The current WWW network is a completely different entity than the network from a decade ago. This new approach creates a more mature environment for social networks and collaboration. In an abstract sense, social networks concern everyone. The widespread adoption of social networking sites indicates an evolution in social interactions among people" (Weaver & Morrison, 2008, pp. 97–100). The development of communication in cyberspace has enabled individuals, groups, and organizations to present themselves in new ways. Informational content spreads across the Internet at tremendous speed and in all directions, which can harm positive reputation and identity in crisis situations (Vrabec & Odziomková, 2018, pp. 321–335). Social media modernize communication systems (Kaplan & Haenlein, 2010, pp. 59–68) and can even serve as a framework for a revolution laying the foundations for the functioning of the global communication economy (Gregor & Stawiszyński, 2011, pp. 209–214). Communication is a constitutive element of all social processes; it constitutes an attribute of every culture. It is a conditio sine qua non of human life and social order (Watzlawick et al., 1974, p. 13). A society where work is based on information becomes a key factor in the economy (Deuze, 2020, pp. 20–22). It also plays a very important role in the innovation ecosystem.

Notes

1 The first includes oral communication (e.g., direct conversation, speech, discussion, consultation), written communication (e.g., report, notes, article, letter), and signaling communication (e.g., report, notes, article using Braille alphabet tools).

The second comprises paralinguistic communication (e.g., intonation, accent, tone of voice, rhythm, sound), non-verbal communication (e.g., gestures, facial expressions, touch, posture), and context (e.g., distance between speakers, appearance, props, interior decor). All these forms of communication take place within the innovation ecosystem.

2 The traditional model advocated the use of material tools in the motivation process, which was intended to compensate for the hardships of work. The human relations model assumed that the most effective way of motivating is to satisfy employees' social needs and create a suitable work atmosphere. The human resources model was based on a systemic approach to motivation issues, emphasizing the need to treat employees subjectively by increasing their responsibilities, self-control, and participation.

3 E. A. Aron et al. examined over 30 individuals who were previously unfamiliar with each other. In pairs, they were tasked with asking each other questions from a list. The session lasted for 60 minutes and was conducted in a windowless room with two chairs set up.

4 Communication noise can have not only external characteristics (e.g., excessively high or low temperature for conducting conversations) or semantic characteristics (e.g., sender's use of the wrong meaning assigned to a given word) but also internal characteristics (e.g., social predispositions of communication participants).

5 Research shows that organizations that attach greater importance to the information transmission process can boast higher levels of employee engagement and a better reputation. See Thomson, K., & Hecker, L. A. (2000). The business value of buy-in. In R. J. Varey & B. R. Lewis (Eds.), *Internal marketing: Directions for management* (pp. 48–55). Routledge; Dortok, A. (2006). A managerial look at the interaction between internal communication and corporate reputation. *Corporate Reputation Review*, *8*(4), 322–338.

6 Many researchers emphasize the inconsistent or even erroneous use of key terms in business communication such as image, reputation, or identity. See: Gilpin, D. (2010). Organizational image construction in a fragmented online media environment. *Journal of Public Relations Research*, *22*(3), 265–287; Barnett, M. L., Jermier, J. M., & Lafferty B. A. (2006). Corporate reputation: The definitional landscape. *Corporate Reputation Review*, *9*(1), 26–38. Brown, T. J., Dacin, P. A., Pratt, M. G., & Whetten, D. A. (2006). Identity, intended image, construed image, and reputation: An interdisciplinary framework and suggested terminology. *Journal of Academy of Marketing Science*, *34*(2), 99–106.

Bibliography

Ackermann, J. M., & Bargh, J. A. (2010). Two to tango: Automatic social coordination and the role of felt effort. In B. Bruya (Ed.), *Effortless attention: New perspectives in the cognitive science of attention and action*. MIT Press Scholarship Online.

Adamus-Matuszyńska, A. (2010). Spokesperson and image of the organization. In Z. Gajdka & W. Widera (Eds.), *Spokespersonship: Theory, practice, contexts*. Wydawnictwo Naukowe Unikat-2.

Aron, A., Melinat, E., Aron, E. N., Vallone, R. D., & Bator, R. J. (1997). The experimental generation of interpersonal closeness: A procedure and some preliminary findings. *Personality and Social Psychology Bulletin*, *23*(4), 363–377.

Barnett, M. J., Jermier, J. M., & Lafferty, B. A. (2006). Corporate reputation: The definitional landscape. *Corporate Reputation Review*, *9*(1), 26–38.

Baruk, A. I. (2006). *Personal marketing as an instrument of creating the company's image*. Dyfin.

Battistona, D., Blanesa I Vidala, J., & Kirchmaiera, T. (2021). Face-to-face communication in organizations. *Review of Economic Studies*, *88*, 575–609.
Bolton, R. (1986). *People skills*. Prentice Hall.
Bough, A., & Condrill, J. (1998). *101 ways to improve your communication skills instantly*. Goalminds.
Budzyński, W. (2008). *Public relations: Strategy and new image creation techniques*. Wydawnictwo Poltext.
Burton, K. (2012). *A study of motivation: How to get your employees moving*[SPEA Honors Thesis, Indiana University].
Byczyk, M. (2022). The essence of team communication: Trend, organization value and affection on management. *Scientific Papers of Silesian University of Technology*, 122–133.
Cameron, K. S., & Quinn, R. E. (2011). *Diagnosing and changing organizational culture: Based on the competing values framework*. Jossey-Bass.
Caruso, D. R., & Salovey, P. (2009). *Emotional intelligent manager*. Dom Wydawniczy "Rebis".
Castells, M. (2007). Network society. In M. Marody (Ed.), *Network society*. Wydawnictwo Naukowe PWN.
Chaffee, S. H., & Metzger, M. J. (2001). The end of mass communication? *Mass Communication & Society*, *4*(4), 365–366. https://doi.org/10.1207/S15327825MCS0404_2
Chandler, M. T., & Grealish, L. D. (2019). *Feedback (and other dirty words): Why we fear it, how to fix*. Berrett-Koehler Publishers.
Christensen, L. T., & Askegaard, S. (2001). Corporate identity and corporate image revisited – A semiotic perspective. *European Journal of Marketing*, *35*(3–4), 292–315.
Clark, H. H. (1996). *Using language*. Cambridge University Press.
Clutterbuck, D., Hirst, S., & Cage, S. (2003). *Talking business: Making communication work*. Butterworth-Heinemann.
Coyle, D. (2023). *The culture code: The secrets of highly successful groups*.Random House.
Cunningham, S. B. (1992). Intrapersonal communication: Review and critique. *Annals of the International Communication Association*, *15*(1), 2–3.
Davis, K. (1969). Management communication and the grapevine. *Personnel Journal*, *4*(48), 43–49.
Davis, K., & Newstrom, J. W. (1989). *Human behavior at work: Organizational behavior*. McGraw-Hill.
Deetz, S. (1995). *Transforming communication: Transforming business: Building responsive and responsible workplaces*. Hampton.
DePaulo, B., Kirkendol, S. E., Kashy, D. A., Wyer, M. M., & Epstein, J. A. (1996). Lying in everyday life. *Journal of Personality and Social Psychology*, *70*(5), 979–995.
Deuze, M. (2020). The role of media and mass communication theory in the global pandemic. *Communication Today*, *11*(2), 4–16.
Do, T. T., & Mai, N. K. (2022). Organizational learning and firm performance: A systematic review. *International Journal of Productivity and Performance Management*, *71*(4), 1230–1253.
Dobek-Ostrowska, B., & Wiszniowski, R. (2001). *Theory of public and political communication. Introduction*.Astrum.
Donjean, Ch. (2006). *La communication interne*. Edi.pro.
Duhigg, Ch. (2024). *The power of communication. Discover the secret of conversations that connect* (M. Guzowska, Trans.). Wydawnictwo Naukowe PWN.
Eysenck, M. W., & Keane, M. T. (2000). *Cognitive psychology*. Taylor & Francis.
Fetoshi, A., & Shahini-Hoxhaj, R. (2023). International communication in organization: The case of the post of Kosovo. *Economic Studies (Ikonomicheski Izsledvania)*, *32*(4), 70–88.

Fisher, B. A. (1985). The pragmatic perspective of human Communications. In F. E. X. Dance (Ed.), *Human communication theory*. Harper & Row.
Frydrychowicz, S. (2005). Modes and dimensions of interpersonal communication and human development. *Developmental Psychology*, *10*(3), 97.
Galambaud, B. (1988). Information: Outil de management? *Revue Personnel*, *292*, 17–20.
Gardner, H. (1989). *Frames of mind: Theory of multiple intelligences*. Basic Books.
Gesell, I. (2007). Am I talking to me? The power of internal dialogue to help or hinder our success. *Journal for Quality and Participation*, *3*, 5–6.
Gibson, C., Hardy III, J. H., & Buckley, M. R. (2014). Understanding the role of networking in organizations. *Career Development International*, *19*(2), 146–161.
Granovetter, M. S. (1973). The strength of weak ties. *American Journal of Sociology*, *78*(6), 1360–1380.
Gregor, B., & Stawiszyński, M. (2011). From e-commerce to social commerce – Changes taking place in e-commerce and the Internet and e-clients (trends and challenges). *Internal Trade*, *9/10*, 209–214.
Grice, H. P. (1980). Logic and conversation. In B. Stanosz (Ed.), *The language in light of the science*. Czytelnik.
Grunig, J. E. (2002). Symmetrical and asymmetrical communication: Conceptual differences and empirical findings. *Journal of Public Relations Research*, *14*(2), 93–124.
Guetzkow, H. (1965). *Communications in organizations*.Rand-McNally.
Guthrie, G. (2021). *Horizontal communication vs vertical communication*. Retrieved February 12, 2024, from https://nulab.com/learn/collaboration/horizontal-communication-vs-lateral-communication/
Hackman, J. R. (1977). Work design. In J. R. Hackman & L. L. Suttle (Eds.), *Improving life at work* (pp. 129–130).Goodyear.
Halloran, J. D. (1983). Information and communication: Information is the answer, but what is the question? *Journal of Information Science*, *7*, 160.
Hardaker, S., & Fill, C. (2005). Corporate services brands: The intellectual and emotional engagement of employees. *Corporate Reputation Review*, *7*(4), 365–374.
Hargie, O., Dickson, D., & Tourish, D. (2004). *Communication skills for effective management*.Palgrave.
Harrison, K. (2019). Effective communication planning: An integral element of business management. *Journal of Business Strategy*, *40*(4), 42–50.
Harrison, T. R., & Williams, E. A. (2020). Engagement in communication: Comparing two-way versus one-way communication methods in health-related organizations. *Journal of Health Communication*, *25*(4), 310–319.
Hickson, M. L., & Stacks, D. W. (1985). *Nonverbal communication: Studies and applications*. Brown.
Hogg, M. A., & Vaughan, G. M. (2005). *Social psychology*.Prentice Hall.
Holstein-Beck, M. (2004). *Managerial positions: Theory and practice*. Oficyna Wydawnicza SGH.
Interview with Agnieszka Pałys – Director of the Legal and Organizational Division of the Wrocław Technology Park, Regarding the Role of Communication in the Innovation Ecosystem, Conducted in 2023 by the Authors of the Book, unpublished.
Interview with David Pitschmann from Lakeside Science & Technology Park GmbH on the Role of Communication in the Innovation Ecosystem, Conducted in 2023 by the Authors of the Book, unpublished.
Jakobson, R. (1989). Poetics in light of the linguistics. In M. R. Mayenowa (Ed.), *In search of the core of language*.PIW.
Janowitz, M. (n.d.). The study of mass communication. *International Encyclopedia of the Social Sciences*. Retrieved August 28, 2020, from www.encyclopedia.com/media/encyclopedias-almanacs-transcripts-and-maps/study-mass-communication
Kaplan, A. M., & Haenlein, M. (2010). Users of the world, unite! The challenges and opportunities of Social Media. *Business Horizons*, *53*(1), 59–68.

Keyton, J. (2011). *Communication and organizational culture: A key to understanding work experience*. Sage.
Kingsbury, L., & Hong, W. (2020). A multi-brain framework for social interaction. *Trends in Neurosciences*, *43*(9), 651–666.
Knapp, M. L. (1979). *Nonverbal communication in human interaction*. Wadsworth. Cengage Learning.
Kocoń, P. (2009). Company's identity and organizational culture – definitions and relations. *Economy and Management*, *1*, 143–152.
Kotler, P. (1994). Differentiation and positioning of marketing offer. In P. Kotler (Ed.), *Marketing: Analysis, planning, implementation and inspection*. Wydawnictwo Gebethner i Wolff.
Kożusznik, B. (2007). *Human's behaviour in organization*. Polskie Wydawnictwo Ekonomiczne.
Leonardi, P. M., Huysman, M., & Steinfield, C. (2013). Enterprise social media: Definition, history, and prospects for the study of social technologies in organizations. *Journal of Computer-Mediated Communication*, *19*(1), 1–19.
Lesika, R. V. (1977). A general semantics approach to communication barriers in organizations. In K. Davis (Ed.), *Organizational behavior*. McGraw-Hill.
Lesly, P. (1998). *Lesly's handbook of public relations and communications*(5th ed.). McGraw Hill.
Leśniewski, M. A., Dziekański, P., & Puchała, J. (2023). The effectiveness of communication in the organization management system – A theoretical study. *Наукові записки Національного університету «Острозька академія»*, *28*(56), 38–43.
Lewin, K., Lippitt, R., & White, R. K. (1939). Patterns of aggressive behavior in experimentally created "social climates". *The Journal of Social Psychology*, *10*(2), 269–308.
Lewis, P., Thornhill, A., & Saunders, M. (2003). *Employee relations: Understanding the employment relationship*. Prentice Hall Financial Times.
Listwan, T. (Ed.). (2004). *Human resources management*. C.H. Beck.
Lunenburg, F. C. (2010). Communication: The process, barriers, and improving effectiveness. *Schooling*, *1*(1), 1–11.
Masip, J., Garrido, E., & Herrero, C. (2004). The nonverbal approach to the detection of deception: Judgmental accuracy. *Psychology in Spain*, *8*(1), 48–59.
McKay, M., Davis, M., & Fanning, P. (2019). *The art of effective communication*. GWP.
McKenna, E., & Beech, N. (1997). *The management of human resources*. Gebethner & Ska.
McQuail, D. (2010). *McQuail's mass communication theory* (6th ed.). Sage Publications.
Michelson, G., & Mouly, V. S. (2000). Grapevine and gossip: A study of informal and unofficial communication in the workplace. *Asia Pacific Journal of Human Resources*, *38*(2), 57–68.
Mintzberg, H. (1973). *The nature of managerial work*. Harper & Row.
Mintzberg, H. (1975). The manager's job: Folklore and fact. *Harvard Business Review*, *53*(4), 5–10.
Mogan, R., Fischer, R., & Bulbulis, J. A. (2017). To be in synchrony or not? A meta-analysis of synchrony's effects on behavior, perception, cognition and affect. *Journal of Experimental Social Psychology*, *72*, 13–20.
Müller, V., Sänger, J., & Lindenberger, U. (2018). Hyperbrain network properties of guitarists playing in quartet. *Annals of the New York Academy of Sciences*, *1423*(1), 198–210.
Narożna, D. (2018). *Determinants of the function of the press spokesman in Poland. Theory and practice*. Wydawnictwo "Silva Rerum".
Narula, U. (2006). *Handbook of communication: Models, perspectives, strategies*. Atlantic.

Ober, J. (2013). Function and role of an effective communication in management. *Scientific Journal of Silesian University of Technology, 65*, 263.
Olson, L. N. (2002). As ugly and painful as it was, it was effective: Individuals' unique assessment of communication competence during aggressive conflict episodes. *Communication Studies, 53*(2), 171–188.
Olsztyńska, A. (1999). The objectives and techniques public relations inside the enterprise. *Personnel, 9*, 32.
Pachori, R. (2023a). Multifaceted role of communication in organizational dynamics. *The IUP Journal of Soft Skills, 17*(4), 29–30.
Pachori, R. (2023b). Multifaceted role of communication in organizational dynamics. *The IUP Journal of Soft Skills, 17*(4), 25–26.
Pearce, C. G., Figgins, R., & Golen, S. P. (1984). *Principles of business communication: Theory, application, and technology*. John Wiley.
Pecukonis, E. V. (1990). A cognitive/behavioral approach to social assertive training. In *Assertive Training for Communication Competence* (pp. 113–143). Charles C. Thomas Publisher.
Potocki, A. (2001). *Internal communication in the enterprise*. Wydawnictwo Akademii Ekonomicznej w Krakowie, pp. 36–37.
Potocki, A., Winkler, R., & Żbikowska, A. (2003). *Communication technics in the economic organizations*. Wydawnictwo Difin, 41.
Quirke, B. (2008). *Making the connections: Using internal communication to turn strategy into action*. Gower Publishing Limited.
Rancer, A. S., & Avtgis, T. A. (2006). *Argumentative and aggressive communication: Theory, research, and application*. Sage Publications.
Reimann, H. (1974). *Kommunikations – Systeme*. J.C.B. Mohr Verlag.
Rencker, E. (2008). *Le nouveau visage de la com' interne: réflexions, méthodes, guide pour l'action*. Éditions d'Organisation Groupes Eyrolles.
Richardson, D. C., Dale, R., & Krikham, N. Z. (2007). The art of conversation is coordination. *Psychological Science, 18*(5), 407–413.
Robbins, S. P. (1998). *Organizational behavior: Concepts, controversies, applications* (8th ed.). Prentice Hall.
Rogala, A. (2013). Determinants of the effectiveness of internal communication in the enterprise. *Poznań*. Retrieved February 16, 2024, from www.wbc.poznan.pl/Content/272466/Anna_Rogala_doktorat.pdf
Rogers, E., & Kincaid, L. (1982). Communication is networks and convergence. *Intermedia, 10*(1), 16.
Rosengren, K. E. (2006). *Communication: An introduction*. Sage Publications Ltd.
Scholes, E. (Ed.). (1997). *Gower handbook of internal communication*.Hampshire Limited: Gower Publishing.
Schulz von Thun, F. (2003). *The art of conversation. The analyze of disorders*. Wydawnictwo WAM, pp. 10–11.
Scott, K. (2019). *Radical Candor: Fully revised & updated edition: Be a kick-ass boss without losing your humanity*.St. Martin's Press.
Śmietańska, J. (2017). Emotional intelligence in business. *Human Resources Management*, nr *1*(114), Instytut Pracy i Spraw Socjalnych, 25–43.
Smith, L., & Mounter, P. (2008). *Effective internal communication*. Kogan Page Limited.
Spitzberg, B. H., Canary, D. J., & Cupach, W. R. (1994). A competence-based approach to the study of interpersonal conflict. In D. D. Cahn (Ed.), *Conflict in personal relationships* (pp. 183–202).Erlbaum.
Stankiewicz, J. (2006). *Communicating within the organization*. Astrum, pp. 56–57.
Stephens, G. J., Silbert, L. J., & Hasson, U. (2010). Speaker-listener neural coupling underlies successful communication. *Proceedings of the National Academy of Sciences, 107*(32), 14425–14430.

Stewart, J. (2002). *Bridges instead of walls. About communication between people.* Wydawnictwo Naukowe PWN, p. 25.
Steyn, B. (2003). From strategy to corporate communication strategy: A conceptualisation. *Journal of Communication Management, 8*(2), 168–183.
Stone, D., & Heen, S. (2015). *Thanks for the feedback: The science and art of receiving feedback well.* Penguin Books Ltd.
Stoner, J. A. F., Freeman, R., & Gilbert, D. (1999). *Management.* PWN, pp. 518–519.
Stoner, J. A. F., & Wankel, Ch. (1994). *Management.* PWE, p. 443.
Sutton, B. (2003). *How to build a network (networking).* Petit, p. 113.
Sypniewska, B. A. (2013). The role and importance of communication in the organization – research report. *Scientific Journal of the PWSZ in Płock, Economic Sciences, XVIII*, 86.
Van Vuuren, M., de Jong, M. D. T., & Seydel, E. R. (2007). Direct and indirect effects of supervisor communication on organizational commitment. *Corporate Communications, An International Journal, 12*(2), 116–128.
Vrabec, N., & Odziomková, J. (2018, January). Online identity and reputation in cyberspace: New trends, strategies and tools to prevent and address crisis communication situations. *Megatrends & Media*, 321–335.
Watzlawick, P., Bavelas, J. B., & Jackson, D. D. (1967). *Pragmatics of human communication, a study of interactional patterns, pathologies and paradoxes.* WW Norton & Company, p. 284, 304.
Watzlawick, P., Beawin, J. B., & Jackson, D. D. (1974). *Menschliche Kommunikation.* Hans Huber Verlag, p. 13.
Weaver, A. C., & Morrison, B. B. (2008). Social networking. *Computer, 41*(2), 97–100.
Weimann, G., Weiss-Blatt, N., Mengistu, G., Tregerman, M. M., & Oren, R. (2014). Reevaluating the end of mass communication? *Mass Communication & Society, 17*(6).
Wójcik, K. (2021). Image and reputation of the organization: Information and management potential – part I. *Media Studies*, tom 22, *4*(87), 1061–1076.
Wood, J. T. (2009). Gender. In W. F. Eadie (Ed.), *21st century communication: A reference handbook* (Vol. 1, pp. 371–389). Sage Publications Inc.
Wright, M. (Red.). (2009). *Gower handbook of internal communication.* Gower Publishing Limited.
Zajkowska, M. (2011). Communication deficits as a determinant of the implementation of enterprise communication integration. In B. Pilarczyk (Red.), *Market communication. Strategies and instruments, scientific journal of the Poznań University of economics and business* (nr 208, pp. 63–72). Wydawnictwo Uniwersytetu Ekonomicznego w Poznaniu.

3 Communication mechanisms, barriers, and challenges – research results

Introduction

This chapter presents a comprehensive exploration of the crucial role that communication plays within European innovation ecosystems. The focus of this study is to analyze and understand the diverse communication mechanisms, trends, and challenges that prevail across organizations linked to the International Association of Science Parks and Areas of Innovation (IASP). Through a detailed survey involving management representatives from various member organizations of IASP, this research aims to shed light on the intricate dynamics of communication at different levels, namely interpersonal, interteam, and interorganizational.

The survey is motivated by the growing recognition of the integral role that effective communication plays in enhancing the dynamism and success of innovation ecosystems. Scholars and practitioners alike acknowledge that robust communication channels and practices not only facilitate the smooth flow of information but also enhance collaboration and synergy among various stakeholders involved in the innovation process. As such, this chapter aims to dissect the communication mechanisms that are operational within these ecosystems, investigate prevalent communication trends, identify common communicative barriers, and highlight the challenges that organizations face in this regard.

Methodologically, the study employs a structured survey approach to gather data from respondents. These individuals are strategically selected to represent a wide array of organizations within the innovation ecosystem in Europe, thereby ensuring that the findings encapsulate a holistic view of the communication landscape across diverse settings.

Furthermore, the chapter delves into the specific challenges that entities face in maintaining and enhancing communication within a complex and often fragmented innovation ecosystem. It examines how organizations navigate communicative hurdles at both the micro (interpersonal and interteam) and macro (interorganizational) levels. The analysis not only sheds light on the commonalities and discrepancies in communication practices across different types of innovation entities but also offers insights into the adaptive strategies that organizations employ to overcome these challenges.

DOI: 10.4324/9781032697802-4

The empirical data collected through the survey is analyzed to draw meaningful conclusions about the state of communication in European innovation ecosystems. This analysis is critical in identifying the leverage points where interventions could be most effective in enhancing communicative efficiency and, by extension, the overall productivity of the innovation ecosystem. The findings from this research are expected to contribute to the broader discourse on the role of communication in fostering successful innovation environments, providing valuable insights for policymakers, managers, and scholars interested in the dynamics of innovation ecosystems.

In sum, this chapter serves as a foundational piece that not only highlights the nuances of communication within innovation ecosystems but also sets the stage for subsequent discussions on strategies to optimize communication for enhanced innovation outcomes. Through a rigorous examination of the data gathered from a representative sample of the European innovation community, the study aspires to offer a comprehensive overview of the critical communicative aspects that underpin the success and vitality of these complex and multifaceted environments.

Research methodology, study objectives, research group

In science, research methods are understood as "recommended or actually used schemes of activities aimed at answering questions formulated in that science" (Nowak, 2012, p. 22). Each of them constitutes "one of the distinguishable ways of knowing" (Fiske, 1986, p. 62). In addition to them, science utilizes research techniques, which serve a supportive role toward the method. These are certain activities through which we conduct research using the assumed method (Łuszczyński, 2005). This process can be supported, among others, by survey research (Wimmer & Dominick, 1983, pp. 14–15).

The scientific method is characterized by objective, rigorous observation, and analysis. It cannot deviate from theory (Hansen & Machin, 2013, p. 1). Therefore, for the purposes of the study entitled "Innovation Ecosystems and the Role of Communication," it was assumed that communication signifies the flow of information (including feedback) circulating within a specified system (Filipiak, 2004, pp. 99–100), and innovation ecosystems should be defined as dynamic and multidimensional networks consisting of diverse actors, actions, artifacts, institutions, and relationships, both collaborative and competitive, operating in an open and dynamic environment conducive to the creation, development, and dissemination of innovation across various industries and areas. This definition emphasizes inclusivity and comprehensiveness, considering a wide range of elements such as actors (ecosystem participants), actions (innovation processes), artifacts (products, services, technologies), institutions (legal, regulatory, educational), and various types of relationships (collaboration, competition). Innovations in such an ecosystem result from interactions among actors who share knowledge, resources, competencies, and technologies, and collectively work on solving problems and challenges (Moore, 1993, 1996). In this arrangement, the environment in which the ecosystem operates is also important, including cultural, political, economic, and technological factors that may influence innovation processes (Adner, 2006). In an innovation ecosystem, the key is to connect all these elements in a way that fosters value creation. This system is characterized by an open and diverse structure that allows for easy entry and exit of various actors, and also encourages collaboration and knowledge exchange among them (Chesbrough, 2003). It is not centrally controlled, which promotes the creation of an environment where innovations can emerge and develop organically and unpredictably.

In reference to the above-defined concepts, our research was conducted using an empirical method, involving activities such as preparing, conducting a survey, and analyzing its results. It was assumed that promising results could be achieved by combining two perspectives: quantitative and qualitative approaches, within a single research project (Krauz-Mozer & Ścigaj, 2013, p. 432).

The inspiration to delve into this topic arose from the growing interest within the international scientific community in the issues surrounding innovation ecosystems, as well as the unprecedented connection between this area and the broader field of communication, which has not been extensively explored in the literature before. Undertaking considerations in this area seems fully justified. It should be emphasized that while there are various publications on innovation ecosystems and relational approaches in the literature, available publications lack the so-called "soft aspects" of ecosystem functioning, particularly the role of communication in the processes occurring within it.

The aim of the study was to demonstrate the role of communication in creating value within innovation ecosystems from the perspective of an international network of technology parks and innovation areas. The theoretical assumptions of the undertaken exploration led to the adoption of a hypothesis suggesting that effective communication is one of the key factors for the successful functioning of innovation ecosystems.

The exploration was conducted based on a prepared questionnaire survey. The subjects of the study were representatives of management from organizations affiliated with the International Association of Science Parks and Areas of Innovation (IASP) located in European countries (territorial scope). The research focused on a wide spectrum of entity types that play a crucial role in innovation ecosystems. Among the respondents were representatives of Science Parks, Technology Parks, Science and Technology Parks, Industrial Parks, Innovation Districts, small and medium-sized enterprises (SMEs), companies acting as research accelerators, entities of Venture Capital, Innovation Areas, Business Support Organizations, Research Groups, Industrial Clusters, Innovation-Driven Business Clusters, National Innovation Agencies, Universities, University Departments, accelerators, and companies. The adopted research sample consisted of 60 innovation centers from across

Europe (including Austria, Belgium, Bulgaria, Croatia, the Czech Republic, Denmark, England, Spain, Estonia, Finland, France, Greece, Germany, Hungary, Iceland, Italy, Lithuania, Luxembourg, the Netherlands, Poland, Portugal, Romania, Scotland, Serbia, Slovenia, Sweden, Switzerland, and Turkey). The number of institutions from each country varied, with the highest number of responses coming from Italy, Poland, and Spain. They represent over 50% of European centers affiliated with this international association with a confidence level of 95.5%. It should be noted that IASP has three membership categories spread across 78 countries: full, associate, and affiliated. However, the exploration only included full members of the association because these are fully operational organizations. At the time of the research, there were only 113 such entities in Europe. Therefore, the adopted research sample provides a basis for considering the conducted research as representative.

The research was conducted in the second half of 2023, and the analysis of the survey results took place in the first part of 2024 (temporal scope). The subject of the research revolved around the theme of communication in innovation ecosystems. The authors of the study formulated questions regarding the evaluation of the communication process in the aforementioned organizations by surveying respondents at the interpersonal, interteam, and interorganizational levels in the following areas: adopted communication mechanisms in the respondent's organizations and other entities, communication problems in such organizations on three levels, their strengths compared to other organizations, identification of communication barriers, and indication of communication challenges (subject scope).

Data collection was carried out through remote completion of the survey questionnaire via the Internet, email, using a Google form. Respondents were asked to fill in its contents. The questionnaire consisted of 24 closed and open-ended questions. It was also indicated that the survey results would serve as research material for the purpose of this publication. Participation in the study was anonymous.

The data obtained from the online survey were analyzed using the developed methodology.[4] The result database was verified to avoid errors resulting from incorrect completion of the questionnaire or the data import process. After this process, the results were presented, and attempts were made to draw conclusions.

The results analysis

The establishment dates of the surveyed entities participating in the research range from 1950 to 2021. They employ anywhere from 50 individuals to over 500 employees (45% of the surveyed organizations). The majority of surveyed institutions are characterized by a mixed ownership model (45% of entities).

The first question concerned the assessment of communication quality within the innovation ecosystem. The results provide valuable insights into the perception of communication effectiveness in these environments.

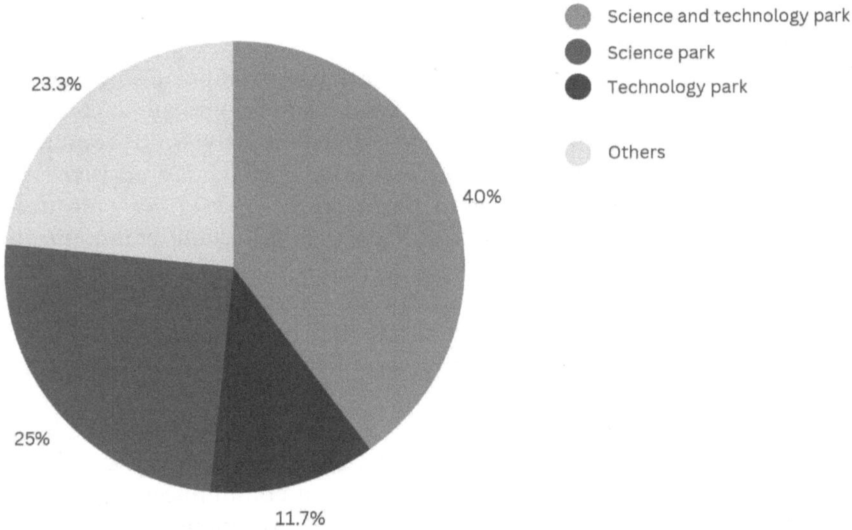

Figure 3.1 The type of institution.
Source: own development

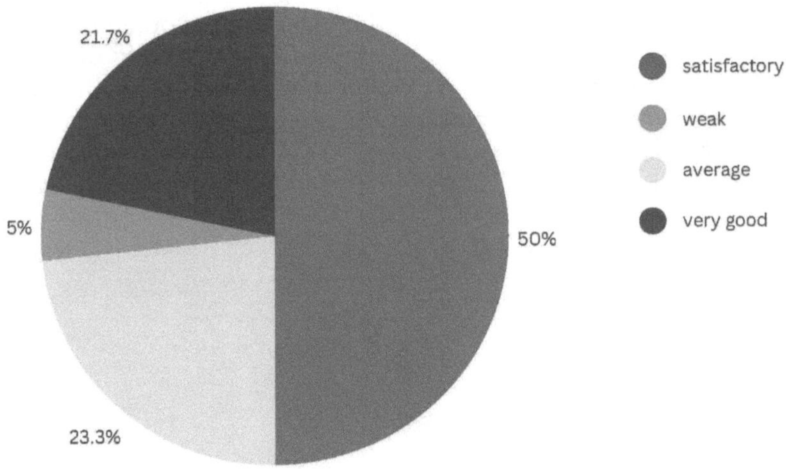

Figure 3.2 The rate of quality of communication in the innovation system.
Source: own development

The majority of respondents, exactly 50%, rated the quality of communication as "satisfactory." This rating, although not indicating outstanding quality, suggests that communication within these organizations meets basic requirements but also leaves room for improvement. This is the predominant perception among the study participants, indicating that most innovation ecosystems operate at a satisfactory level of communication, yet they have not fully reached their potential. The next group, 23.3% of respondents, rated communication as "average." This rating may indicate some deficiencies in communication, which, however, are not serious enough to completely disrupt the functioning of the ecosystem. Approximately 1/5 of respondents (21.7%) regarded communication as "very good," which is a positive signal, but considering the total number of participants, it does not constitute a majority. This suggests the existence of ecosystems where communication is at a high level, but these are rather exceptions than the rule. Only 5% of respondents rated communication as "poor." Although this is the smallest group, its existence is an important signal that in some innovation ecosystems, communication may be a serious problem requiring immediate attention and improvement.

Participants were also asked to assess communication within the institutions they represent. They could indicate their opinions on the quality of communication in three key areas: interpersonal communication, organizational communication (between teams), and external communication. In the first area – interpersonal communication, the majority of respondents perceived it positively. Close to half of the respondents rated it as "very good" (48.3%), and over 40% as "satisfactory" (43.3%). Only five respondents rated interpersonal communication as "average."

The obtained results suggest that within the analyzed organizations, there is a sense of strong and effective communication at the individual level, which is a fundamental element in building a healthy work environment and good relationships among employees. However, responses were much more diverse in the context of organizational communication (between teams).

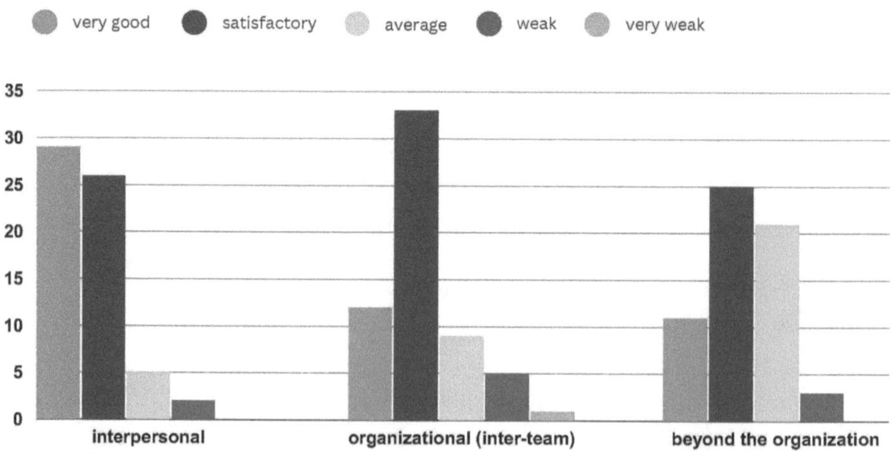

Figure 3.3 The rate of the level of communication in the organization.

Source: own development

The majority, 55% of respondents, rated it as "satisfactory," 20% as "very good," and 15% as "average." An important signal is that over 8% of respondents (result: 8.3%) considered communication between teams to be "poor" and just under 2% (result: 1.6%) – "very poor." Such results indicate the existence of challenges in the flow of information and cooperation between different groups within the organization, which may affect its overall effectiveness.

In terms of communication outside the organization, close to 20% of respondents (result: 18.3%) rated it as "very good," over 40% (result: 41.6%) as "satisfactory," and 35% as "average." Only 5% of individuals rated it as "poor."

In the question focusing on the assessment of the activity and engagement of key stakeholders in innovation ecosystems, respondents were tasked with evaluating three main groups: startups,[1] small and medium-sized enterprises,[2] research institutions, and universities, as well as public administration.

In the first category – startups and small and medium-sized enterprises (SMEs), they were rated as very active and engaged. The majority of respondents gave them high ratings, especially in the range from 6 to 8 on the scale, resulting in an average score of about 5.53. This indicates a strong and positive perception of these entities as key players in the innovation ecosystem. Research institutions and universities were also positively rated, although slightly lower than startups and SMEs, with an average score of about 5.33. They received many ratings in the middle and upper parts of the scale, suggesting that they are important but somewhat less dynamic participants in the ecosystem. Compared to the other two groups, public administration was

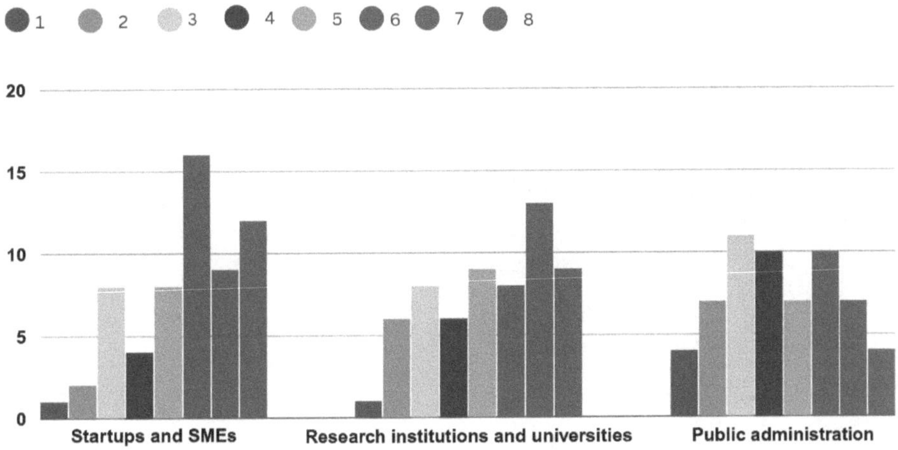

Figure 3.4 The most active and engaged stakeholders within the innovation ecosystem.
Source: own development

rated as less active and engaged, with an average score of about 4.33. These results may suggest that although it plays a role in the innovation ecosystem, its contribution is perceived as smaller compared to the private and academic sectors.

In the study focused on the role of institutions in the innovation ecosystem, respondents had the opportunity to specify what function their organizations serve, according to them. The results show a diversity of roles these institutions play, reflecting the complexity and dynamics of innovation.

More than 50% of respondents (result: 51.6%) identify their institutions as "a facilitator" (Adner & Kapoor, 2010). This suggests that the predominant role of many institutions is to facilitate collaboration and development in the innovation ecosystem. This may include actions such as creating platforms for knowledge exchange, supporting cooperation networks, or organizing events aimed at stimulating innovation. Another significant group, comprising over 23% of respondents (result: 23.3%), see their institutions as "brokers." This role may involve activities focused on connecting various entities in the ecosystem, such as companies, research institutions, and investors, which is crucial for the flow of knowledge and resources. 20% of respondents identify their institutions as "leaders" in the innovation ecosystem. This indicates the presence of institutions that not only participate in this ecosystem but also actively shape its direction and dynamics, perhaps by initiating new projects or leading strategic initiatives. Three respondents indicated other roles, such as "observers," "investors," or "enablers."

The question focused on the role of communication in innovation ecosystems forced respondents to indicate the two main objectives that, in their opinion, communication fulfills in their environment. The results show that

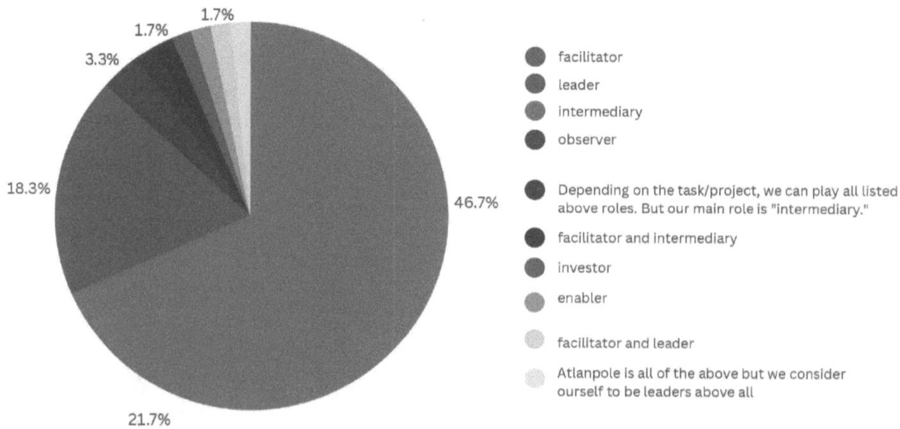

Figure 3.5 The role of institutions in the innovation ecosystem.

Source: own development

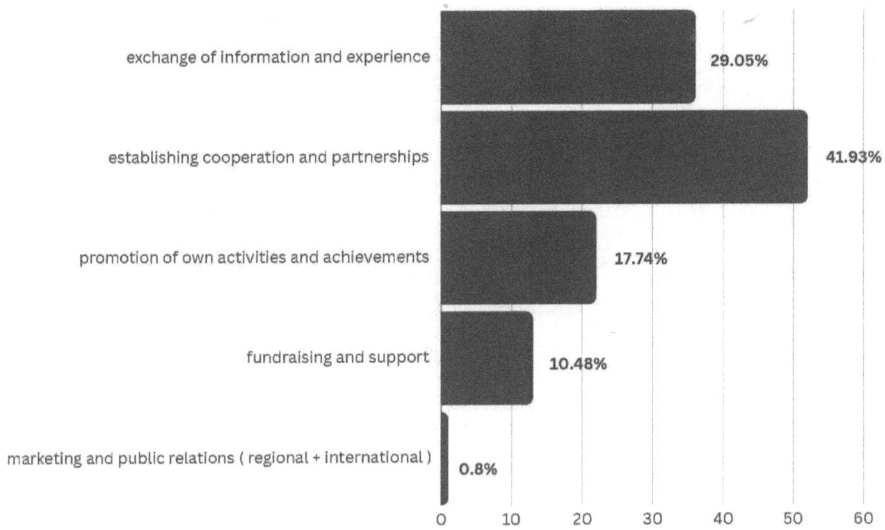

Figure 3.6 The main objectives of communication within the innovation system.
Source: own development

out of all the proposals, there are two dominant ones, which are most frequently emphasized by the participants.

"Establishing cooperation and partnerships" is a goal identified by the largest number of respondents (result: 41.93%). This suggests that communication in innovation ecosystems is primarily perceived as a tool for building cooperation networks, creating partnerships, and working together for innovation. This is crucial for the development and effectiveness of the ecosystem because it enables the exchange of resources, knowledge, and experiences. The second most frequently mentioned goal, indicated by 29.05% of respondents, is "exchange of information and experiences." This demonstrates that communication serves as a platform for sharing knowledge, experiences, and best practices, which is crucial for the development and effectiveness of innovation ecosystems. For nearly 18% of respondents (result: 17.74%), "promoting one's own activities and achievements" is also considered an important communication goal. This emphasizes the role of communication in building reputation and presenting successes, which can contribute to increasing visibility and prestige in the ecosystem. Meanwhile, for close to 11% (result: 10.48%) of respondents, "acquiring funds and support" is also considered important, although to a lesser extent. Communication can serve as a tool for securing financial resources and other forms of support. Only one respondent indicated "marketing and public relations" (both regional and international) as the main communication goal. This suggests that these aspects are less important to the respondents in the context of innovation ecosystems, or that they are perceived as less prioritized compared to other goals.

The study also analyzed whether companies have a communication plan with specific goals and actions. Respondents were asked "whether their institutions have a defined communication strategy or plan."

The results shed light on how institutions approach planning and organizing their communication activities. Out of 60 respondents, the majority, over 70% (result: 73.3%), confirmed that their institutions have developed a communication strategy or plan. This indicates a conscious approach, where these institutions actively plan and organize their communication activities. Having such a strategy is crucial because it allows for effective management, achieving specific communication goals, and building and maintaining relationships within the ecosystem. On the other hand, a significant minority, close to 27% of respondents (result: 26.6%), indicated that their institutions do not have a defined communication strategy. The lack of such a strategy can be a barrier to effective communication management and may indicate potential gaps in the communication of these institutions. This may mean that their actions are less coordinated or intentional, which can affect their ability to achieve goals and operate effectively within the ecosystem.

The survey also included a question about available forms of support in the region for stakeholders aimed at improving the quality of the innovation ecosystem.

The majority of respondents, a staggering 80%, confirmed the existence of support within the ecosystem. This indicates active efforts, at both the governmental and possibly private levels, aimed at supporting innovation.

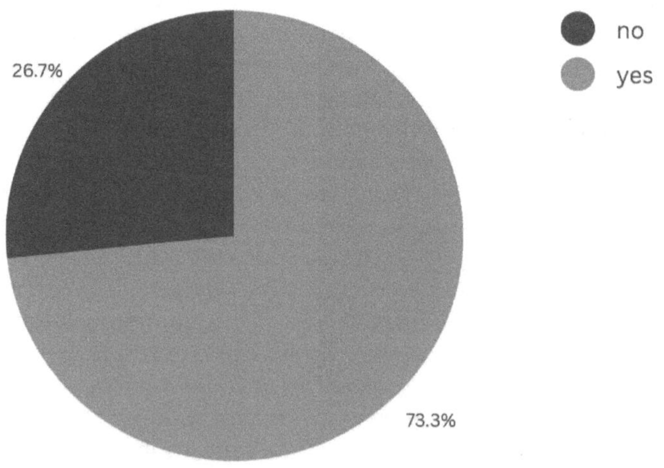

Figure 3.7 A communication strategy/plan with defined objectives and actions.
Source: own development

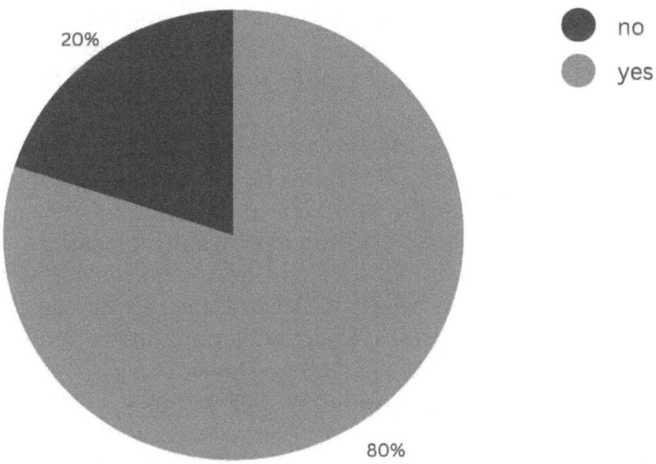

Figure 3.8 Forms of support or resources (e.g., specific government programs) available to stakeholders in regions to improve the quality of the innovation ecosystem.

Source: own development

This may include various programs, initiatives, funding, or training. On the other hand, 20% of respondents indicated that there is no available support in their regions or they are not aware of its existence. This may indicate gaps in communication or the availability of support programs, as well as regional differences in the availability of such resources. Those who confirmed the availability of support mentioned various forms of assistance, with the most commonly mentioned are as follows:

1 On-demand programs and training – many responses indicate the existence of on-demand programs, training funded by regional governments, international programs, study visits, and exchanges.
2 Financing infrastructure and the ecosystem – respondents mentioned financing infrastructure and access to ecosystem funds upon successful application.
3 Financing projects and initiatives – responses indicate the existence of project financing programs, which are often independently defined by institutions.
4 Support at the national and regional levels – many responses refer to support at the national level, including the creation of science and technology parks and other initiatives.
5 European and government funds – the European Regional Development Fund (ERDF) was mentioned, co-financing by the European Union, regional economic development schemes, and government programs.
6 Grants, associations, competence centers – respondents mentioned various forms of grants, associations, and competence centers as sources of support.

7 Programs supporting innovation and collaboration – many responses refer to programs supporting innovation, collaboration between startups and SMEs, as well as collaboration between universities and industry.

A somewhat different, yet still integral issue regarding communication in the innovation ecosystem, is the topic of barriers. The knowledge of the respondents was utilized to gather information about them.

In this question, respondents had the opportunity to indicate three main communication barriers. Over 21% of participants in the study pointed out that the main communication barrier is "lack of time." This suggests that time constraints are the primary obstacle to effective communication, which may result from the intense pace of work and numerous responsibilities in innovation ecosystems. The "lack of human resources" identified by 17.05% of respondents is another key barrier. Institutions often struggle with a shortage of staff or appropriate competencies, which hinders effective communication. Close to 18% of respondents (result: 17.61%) suggested that "poor coordination of activities" is also a significant obstacle. This may indicate problems with organizing work, project management, and coordination between different teams or departments. Other responses included in this question were: "rigid organizational structure," "resistance to change," "lack of shared values and goals," "competition," as well as "generational, language, and cultural differences." However, these barriers were mentioned much less frequently.

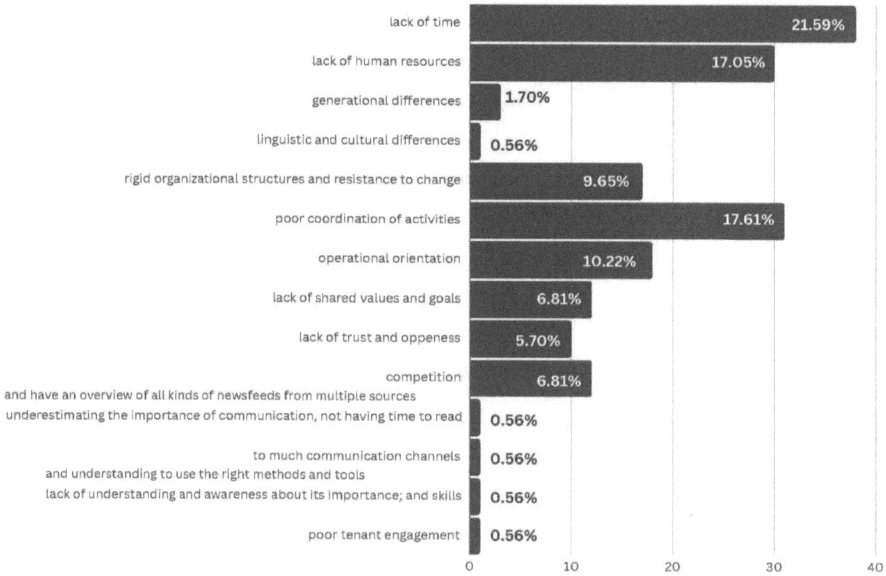

Figure 3.9 The main communication barriers within the innovation ecosystem.

Source: own development

Participants were asked what is a greater barrier in communication: human or technical factors. The overwhelming majority of respondents, 98% of the total surveyed, pointed to "human factors" as the main barrier in communication. This suggests that behaviors, attitudes, and other interpersonal aspects have a crucial impact on the effectiveness of communication. Issues such as lack of empathy, poor listening skills, resistance to change, or interpersonal conflicts can significantly hinder effective information exchange and collaboration. Only one respondent identified "technical factors" as the main barrier. This may indicate that tools and technologies, while important, are not perceived as the main obstacles in communication. Most institutions have the necessary technological tools, but the challenge remains in their effective utilization in a human context. These results emphasize the importance of interpersonal relationships and communication skills in creating effective communication. This indicates the need to focus on the development of soft skills among employees and leaders in innovation ecosystems.

Respondents pointed out various actions that their organizations undertake to overcome communication barriers. Among the most commonly mentioned is encouraging collaboration through events, especially through their organization – indicated by nearly 24% of respondents (result: 23.91%). Creating spaces for building relationships, exchanging knowledge, and collaboration are crucial for improving communication. Building trust and clear communication of goals and vision, indicated by 14.67% of respondents, are also important for the surveyed. Another frequent response (14.67% of respondents) turned out to be adapting communication to different stakeholder groups. This is essential for understanding and reaching diverse audiences. Undertaking joint projects, including cross-sector collaboration, is an action that highlights the importance of collaboration between different sectors and institutions within the innovation ecosystem. On the other hand, highlighted by over 9% of respondents (result: 9.25%), "investments in education and training" emphasize that communication skills are crucial and can be developed. The use of modern tools and technologies can support better communication, as recognized by over 7% of respondents in the survey (result: 7.06%).

Respondents in the study also expressed opinions about the role that technology and digital tools play in overcoming communication barriers in innovation ecosystems. 45% of them believe that technology and digital tools play a significant role in overcoming communication barriers. A significant portion of the study participants perceive it as a key element in improving communication. Close to 42% of respondents (result: 41.6%) consider the role of technology to be moderate, which may suggest that although it is helpful, it is not the only or dominant solution in overcoming communication challenges. On the other hand, over 13% of respondents believe (result: 13.3%) that the role of technology is limited.

In the survey, respondents indicated various digital tools and technologies that organizations use to improve communication. The most frequently

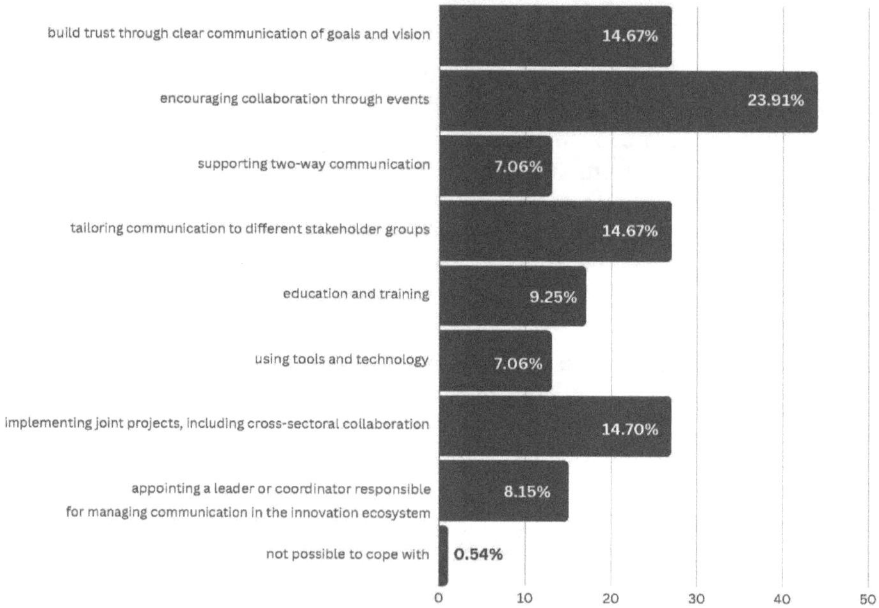

Figure 3.10 The key actions to address the communication barriers in order to improve communication in the innovation ecosystem.

Source: own development

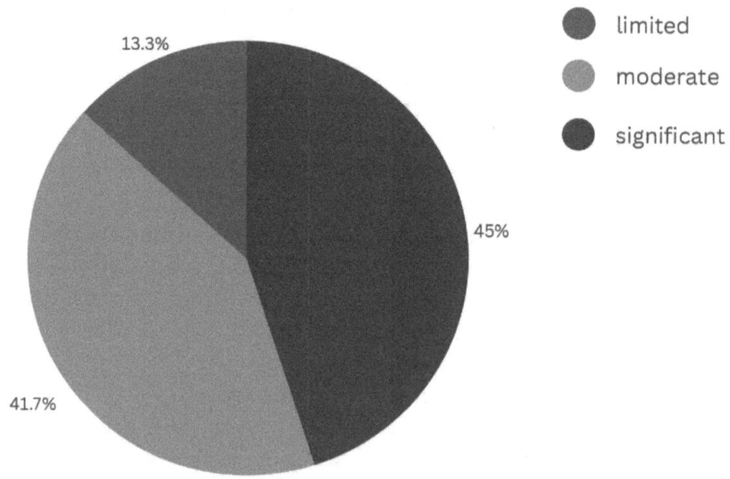

Figure 3.11 The role of technology and digital tools in overcoming communication barriers in the innovation ecosystem.

Source: own development

mentioned were online collaboration platforms such as Microsoft Teams, Slack, and Trello, cited by 47 respondents. This indicates their crucial role in enabling effective communication and collaboration. Cloud services for data sharing were also highlighted. Mentioned by 29 respondents, this underscores their importance in data sharing and management. Knowledge management systems like SharePoint, mentioned by 28 respondents, suggest their role in organizing and distributing knowledge. Understanding trends and making data-driven decisions require the use of data analysis, mentioned by 24 respondents. Only 4 respondents believed that tools for managing innovative projects, such as IdeaScale or Spigit, contribute to improving communication.

Respondents of the study also expressed their opinions on whether there is a need for introducing new tools or technologies to improve communication among stakeholders in their innovation ecosystems. The results of this question are presented in the chart below (Figure 3.13).

The majority of respondents, 37 out of 60 (approximately 62%), do not believe that the introduction of new tools or technologies is necessary. The current ones are considered sufficient, or respondents indicate that there are other, more significant barriers to overcome in communication. A slightly

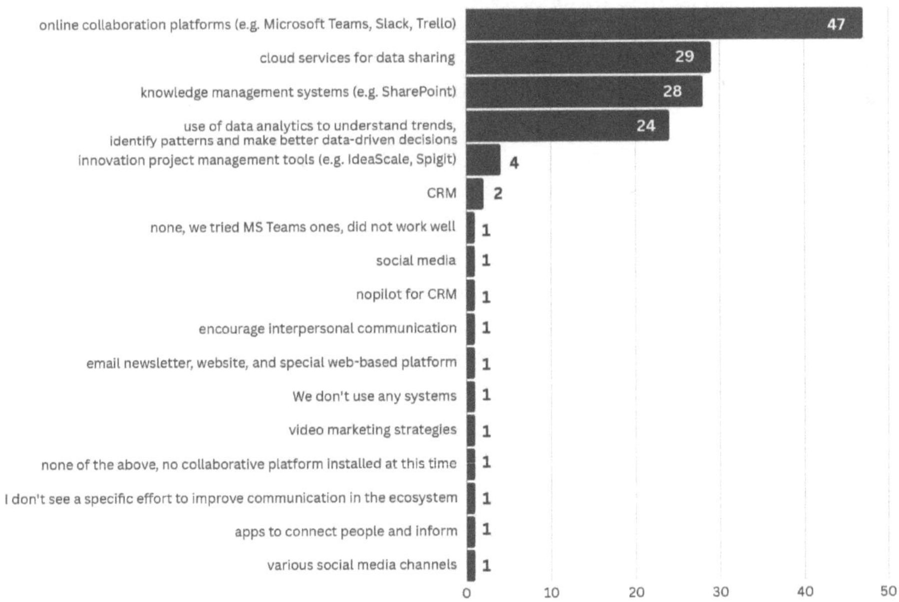

Figure 3.12 Digital tools and technologies used by organizations to improve communication in the innovation ecosystem.

Source: own development

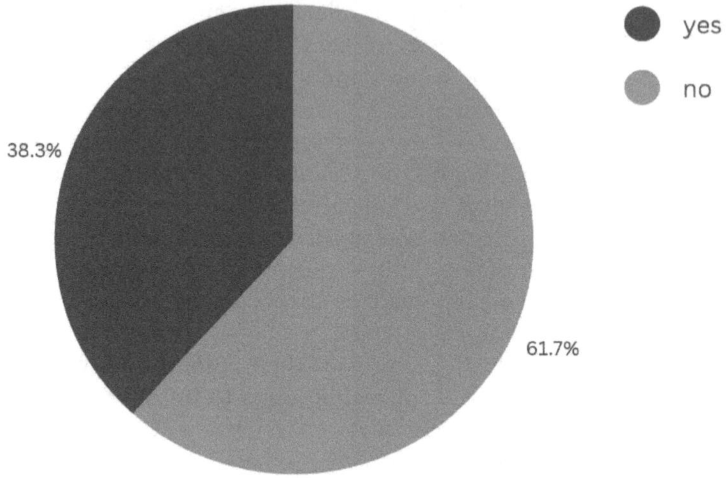

Figure 3.13 New tools or technologies that could be introduced to improve communication between stakeholders in the innovation ecosystem.

Source: own development

smaller group, 23 respondents (about 38%), believe that there is room for the introduction of new tools or technologies. This means that there is a certain group of stakeholders who see potential in technological innovations for further improving communication.

In seeking detailed information, those who responded that there are new tools and technologies that could be introduced to improve communication were asked to list the proposed solutions. Based on the responses provided, the main areas in this regard were identified:

1 Utilization of data and visualization: digital twins, other forms of visualization, digital learning systems – these responses indicate a growing interest in using advanced data visualization techniques for better understanding and communicating information.
2 Platforms and applications: TRIPOLIS Platform, a mobile application with various programs, Miro, Notion, Slack, Microsoft Teams – these tools are already widely used and recognized as effective in improving communication and collaboration.
3 Artificial intelligence (AI) – mentioned several times as a tool for improving communication, indicating the potential of AI in analyzing and processing communication data.
4 Dedicated mobile applications – applications specially designed for communication in innovation ecosystems, indicating the need for more personalized solutions.

5 Time and calendar management tools – indicating the importance of organization and coordination in communication.
6 Chat GPT – mentioned as a tool for improving communication, which may indicate a growing interest in using advanced language technologies.
7 Digital collaboration platforms – platforms for improving communication and collaboration among stakeholders, consistent with current trends in digital communication.
8 Centralization of innovation funding search – a tool for centralizing the search for innovation funding, indicating the need for better resource management.
9 Virtual platforms – for organizing virtual events and meetings, which has become particularly important in times of pandemics.
10 Events calendar for stakeholders – a shared events calendar for stakeholders in the innovation ecosystem, emphasizing the importance of event and meeting coordination.
11 Read.ai – for quick notes and memos, indicating the need for more efficient information management.

Giving respondents the option of more than one choice in the survey, various communication channels were indicated that they use in contacts with stakeholders in the innovation ecosystem. The most frequently mentioned are email and instant messengers – indicated by 59 respondents. They play a key role in everyday communication. The telephone was indicated by 27 respondents – it is still a popular means of communication, especially in situations requiring quick contact. 50 respondents noticed the dynamically developing social media, which maintain their importance as important channels for maintaining contacts and fast communication. Online platforms were mentioned by 26 individuals, and face-to-face meetings were considered crucial for direct interactions and relationship building (result: 53 respondents). Events are also crucial for networking and building communities around the innovation ecosystem, with only 2 respondents indicating artificial intelligence. Drop-by/Open Doors called informal visits represent a solution mentioned by 1 person.

Survey respondents had the opportunity to express their opinions on whether they consider artificial intelligence as an opportunity or a threat to the development of communication, and the answer to this question is presented in Figure 3.15.

The majority, 50 out of 60 (approximately 83%) individuals perceive artificial intelligence as an opportunity for the development of communication. This optimistic approach toward the potential of AI is enhancing, facilitating, and innovating communication. A smaller group, 10 respondents (about 17%), view AI as a threat. This may reflect concerns related to automation, loss of privacy, communication errors based on AI, or other potential negative consequences.

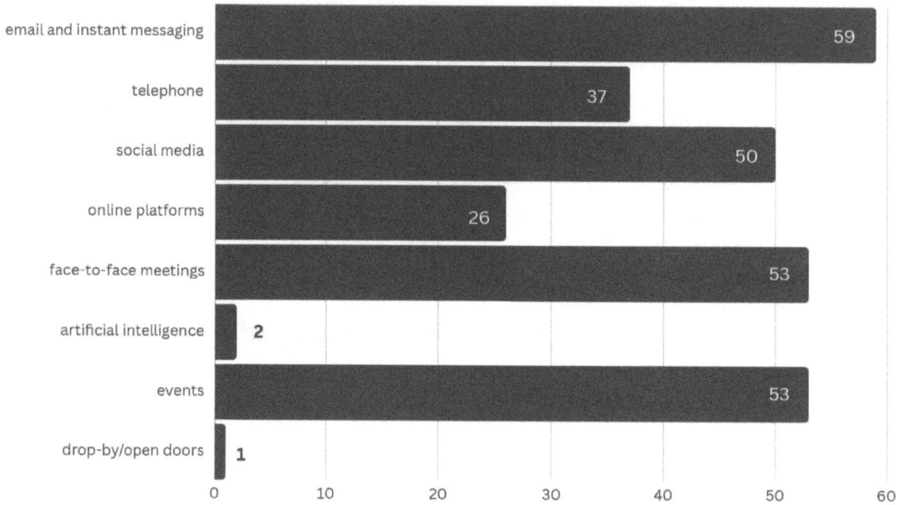

Figure 3.14 Communication channels to contact stakeholders in the innovation ecosystem.

Source: own development

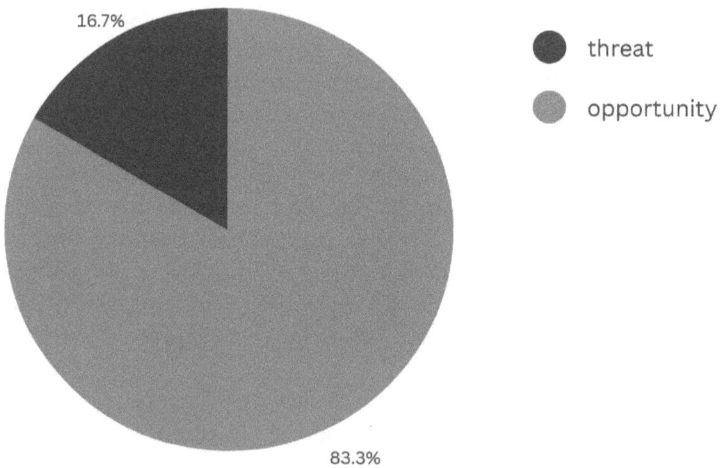

Figure 3.15 Artificial intelligence – an opportunity or a threat for the development of communication.

Source: own development

Among the goals of the conducted study was also the desire to verify which of the interactions drawn from the natural ecosystem are considered most common in innovation ecosystems in Europe. The responses are presented in Figure 3.16.

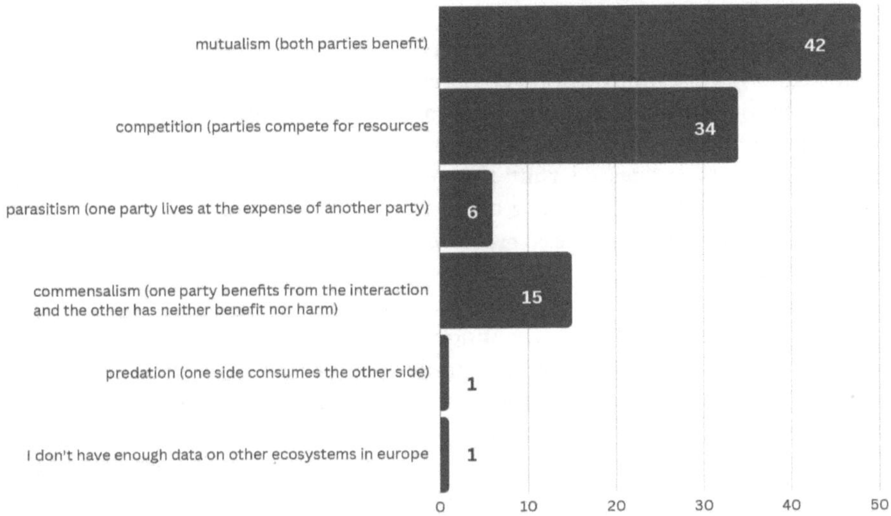

Figure 3.16 The most common interactions from the natural ecosystem to innovation ecosystems in Europe.

Source: own development

Respondents of the study indicated various forms of interactions[3] that they consider most common in innovation ecosystems in Europe. With the option to select two answers, they most frequently mentioned:

1 Mutualism (both parties benefit) – indicated 42 respondents. It is perceived as the dominant form of interaction. Collaboration and mutual benefits are key elements of these ecosystems.
2 Competition (parties compete for resources) – mentioned by 34 respondents. It is also perceived as common. Competition for resources is an important aspect of innovation ecosystems.

   Other forms of interaction such as parasitism, commensalism, and predation were mentioned, but to a much lesser extent, which may indicate that they are less characteristic of these environments.

For respondents, collaboration and seeking common benefits are central aspects of innovation ecosystems in Europe. Relationships based on mutual benefits are crucial for development and success in these environments. The presence of competition as a common form of interaction indicates the dynamic nature of innovation ecosystems, where competition for resources and market position is an important element. Other forms of interaction, although present, seem to play a lesser role, which may reflect the specificity of innovative environments, where collaboration and competition dominate over one-sided benefits or negative interactions.

In response to the questions, respondents had the opportunity to indicate various methods and indicators they use to assess the effectiveness of communication in their innovation ecosystems.

Among the most common responses are surveys conducted among tenants/customers/stakeholders. This solution was indicated by 41 respondents. 40 respondents suggested that the number of participants in events is used as a quantitative measure of activity effectiveness assessment. Customer satisfaction with the services offered was an option indicated by 30 respondents.

In reference to the previous question, actions aimed at improving the effectiveness of communication in the innovation ecosystem were also analyzed.

There are several diverse actions undertaken to improve communication in innovation ecosystems. In the next question, respondents had the opportunity to indicate all actions occurring in their ecosystem. In the study, the most frequently mentioned response indicated by respondents was staff training. As many as 33 respondents stated that the development of the employees' communication skills is perceived as crucial for the improvement of communication, in general. 24 respondents acknowledged that the introduction of new tools and technologies is evidence of organizations' efforts toward innovation and adapting their communication approaches. Changing communication strategies is also a frequently mentioned response, indicating the need to adapt strategies to changing conditions and needs. Only one respondent pointed out at the customized events and activities based on

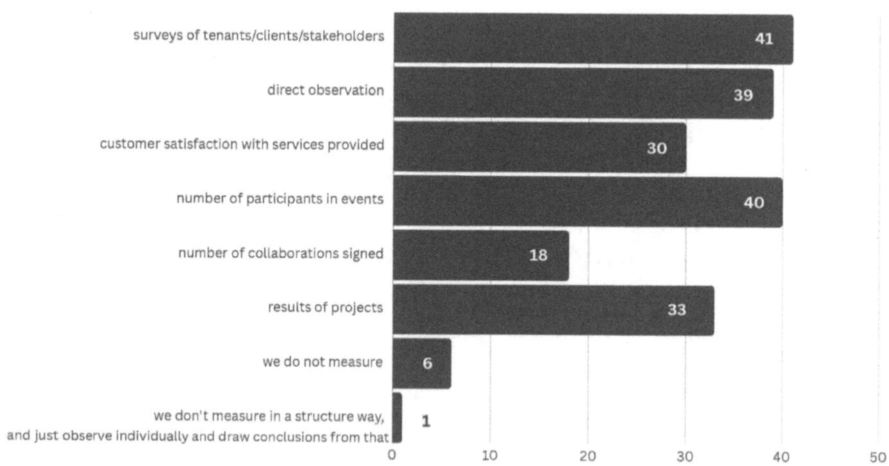

Figure 3.17 Methods/indicators used to measure the effectiveness of communication within the innovation ecosystem.

Source: own development

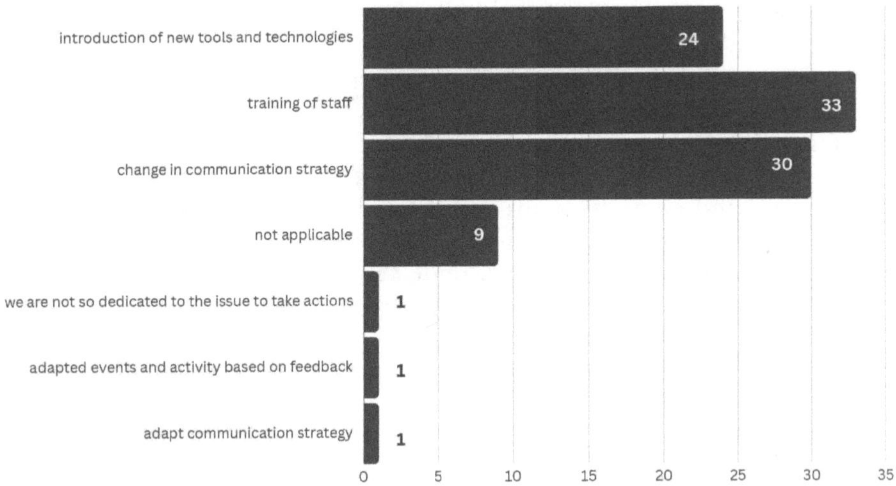

Figure 3.18 Actions taken on the basis of the measurement results to improve the effectiveness of communication in the innovation ecosystem.

Source: own development

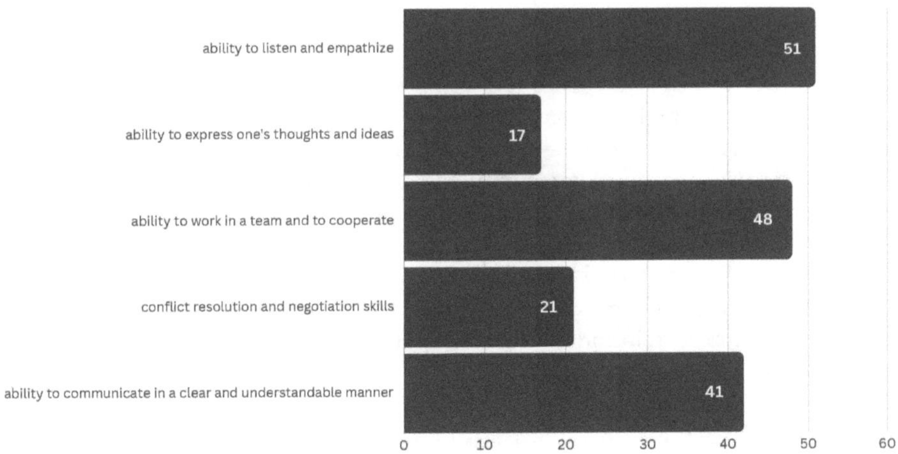

Figure 3.19 The most important communication skills for people working in the innovation ecosystem.

Source: own development

the feedback. Some organizations respond directly to specific feedback from stakeholders. A small number of individuals indicate a lack of engagement in improving communication, which may indicate limited resources or other priorities.

One of the questions in the survey verified the competency skills considered as the most important for individuals working in innovation ecosystems.

Respondents of the study identified three key communication skills that they consider the most important in working at the innovation ecosystems. The most frequently mentioned ones are:

1 Listening and empathy skills – indicated by 51 respondents, it is the most commonly cited response. This underscores its importance in building effective relationships, understanding needs, and perspectives of others.
2 Teamwork and collaboration skills – mentioned by 48 respondents, it emphasizes that the ability to effectively interact and cooperate in a group is crucial in innovation ecosystems.
3 Clear and understandable communication skills – indicated by 41 respondents. This is recognized as important, suggesting the need for clear communication of information and ideas.
4 Other mentioned skills – these include the ability to express one's thoughts and ideas and conflict resolution and negotiation skills.

The conducted study revealed that there are numerous challenges that respondents encounter in the context of communication in their innovation ecosystems. In the given question regarding this issue, they could have indicated all the variants that were related to them.

"Information overload" has become the most commonly mentioned challenge and was indicated by 46 respondents. Meanwhile, the need for the development of communication skills was mentioned by 26 respondents. A similar number pointed out that the increased competition and pressure for speed are the adaptations to a dynamic and often demanding environment. Other challenges included changing communication technologies, growing globalization and cultural diversity, generational differences, increasing customer and market demands, as well as identifying relevant information for the other party.

Respondents of the study identified three key actions each that can contribute to improving communication in innovation ecosystems.

According to the respondents, such actions should include:

1 Building tolerance, trust, and openness to collaboration – indicated by 30% of respondents. This suggests that interpersonal relationships and building trust are crucial for effective communication.
2 Supporting the development of communication skills – indicated by over 29% of respondents (result: 29.33%) emphasizes the need for continuous improvement of these skills in a dynamic environment.
3 Establishing clear communication rules – mentioned by nearly 19% of respondents (result: 18.66%) is perceived as important and signals the need for clarity and coherence in communication processes.

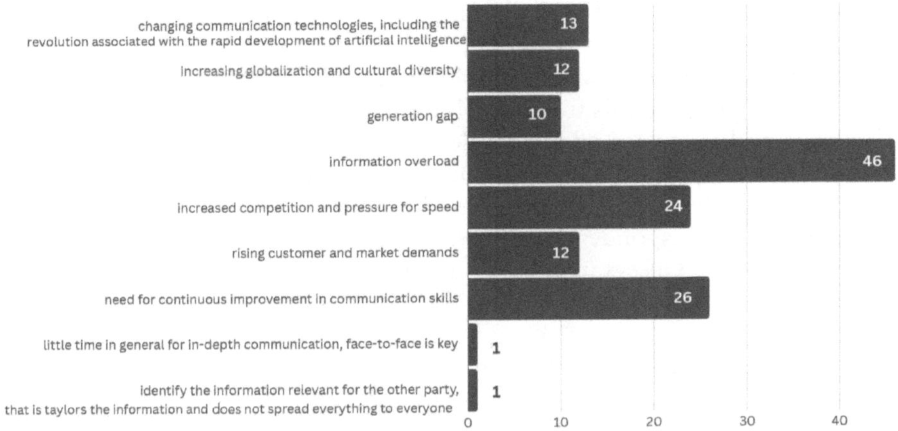

Figure 3.20 Key communication challenges in your innovation ecosystem.

Source: own development

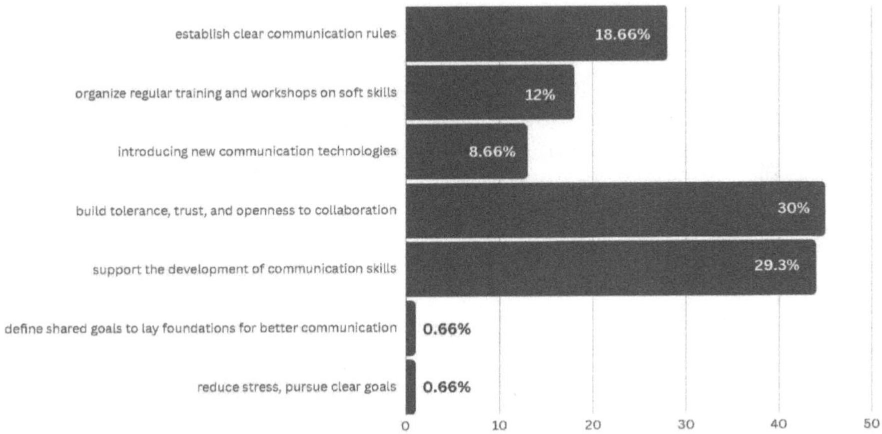

Figure 3.21 The key actions that can be taken to improve communication between actors in your innovation ecosystem.

Source: own development

4 Other actions included organizing regular training and workshops on soft skills and introducing new communication technologies.

At the request formulated in the question, respondents of the study pointed out two main trends that, according to them, will have the greatest impact on the communication process in their innovation ecosystems.

Respondents identified the following two main trends:

1 Rapid development of artificial intelligence and the transition of life into the virtual world – this trend was indicated by 33 respondents, suggesting that AI technologies and the development of the virtual world will have a significant impact on how we communicate and collaborate.
2 Sustainable development, including the climate crisis – an argument mentioned by 38 respondents emphasizes the growing ecological awareness and the need to integrate these issues into communication and innovative actions.

Other trends included demographic changes, the era of biotechnology, and the multi-polarization of the world.

Research conclusions

In the era of rapidly advancing globalization and dynamic technological changes, innovation ecosystems play a crucial role in shaping the economic and social future of Europe. Central to these ecosystems is communication, which enables the exchange of knowledge, ideas, and resources among diverse actors. The purpose of the above study was to examine and understand the role that communication plays in innovation ecosystems in Europe. The aim was to answer the question of how effective communication can contribute to the success of innovation ecosystems.

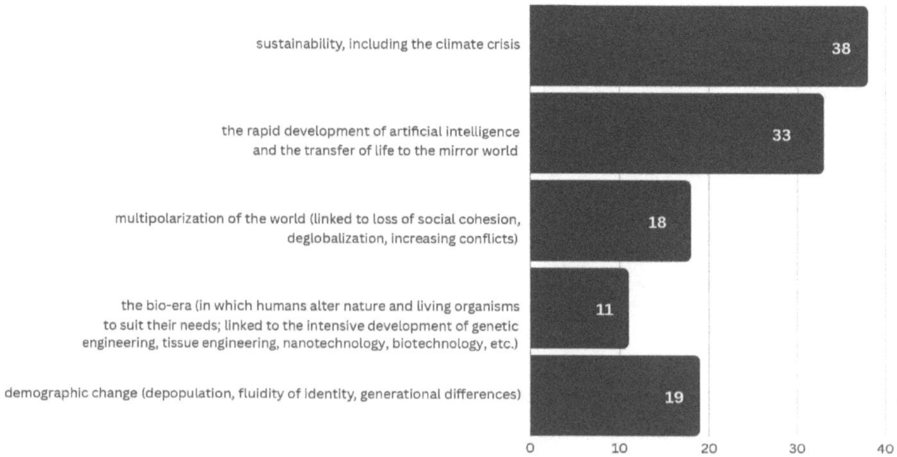

Figure 3.22 Key trends for the next five years that will impact the communication process.

Source: own development

It turns out that the majority of respondents participating in the study evaluate communication in innovation ecosystems as at least average, with a predominance of "satisfactory" ratings. However, there is significant potential for improvement, especially considering that only a small percentage considered communication to be "very good." These results indicate the need for further improvement of communication processes to increase the effectiveness and efficiency of innovation ecosystems.

The conducted study indicates that although organizations generally perform relatively well in external communication, there are certain areas that require improvement, especially in the context of building and maintaining relationships with external partners and stakeholders. Despite the relatively high evaluation of interpersonal communication within the surveyed entities, organizational and external communication presents a diversity of responses. This suggests the need to focus on improving information flow and collaboration both within the organization and in its external relations. It seems particularly important to pay attention to communication between teams and external partners, which can contribute to increased effectiveness and efficiency of the organization.

There is no doubt that start-ups and SMEs are perceived as the most active stakeholders in the eyes of the surveyed entities within the innovation ecosystem. Their involvement underscores their key role in promoting innovation and development. There is a clear difference in perceived activity between groups, with public administration rated as the least active. This may indicate the need to increase engagement from the public sector. It also highlights areas where individual stakeholder groups can increase their involvement and activity to further contribute to development.

The innovation ecosystem consists of diverse entities that can play specialized or niche roles, with each contributing a unique input. This diversity is crucial for the dynamics and adaptability of the ecosystem. It enables effective collaboration and exchange among different entities. The dominance of "a facilitator" role in the conducted study underscores the importance of creating conditions conducive to cooperation and innovation. Facilitators play a crucial role in connecting various elements of the ecosystem, which is essential for its healthy development. On the other hand, while the presence of leaders is smaller, it is significant for directing and inspiring changes within the ecosystem. They can be a driving force for innovation, introducing new ideas and directions for development.

Respondents participating in the study believe that building cooperation and exchanging knowledge are priorities in innovation ecosystems. This underscores that communication is crucial for supporting innovation and development. Its various goals reflect the complexity and multidimensionality of innovation ecosystems, where different entities may have different communication priorities and needs. Areas such as marketing and PR, although currently less emphasized, may offer potential for further development, especially in the context of promoting innovation on a broader scale and building stronger market visibility.

The significance of having a defined communication strategy in institutions operating within innovation ecosystems is immense. Most institutions recognize the benefits of planning and organizing communication activities. At the same time, there is room for those institutions that have not yet developed their strategy to increase their communication effectiveness through its development and implementation. Such action can help them better manage their activities and achieve their goals within the ecosystem.

At large, according to the respondents, there is a wide range of support in innovation ecosystems, from funding infrastructure and projects to training, exchanges, and on-demand programs. This shows that support is tailored to the various needs and operating models of institutions. Many innovation-supporting programs are initiated and funded by national and regional governments, emphasizing their role in promoting innovation. There is a need for better informing stakeholders about available resources and support, especially in regions where respondents are unaware of such possibilities. This can help utilizing fuller use of available resources or support.

According to the respondents, resource and organizational constraints are the main obstacles to effective communication. This underscores the importance of time management, human resources, and coordination of activities in innovation ecosystems. The diversity of mentioned barriers shows that communication in innovation ecosystems is a complex process that can encounter various obstacles, from structural to cultural ones. Focusing on time management, human resources, and coordination of activities can bring significant benefits, and improvement in these areas can help overcome barriers and facilitate effective information exchange. The lack of human resources emphasizes the need for investment in personnel and competence development, which is crucial for improving communication effectiveness. The diversity of barriers indicates the need for an individualized approach to solving communication problems in different organizations and contexts. This may involve adapting communication strategies to the specific needs and challenges of each institution.

Focusing on the development of soft skills such as empathy, active listening, and conflict management can be crucial for improving communication in innovation ecosystems. Similarly, technology can serve as a supportive tool, but it does not replace the need for the development of interpersonal and communication skills. It can be considered whether there is a relationship between these barriers and previously identified communication goals or communication strategies. It is possible that institutions with well-defined communication strategies are better prepared to deal with interpersonal challenges.

The respondents' indication of appointing individuals responsible for communication can help in better managing and coordinating communication activities. The high value placed on collaboration and events suggests that creating opportunities for interaction and collaboration is crucial for improving communication. Focusing on building trust and adapting communication to different stakeholder groups shows that understanding and reaching diverse audiences are important for effective communication, and investments in education and training indicate an understanding that communication skills are crucial and can be developed. Organizations employ various strategies, from building relationships and trust to leveraging technology to overcome communication barriers. The high value placed on collaboration and events suggests that creating opportunities for interaction and collaboration is crucial for improving communication. Appointing individuals responsible for communication can help in better management and coordination.

Most respondents consider technology to be an important element in overcoming communication barriers. Digital tools can significantly support communication processes, facilitating the exchange of information and collaboration. The group viewing the role of technology as limited may perceive other aspects, such as human or organizational factors, as more significant in communication. Technology and digital tools are considered important in overcoming communication barriers, although their role varies depending on the context and specific needs. Furthermore, while technology is important, it is not seen as a panacea for all communication challenges. Other aspects such as interpersonal skills and management also play a crucial role. There is potential for further use of technology to improve communication, especially in areas where its role is currently perceived as limited. This may involve the development of new tools, training in their effective use, and integration of technology with other communication methods.

The aforementioned results indicate that online collaboration platforms are, for respondents, a crucial tool in enabling effective communication and collaboration in innovation ecosystems. Organizations use various tools, demonstrating that communication in innovation ecosystems requires a diversified approach and the utilization of different technologies. Tools such as CRM and social media are less frequently mentioned, which may indicate their limited application in the context of communication. Digital technologies, especially online collaboration platforms, play an important role in improving communication in innovation ecosystems, but the choice of tools depends on the specific needs and context of each organization. There is potential for further development and integration of different digital tools to increase communication effectiveness. This may include better utilization of data analysis, knowledge management systems, and project management tools.

Survey results also indicate that current tools and technologies are considered mainly sufficient by the majority of respondents. Existing solutions are effective in the current ecosystem, or focusing on other aspects such as interpersonal skills or management may be more important. However, there is a group of respondents who see opportunities for improvement and innovation in communication tools. This is a very important signal of specific gaps or needs that are not currently being met by existing solutions. Decisions regarding the introduction of new tools should be made after considering current needs and the capabilities offered by existing solutions. This may include analyzing the effectiveness of current tools and identifying areas where new technologies could bring additional value.

Respondents participating in the study identified a wide range of tools and technologies, from advanced AI-based solutions to more traditional collaboration and communication platforms. This is evidence of diverse needs and possibilities regarding communication in innovation ecosystems. Many of the suggested tools aim to tailor communication to the specific needs and contexts of different stakeholder groups, which corresponds to the need for personalization and flexibility in communication. Artificial intelligence and digital data visualization tools are perceived as promising areas to explore in order to improve communication. This indicates openness to innovation and the use of new technologies to enhance communication processes.

The results obtained in the study indicate that e-mail and internet messengers are considered by respondents as essential tools in daily communication, offering convenience and speed in exchanging information. Despite the growing role of digital technologies, direct interactions still play a crucial role in building strong relationships and effective collaboration.

The above research also suggests that most respondents see AI as a tool that can bring benefits to communication, such as efficiency, personalization, and the ability to analyze large datasets. The group considering AI a threat may perceive risks associated with excessive automation, loss of control over communication processes, or ethical and privacy issues.

It turns out that collaboration and seeking mutual benefits are central aspects of innovation ecosystems in Europe. Building relationships based on mutual benefits is crucial for success in these environments. There is a dynamic balance between collaboration and competition, which is typical of healthy innovation ecosystems. This indicates the need for skillful balancing between these two aspects. Innovation ecosystems are characterized by a diversity of interactions, referring to the complexity and multidimensionality of these environments. This underscores that different forms of interaction can coexist and contribute to the overall health and dynamics of the ecosystem.

The research findings demonstrate that the development of employees' communication skills is highly significant for respondents. Organizations aim to innovate and adapt their communication approaches to better meet the needs and challenges of innovation ecosystems. Entities also employ various strategies, from staff training to the introduction of new tools, to improve communication in innovation ecosystems. Continuous training and adjusting communication strategies are crucial for maintaining effective communication in dynamic innovation ecosystems. On the other hand, responding to feedback and adjusting actions based on it is important to ensure that communication is effective and meets the needs of stakeholders.

The surveyed organizations employ various methods to assess the effectiveness of communication, reflecting the complexity and multidimensionality of communication in innovation ecosystems. Direct feedback from stakeholders and observation are crucial for assessing the effectiveness of communication. There is a need for a systematic approach to measuring this kind of effectiveness to better understand its impact on the innovation ecosystem.

It turns out that the ability to listen and show empathy is perceived as crucial in building effective relationships and understanding the needs of others, which is essential in innovative environments. The ability to work in teams and collaborate is highly valued, emphasizing the importance of synergy and collective action in innovation ecosystems. Meanwhile, the ability to communicate clearly and understandably is crucial for effectively conveying and exchanging information. Soft skills such as empathy, listening, and collaboration are incredibly important in innovative environments. Effective communication, in both expressing ideas and understanding others, is crucial for success in ecosystems. There is a need for continuous development of communication skills among employees in innovation ecosystems to support collaboration, innovation, and problem-solving.

The above exploration results indicate that information overload is the main challenge for respondents, which means that there is a need for better information management and the avoidance of information overload. The challenge associated with the need for continuous improvement of communication skills points out that adaptation to changing conditions and communication tools is crucial. Increased competition and pressure for speed indicate a dynamic and often demanding environment where fast and effective communication essential. There is a need for better information management to prevent overload and improve communication effectiveness. Changing technologies, including AI, require continuous adjustment and development of communication skills. Growing customer and market demands require flexibility and the ability to quickly respond in communication.

Establishing clear communication rules indicates the need for clarity and consistency. The results emphasize that effective communication in innovation ecosystems is based on strong interpersonal relationships and well-developed soft skills. Regular training and workshops can help develop and maintain a high level of communication skills. Clear communication rules and structures can help ensure that communication is effective and understandable for all parties involved.

It turns out that the rapid development of AI and the shift of activities to the virtual world will be crucial – according to respondents – for the future of communication in innovation ecosystems. Sustainable development and the climate crisis are recognized as important trends, indicating the need to address these issues in communication and innovation strategies. Organizations will need to adapt their communication strategies to rapidly evolving technologies such as AI, which may include the use of new communication tools and platforms. Sustainable development and climate issues will increasingly impact communication and actions in innovation ecosystems, requiring the integration of these issues into communication strategies. Demographic and geopolitical changes will require flexibility and adaptability in communication, which may involve considering cultural and generational diversity.

As part of understanding the dynamics of communication in innovation ecosystems, a detailed analysis of the survey results targeting participants in these ecosystems was conducted. The aim of the study was to identify key aspects, challenges, and trends influencing the effectiveness of communication in an environment characterized by continuous development and innovation. The analysis of respondents' answers revealed a moderate assessment of the quality of communication in innovation ecosystems, with a predominance of perceptions as "satisfactory," indicating potential areas for improvement.

Notes

1 A startup is a young, innovative company focused on rapid growth and scalability, often operating in conditions of uncertainty and exploring new markets or technologies.

2 Small and medium-sized enterprises (SMEs), according to EU Recommendation 2003/361/EC, are companies that employ fewer than 250 people and have an annual turnover not exceeding 50 million euros or an annual balance sheet total not exceeding 43 million Euros, provided that they are independent companies, meaning that 25% or more of their capital or voting rights are not owned by a single enterprise or jointly by several enterprises that do not meet the SME criteria.

3 The identification of types of interactions in the survey questionnaire was based on J.F. Moore's classification (Moore, 1993), who introduced the concept of business ecosystems, analyzing various forms of interaction between organizations (including mutualism as a form of cooperation benefiting all parties involved).

4 When respondents answer questions with multiple possible responses, it is possible for the total percentage to exceed 100%. To adjust these percentages so that they sum to 100%, the following methodology is applied:

Adjusted Percentage (X) = (Number of respondents who selected a given response/Total number of respondents) × 100%

This formula ensures that the percentage for each response is proportionate to the total number of respondents, thereby adjusting the figures to fit within a 100% scale.

Alternatively, the authors provide the number of respondents selecting each possible response.

Bibliography

Adner, R. (2006). Align your innovation strategy with the innovation ecosystem. *Harvard Business Review*, *84*(4), 98–107.

Adner, R., & Kapoor, R. (2010). Creating value in innovation ecosystems: How the structure of technological interdependence influences firm performance in new generations of technology. *Strategic Management Journal*, *31*(3), 306–333.

Chesbrough, H. W. (2003). *Open innovation: The new imperative for creating and profiting from technology*. Harvard Business Press.
Filipiak, M. (2004). *Homo communicans. Introduction to the theory of mass communication*. Maria Curie-Skłodowska University Publishing House.
Fiske, D. W. (1986). Specificity of method and knowledge in social sciences. In D. W. Fiske & R. A. Shweder (Eds.), *Metatherapy in social science*. The University of Chicago Press.
Hansen, A., & Machin, D. (2013). *Media and communication research methods*. Red Globe Press.
Krauz-Mozer, B., & Ścigaj, P. (2013). Does Polish political science need a quantitative approach? In B. Krauz-Mozer & P. Ścigaj (Eds.), *Research and methodological approaches in political science*. Jagiellonian University Publishing House.
Łuszczyński, A. (2005). *Methodological foundations of political science research*. Publishing House of the University of Rzeszów.
Moore, J. F. (1993, May–June). Predators and prey: The new ecology of competition. *Harvard Business Review*, pp. 75–86.
Moore, J. F. (1996). *The death of competition: Leadership and strategy in the age of business ecosystems*. Harper Paperbacks.
Nowak, S. (2012). *Social research methodology*. PWN.
Wimmer, R. D., & Dominick, J. R. (1983). *Media research. Introduction* (2nd ed.). Wadsworth Cengage Learning.

4 New concept for strong communication mechanisms within innovation ecosystems

Introduction

This chapter introduces a novel concept aimed at fostering robust communication mechanisms within innovation ecosystems. It emphasizes the critical need for resolute and reliable channels of communication to cultivate collaborative environments where stakeholders can effectively exchange resources and ideas. The overarching objective of this chapter is to develop a fully integrated theoretical-empirical framework. This approach combines an understanding of necessary conditions with existing barriers to innovation. By elucidating the underlying framework beforehand, the chapter aims to facilitate communication among various stakeholders in a manner conducive to creating a favorable atmosphere for collective technological change. The ultimate goal is to provide interested parties with a well-organized explanation of how to navigate communication challenges and implement a collaborative innovation strategy effectively.

The chapter provides a systematic exploration of the multifaceted nature of communication within these systems, viewing communication as an energizing agent for innovation and as a bridge that brings various groups together to pursue common goals. The central theme of this discourse is that communication in innovation ecosystems can be more effective than ever before. With the rapid development of electronic communication, it is now possible to connect with a larger number of people over greater distances at reduced costs. However, the chapter also acknowledges the downsides of technological dependence, such as digital divisions and information overload, which can impede effective communication. The chapter proceeds to examine the inherent barriers to effective communication within innovation ecosystems. These barriers extend beyond intra-organizational communication and also hinder interorganizational and regional collaborations, thereby directly impacting the entire innovation ecosystem across time and space. To address these challenges, the chapter introduces a systematic and empirically verified framework rooted in theory. This framework is designed to facilitate communication within and among innovation ecosystems by emphasizing several key pillars.

DOI: 10.4324/9781032697802-5

First and foremost, this chapter establishes that effective communication is not merely a functional aspect of innovation ecosystems but a strategic imperative. It serves as the cornerstone upon which the success of collaborative ventures and the effectiveness of innovation processes are built. Given the multifaceted nature of these ecosystems, characterized by heterogeneous groups of stakeholders with varying goals, backgrounds, and expertise, inclusive, transparent, and adaptable communication are essential. This approach is vital for aligning objectives, exchanging knowledge, and fostering a culture of trust and mutual respect among participants.

Moreover, the chapter highlights the significant impact of communication barriers, such as organizational silos, cultural differences, and technological disparities. If left unaddressed, these barriers can hinder the exchange of information and ideas, impede collaborative efforts, and ultimately limit the innovation potential of the ecosystem. To overcome these barriers, the chapter advocates for a proactive and strategic approach that prioritizes the removal of silos and the promotion of open communication.

Furthermore, the chapter emphasizes the pivotal role of technological advancements in shaping the communication landscape within innovation ecosystems. Digital technologies, including AI-driven platforms, have profoundly transformed how stakeholders communicate and collaborate, enabling distance-independent, real-time interaction irrespective of physical location. While these technologies offer opportunities for quicker and easier information exchange, a balanced approach is necessary to capitalize on their benefits while mitigating potential shortcomings, such as digital exclusion and the loss of the human touch in communication.

Lastly, the chapter underscores the broader implications of communication in the regional and global context of economic development within innovation ecosystems. Enhanced communication and collaboration can accelerate innovation, drive economic growth, and promote sustainable development. Thus, this consideration not only advances scholarly discussions on innovation ecosystems but also provides valuable insights for policymakers, businesses, and other stakeholders interested in fostering innovation-driven growth. In conclusion, the insights derived from this chapter significantly contribute to understanding innovation ecosystems and provide a roadmap for building more connected, innovative, and resilient communities.

Necessary conditions

The essence of innovation ecosystems lies in their capacity to cultivate collaborative environments wherein stakeholders engage in the exchange of knowledge, ideas, and resources. Central to the success of such ecosystems is the establishment of robust communication mechanisms. The literature highlights the multifaceted nature of communication within innovation ecosystems and underscores the significance of various necessary conditions for its effectiveness. By integrating these insights into a comprehensive framework, stakeholders can navigate the complexities of communication, thereby fostering an environment conducive to collaborative innovation.

Authors have long emphasized the pivotal role of communication in innovation ecosystems. Chesbrough (2003) posited that open innovation thrives on effective communication and collaboration among diverse entities, transcending organizational boundaries to harness external ideas. Additionally, Powell et al. (1996) highlighted the significance of communication networks in the dissemination of tacit knowledge, asserting that strong communication channels facilitate the transmission of valuable insights critical for innovation.

Integration of diverse perspectives has also garnered attention as a crucial condition for effective communication. Dahlander and Gann (2010) emphasized the value of diverse perspectives in spurring creativity and innovation, asserting that heterogeneous inputs lead to richer problem-solving approaches. Moreover, Bosch-Sijtsema et al. (2014) advocated for the integration of various stakeholder viewpoints to enhance the resilience and adaptability of innovation ecosystems.

This comprehensive framework amalgamates theoretical insights from the literature with empirical findings derived from the authors' research endeavors. By integrating these essential pillars (open communication, diverse perspectives, collaborative approach), it provides a structured approach to cultivate robust communication channels within innovation ecosystems, aiming to foster an environment conducive to collaborative innovation. The establishment of effective communication within innovation ecosystems hinges upon foundational elements that serve as bedrocks for the facilitation of seamless and meaningful communication among diverse stakeholders. The diagram provided below depicts the necessary conditions essential for cultivating robust communication mechanisms within innovation ecosystems.

Establishing and maintaining trust is crucial for effective communication and collaboration across different organizations and regions. Within the realm of interorganizational communication, trust serves as the cornerstone upon which successful partnerships and collaborations are built (Mayer et al., 1995). It facilitates seamless transactions, mitigates perceived risks inherent in cooperative endeavors (Zhu et al., 2020), and cultivates an environment conducive to transparent and efficacious exchange of information (Ansell & Gash, 2008).

In the sphere of regional communication, trust assumes an even broader significance, transcending organizational confines to encompass cultural and societal norms (Huxham & Vangen, 2005). Cultivating trust within this domain necessitates a profound comprehension of local customs, a reverence for regional idiosyncrasies, and a steadfast dedication to transparent and ethically sound communication protocols (Koschmann, 2012). Typically, trust at the regional level is nurtured over time through consistent and dependable actions that underscore a genuine commitment to the well-being and interests of regional communities (Owen-Smith & Powell, 2004).

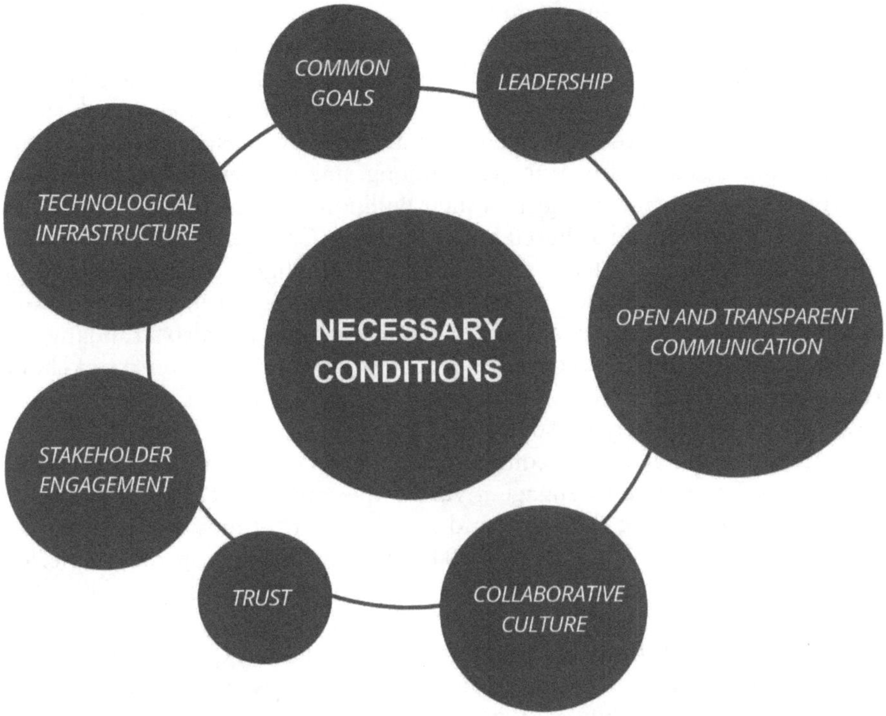

Figure 4.1 Key elements for fostering effective communication in the innovation ecosystem.

Source: own development

Effectively engendering trust in both interorganizational and regional contexts demands adept management and alignment of the varied interests harbored by diverse stakeholders (Tsai & Ghoshal, 1998). It entails a strategic approach that acknowledges and addresses the multifaceted dynamics inherent in fostering trust across organizational and regional boundaries. The establishment of trust among various stakeholders in Silicon Valley has been linked to its culture of openness and knowledge sharing (Etzkowitz & Leydesdorff, 2000). This environment of transparency and collaborative exchange fosters mutual trust among different players within the ecosystem, contributing significantly to its success as an innovation hub.

Fostering a culture of trust and mutual understanding among stakeholders is critical in cultivating a shared commitment to common goals (Murray et al., 2010). Open dialogue, transparency, and acknowledging the value of each stakeholder's contributions contribute significantly to building a cohesive ecosystem with aligned objectives (Bason, 2010). Efforts to promote trust, such as transparent communication, recognition of diverse contributions, and inclusive collaboration, foster a conducive atmosphere for joint endeavors (Murray et al., 2010). Transparent decision-making processes, the dissemination of relevant information, and the validation of each stakeholder's viewpoint foster inclusivity and collective responsibility toward overarching goals. Cultivating trust among stakeholders helps to mitigate potential conflicts and strengthens their willingness to engage in cooperative ventures directed toward shared aims (Ansell & Gash, 2008).

The importance of trust-building activities highlights their crucial role in promoting positive interactions and driving collaborative efforts toward successful outcomes (Mayer et al., 1995). Common goals are also a fundamental aspect of any innovation ecosystem. It fosters trust among diverse stakeholders by aligning their visions and goals, leading to a collective commitment toward a shared objective (Adner, 2017).

To identify and articulate common aspirations within an innovation landscape, it is imperative to engage a varied spectrum of actors, including industry representatives, academic and research institutions, and government entities (Owen-Smith & Powell, 2004). Innovation hubs, for example, offer invaluable insights into prevailing market trends, industry-specific challenges, and burgeoning opportunities (Cohen & Levinthal, 1990). Academic and research institutions contribute their specialized expertise in research, development, and innovation, augmenting the ecosystem's knowledge base with cutting-edge capabilities (Etzkowitz & Leydesdorff, 2000). Government entities bring forth regulatory perspectives, funding avenues, and policy support, ensuring adherence to regulatory frameworks, and facilitating access to public resources (Borrás & Edquist, 2013).

The participation of various stakeholders guarantees a comprehensive assessment of different perspectives in setting goals and meeting needs within the innovation ecosystem (Chesbrough et al., 2006). This joint effort not only enhances the decision-making process but also strengthens the ecosystem's ability to innovate and adapt to changing environments. Promoting a collaborative culture and prioritizing cooperation over competition further foster trust among stakeholders (Tsai & Ghoshal, 1998). Clear and comprehensive policies on intellectual property rights are essential in fostering trust among innovators and investors (Hagedoorn, 2002). In addition, government policies that promote innovation and protect stakeholder interests significantly contribute to nurturing trust within the ecosystem (Kemp & Pearson, 2007).

Establishing common goals within an innovation ecosystem is an intricate process pivotal to its functionality and success. The literature underscores several effective strategies to cultivate shared objectives among diverse stakeholders within these dynamic environments (West & Bogers, 2014). Freeman (1984) emphasizes the key role of shared goals in fostering collaboration and collective action. One fundamental approach involves facilitating collaborative dialogue and consensus-building processes among stakeholders to articulate and define overarching goals that resonate across the ecosystem (Ansell &

Gash, 2008). This process often entails inclusive decision-making forums, effective communication channels, and participatory mechanisms that ensure representation of diverse perspectives and interests (Dahan et al., 2010). Additionally, strategic leadership and governance mechanisms play a crucial role in guiding the establishment and realization of common goals, providing direction and steering collaborative efforts toward shared outcomes (Westley et al., 2007a).

For communication to be effective within innovation ecosystems, transparency and openness are identified as foundational conditions. Aral and Weill (2007) note the centrality of transparency in generating trust and collaboration, stating, "For communication to be effective, agents must have a basis of shared knowledge and a degree of trust that conveyed information is accurate and truthful. Transparency is important in facilitating a free flow of information" Van den Ende et al. (2014) further support this by underlining the essential role of openness in stimulating knowledge-sharing behaviors among ecosystem participants. Many of the necessary conditions for increased collaboration and innovation within an innovation ecosystem are facilitated through the establishment of open and transparent communication practices.

The generation of synergy is a fundamental example, where this is promoted through the sharing of ideas and the refinement of these ideas among agents, resulting in more innovative solutions (Chesbrough, 2003). The cross-pollination of differing perspectives among agents is also critical, as this aids in the generation of novel and breakthrough innovations (Cohen & Levinthal, 1990). These and many other such conditions speak to the critical role of openness in communication for driving innovation within an ecosystem.

This form of communication also has important trickle-down outcomes that serve to strengthen the ecosystem. An example of these involves trust and stakeholder engagement, which are generated through transparency. Trust building is driven through transparent operation in the processes and decision-making engaged in, forming an important base for longer-term arrangements between agents and the deeper or more robust forms of collaboration that generally lead to more successful outcomes (Mayer et al., 1995). Stakeholder engagement, and through this, the valuing of the contributions of stakeholders and their active participation from the starting moment of an endeavor, are also critical in creating the environment where such stakeholder contributions will be successful (Ansell & Gash, 2008). Such trust and engagement are critical in underpinning the broader aspect of collaboration and innovation sought within an ecosystem.

Improved project outcomes are a critical facet driven by a more open set of communicative channels. The informed and inclusive decision-making processes stemming from this communication pave the way for better and more sustainable decisions. Identifying and addressing risks in the earliest phases allow for mitigation of potential risk factors that could otherwise significantly threaten an organization's viability (Kogut & Zander, 1992). These outcomes underscore how open communication drives both project success and long-term sustainability and resilience.

Another important aspect is fostering an adaptive and resilient ecosystem. A communication-rich environment encourages greater interaction among agents, enabling a more flexible response to change and potentially faster adaptation to new information or market shifts (Brown & Eisenhardt, 1997). Moreover, clear communication among agents is crucial for responding to the crises that organizations within an ecosystem frequently face, facilitating swift coordination and intervention when unforeseen challenges arise (Owen-Smith & Powell, 2004). These factors illustrate how open communication within an ecosystem contributes to organizational and broader success in a dynamically changing and unpredictable context.

Open communication practices play a central role in enabling knowledge sharing and learning. A continuous exchange of information fosters a culture of learning and knowledge sharing among stakeholders, enriching the skill set and expertise within the ecosystem (Tsai & Ghoshal, 1998). The transparent sharing of successes and failures provides invaluable insights into effective practices and contributes to the establishment of best practices (Hargadorn & Sutton, 1997). These learning dynamics underscore the role of open communication in fostering a culture of continuous improvement and knowledge dissemination.

Moreover, open communication channels are instrumental in facilitating community and network building. Regular interaction and engagement among stakeholders deepen their sense of community within the ecosystem, fostering stronger bonds and a shared sense of purpose (Adner, 2017). Open forums and collaborative platforms provide ample networking opportunities, potentially leading to the formation of new partnerships and ventures (Powell et al., 1996). These aspects highlight the pivotal role of open communication in strengthening community ties and expanding the ecosystem's network.

Additionally, open communication practices substantially contribute to enhancing reputation and attractiveness. A positive public image, nurtured by transparent and open communication, increases the project's appeal to potential investors, partners, and talent (Kemp & Pearson, 2007). Furthermore, a vibrant, collaborative, and transparent ecosystem becomes a magnet for high-quality talent and additional resources, fueling its growth and development (Chesbrough et al., 2006).

Finally, long-term sustainability is a critical outcome facilitated by open communication practices. An environment that supports open communication and collaboration sustains and grows over time by continuously adapting and innovating in response to changing dynamics (West & Bogers, 2014). These essential conditions underscore the indispensable role played by open communication in fostering collaboration, innovation, and the sustained growth of an innovation ecosystem.

Leadership commitment and governance mechanisms are keys to establishing and realizing common goals within an innovation ecosystem. Leadership provides direction, sets the tone, and mobilizes stakeholders toward common aspirations (Westley et al., 2007b). Leaders also catalyze collaboration and create a space where stakeholders feel empowered to contribute in a manner that adds genuine value and contributes to the shared goals.

Governance structures provide a means to ensure accountability, establish decision-making frameworks, and set up mechanisms for ongoing evaluation and adaptation as common goals develop and their relevance and progress realization are required. These frameworks also play a significant role in shaping the organizational culture within which employees operate, engaging them, and steering organizational work and direction.

Leadership commitment encompasses the dedication and respect that leaders demonstrate toward the goals, values, and members of their organization. Employee commitment, on the other hand, reflects the extent to which employees engage with the organization's mission and proactively contribute to achieving its goals. Research by Jackson et al. (2012) has revealed a positive correlation between respect and transformational and charismatic leadership styles and affective and normative employee commitment. This suggests that employees are inspired and motivated by such leadership styles, leading to a strong loyalty to the organization's mission.

Moreover, leadership commitment plays a crucial role in fostering and maintaining collaborative efforts across organizations. Leaders are tasked with proactively reaching out to create communication opportunities and maintaining ongoing dialogues with external entities. Recent studies highlight the importance of building leadership capacity and sharing leadership responsibilities across organizations to enhance adaptive capacity within complex social-ecological systems (Folke et al., 2005). This is particularly crucial in interorganizational settings where leaders must navigate complex interdependencies and potential conflicts of interest among diverse institutional arrangements, laws, histories, and local values.

Effective leadership in such contexts involves creating a conducive environment for decentralized communication, fostering broad awareness of the situation across the system, and empowering teams to make sense of and decisions in real time. Leaders must ensure that teams can justify their actions and continuously learn from small, stepwise experiments. Additionally, leaders need to be adept at understanding and integrating into the specific vernacular, history, and culture of different regions, showcasing that leadership is not a singular trait but a multifaceted capability.

Stakeholder engagement within an innovation ecosystem is crucial for shaping the direction, depth, and success of transformative initiatives. Freeman introduced the term "stakeholder engagement" as "a process of participation of a range of stakeholders, including business, government, academia, and the local community in a collaborative environment linking research, innovation, and venture creation" (Freeman, 1984, p. 31). It reflects a symbiotic relationship among stakeholders – businesses, government entities, academic institutions, and communities – contributing resources, expertise, and perspectives that create a fertile ground for ideation, experimentation, and implementation.

The literature emphasizes the critical importance of stakeholder engagement and various approaches that underpin effective stakeholder engagement within innovation ecosystems. The dynamism of innovation ecosystems, often characterized by complexity and interconnectedness, requires a comprehensive understanding of how stakeholder engagement is effectively shaped (Etzkowitz & Leydesdorff, 2000).

The literature illustrates numerous mechanisms that reflect stakeholder engagement within innovation ecosystems. The concept of open innovation platforms, as advocated by Chesbrough (2003), serves as a mechanism for the exchange of ideas and knowledge across traditionally siloed boundaries. By broadening the aperture and embracing external ideas, as well as sharing internal innovations, organizations can tap into a broader pool of resources and expertise, extending beyond traditional sectoral boundaries and enhancing the innovation capabilities of the organization.

Co-creation initiatives are fundamental for engaging stakeholders in innovation ecosystems. Collaborative efforts that span multiple stakeholders create a sense of ownership and commitment, which are determinants of innovations that have relevance and impacts. In other words, such efforts dissolve the distinctions between producers and consumers, inviting stakeholders to actively engage in the design and development of products or services (Prahalad & Ramaswamy, 2004) – sometimes with or without a guarantee of ownership. Not only does this inclusive approach lead to innovative outcomes that reflect the needs of stakeholders, but it also creates ties across stakeholders and fosters a culture of innovation and collaboration that they can all become a part of.

Strategic partnerships are integral to the notion of stakeholder engagement within innovation ecosystems. Organizations often partner with a myriad of stakeholders to leverage their complementary strengths, mitigate risk, and access new markets (Belderbos et al., 2004). Such collaborations often lead to knowledge sharing and access to resources, accelerating the process by which ideas become commercially viable innovations. Moreover, strategic partnerships contribute to making the ecosystem resilient by creating interconnected networks that can respond to dynamic market forces and advances in technology, thus promoting mutual adaptation and the co-development of new technologies and organizational forms by partners (Lorenz et al., 2015).

The development of a shared vision is underpinned by a discourse characterized by its participatory nature, which encompasses the perspectives and aspirations of stakeholder groups toward a shared vision within the innovation ecosystem (Ansell & Gash, 2008). Ansell and Gash (2008) highlighted the effectiveness of inclusive decision-making forums, often comprised of stakeholders from various sectors, coming together to deliberate and co-create shared goals. These forums serve as platforms for stakeholder exchange in opportunities and resources, where stakeholders convene to argue, utilize each other's perspectives, and negotiate common ground, effectively "developing a shared understanding and commitment to a set of goals and aspirations" that reflect the desires, concerns, and priorities of all stakeholders involved (Ansell & Gash, 2008, p. 546).

Expanding upon this framework, the concepts of quadruple and quintuple helix collaboration introduce a more comprehensive approach to stakeholder engagement within innovation ecosystems. These models emphasize the importance of integrating academia, industry, government, civil society, and the environment into the innovation process (Carayannis & Campbell, 2012; Carayannis & Rakhmatullin, 2014). The quadruple helix model adds the dimension of "civil society" to the traditional triple helix of university-industry-government relations, advocating for a societal approach to innovation that includes users, communities, and social entrepreneurs. The quintuple helix further incorporates the "environment" as a critical element, highlighting the need for sustainable development and the consideration of ecological perspectives in innovation practices.

These models promote a more holistic and sustainable approach to innovation, where collaboration among diverse stakeholders leads to socially responsible and environmentally sustainable outcomes. By embracing the principles of the quadruple and quintuple helix models, innovation ecosystems can foster a culture of cooperation that not only drives technological advancement and economic growth but also addresses societal challenges and promotes environmental stewardship.

Technological infrastructure plays a pivotal role in enabling communication. As Constantiou and Kallinikos (2015) posited, digital platforms have undergone a profound transformation and are crucial in communication dynamics within ecosystems, allowing them to overcome geographical constraints and enabling the kind of real-time collaboration highlighted by Bagherzadeh et al. (2019).

A strong trend in this space that is revolutionizing technology infrastructure and shaping communication dynamics within innovation ecosystems is artificial intelligence (AI). Its impacts on the transformation of digital platforms have been pointed out by several scholars, outlining how it has become an instrumental technology in creating effective channels that facilitate collaboration among ecosystem actors. As Constantiou and Kallinikos (2015) explained, its introduction has reshaped communication dynamics, particularly within ecosystems, by allowing them to transcend geographical limitations and enable unprecedented levels of connectivity and interaction that these newly evolved digital platforms have brought into play.

Using AI algorithms, these platforms are able to process large volumes of data and enable the seamless flow of information across continents. Bagherzadeh et al. (2019) shed light on how AI-enabled communication solutions have helped streamline workflows, making data more accessible and thus making ecosystems more efficient in how they exchange information.

In this context, AI is not just facilitating the seamless flow of information across geographical boundaries or increasing speed and lowering thresholds for participation. Instead, it offers a more holistic view where AI augments communication. It enables platforms to offer predictive and personalized communication, with machine learning algorithms analyzing patterns in users' engagement and content consumption to offer predictive insights and tailored content. This enriches the nature of engagement within ecosystems, driving richer collaboration and innovation processes.

As AI continues to progress, we can expect this impact to magnify, revolutionizing communication technologies within innovation ecosystems. The convergence between AI and communication technologies holds promises for increased speed in transmitting information globally, diminished barriers to participating in innovation processes, and embedded intelligence into the channels that ecosystems depend on to create sustainable value in the digital economy.

AI technology infrastructure within communication infrastructure is thus the cornerstone of a revolution in communication dynamics within innovation ecosystems, ushering in a new era of connectivity, accessibility, and intelligence.

Defined barriers

The authors offer a panoramic view of the barriers to effective communication and collaboration within and across organizational boundaries. By addressing these barriers systematically, organizations can aspire to tear down communication silos, fostering a culture of transparency, cooperation, and innovation. A blueprint is provided to develop a comprehensive understanding of these barriers and to delineate strategic interventions tailored to address them, ensuring equitable opportunities and an environment conducive to effective communication and collaboration. This approach is important as the hallmark of the fresh competitive collaborative landscape lies in sustaining a lean, distributed, cost-effective, and innovative organization within a constantly shifting economic environment.

The prevalence of communication silos within various organizations and ecosystems underscores the intricate nature of contemporary communication dynamics. The authors delve into the root causes of these enduring silos, scrutinizing their effects in both intra- and interorganizational settings. Leveraging relevant academic insights, the analysis transcends organizational limits to consider the wider repercussions of communication silos and the necessary measures for their alleviation.

In the sphere of interorganizational cooperation, communication silos present formidable obstacles, curtailing the seamless exchange of ideas and knowledge, thereby hampering innovation (Tsai & Ghoshal, 1998). This segment of the chapter investigates assorted tactics designed to dismantle these barriers, focusing on the cultivation of networks, the formation of alliances, and participation in joint ventures (Powell et al., 1996).

Adding to the complexity of communication silos is the regional dimension, further complicated by geographical distances and cultural heterogeneity.

This section tackles the hurdles introduced by these elements, emphasizing the necessity for approaches that capitalize on technological progress and solid communication frameworks (Hargadon & Sutton, 1997). Moreover, it underscores the significance of cultural awareness and educational initiatives, highlighting their effectiveness in enhancing mutual comprehension and diminishing the effects of cultural disparities on communication (Stahl et al., 2010).

The organizational structure significantly influences communication dynamics, with conventional frameworks often inadvertently promoting compartmentalized work settings. This portion of the chapter explores how departmental segmentation and hierarchical divisions contribute to the emergence of communication silos, proposing strategies to stimulate interdepartmental cooperation and the free flow of information (Ansell & Gash, 2008). Technological limitations and management styles are also significant contributors to the prevalence of communication silos within organizations. The authors explore the impact of incompatible systems, inadequate collaborative tools, and top-down communication approaches on the dissemination of information and collaboration.

The barriers identified within the regional framework pose significant challenges that demand strategic measures to enhance communication and cooperation effectively. A principal barrier is the existence of communication silos, with regional disparities in economic growth, technological access, and levels of educational achievement.

Communication silos serve as a major barrier to the exchange of information and collaborative efforts within organizational settings, extensively discussed in organizational theory literature. Described as structural barriers by Katz and Kahn (1978), communication silos manifest as a consequence of rigid organizational hierarchies and the categorization of departments, leading to isolated pools of information and segmented streams of communication. This process was further elaborated upon by Tushman and Scanlan (1981), who found that the lack of cross-functional communication, along with the manner in which information was transmitted and received, played a significant role in perpetuating communication silos.

As a result, communication silos create barriers to information exchange not only within organizations but also exacerbate challenges in aligning efforts in interorganizational collaborative configurations. These silos, characterized by segmented communication channels and isolated pools of information (Tsai & Ghoshal, 1998), are further perpetuated by organizational hierarchies and inadequate information-sharing protocols. It is necessary to comprehensively understand these various factors contributing to the perpetuation of communication silos; the reasons for their endurance may vary, but several factors – including organizational hierarchies, inadequate information-sharing protocols, departmental objectives, communication styles, and technological barriers – continue to sustain the challenge of removing them (Cohen & Levinthal, 1990).

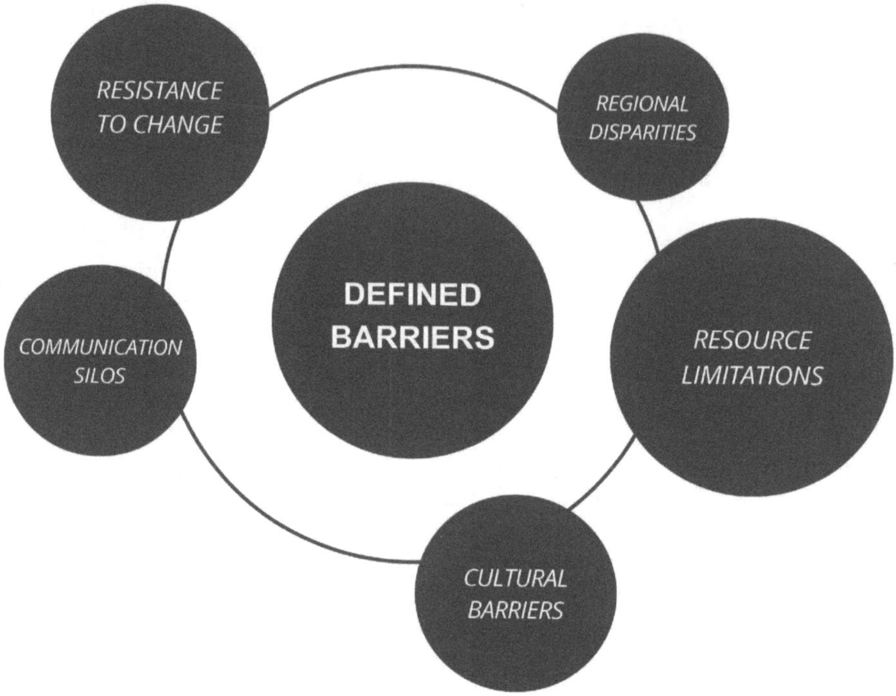

Figure 4.2 Defined barriers to effective communication in the innovation ecosystem.
Source: own development

Such factors not only hinder internal organizational communication but also complicate the communication of organizational staff in larger interorganizational or regional contexts (Powell et al., 1996), where the intertwining of these contexts poses further challenges in aligning innovative initiatives, problem-solving, and the exchange of valid and valuable information. In this academic discourse, special attention has been given to literature and research extending beyond the confines of organizations, allowing an examination of how communication silos permeate academic literature, thus impacting a broad spectrum.

Additionally, exploration of potential strategies and solutions aimed at mitigating these barriers is crucial for fostering improved communication and collaboration across diverse organizational and regional landscapes. Communication silos within an interorganizational framework can pose significant challenges that impede effective collaboration and innovation across different entities. Communication barriers can restrict the free flow of ideas and knowledge, stifling innovation as valuable insights remain confined within organizational boundaries (Hargadon & Sutton, 1997).

To address these challenges, several strategies have been proposed to overcome interorganizational silos. Initiatives that focus on building networks and fostering alliances among diverse entities are advocated to facilitate seamless information sharing and promote collaborative efforts (Ansell & Gash, 2008). Engaging in joint ventures and collaborative projects is a promising approach to breaking down silos and encouraging cooperation and synergy among participating organizations (Chesbrough, 2003). These strategies aim to mitigate the challenges posed by communication silos and enhance collaborative endeavors within interorganizational landscapes.

In regional contexts, communication silos can be compounded by several factors, notably geographical barriers and cultural diversity, which present significant obstacles to the effective exchange of information and collaboration. The presence of larger geographical distances in regional contexts often exacerbates communication silos, undermining the free flow of information and resources between different locales (Stahl et al., 2010). Additionally, linguistic and cultural diversity among different regional constituents only serves to further complicate matters, inciting obstacles to communication and the formation of silos (Stahl et al., 2010).

Cultural factors wield significant influence on enduring communication silos within organizational settings. One central component of this picture is a culture that is high in resistance to change, as it sustains silos by perpetuating an environment where both employees and management are accustomed to old and deeply rooted work practices (Schein, 2010). This resistance can impede the adoption of new collaborative methodologies, stymieing the breaking down of communication barriers. Further, a dearth in interdepartmental or interteam trust will also serve to magnify the silo effect within the organization (Mayer et al., 1995). Where trust is lacking between various units, it can trigger reluctance in sharing information – further solidifying barriers between departments or teams. The dearth of trust in this context becomes a profound obstacle to free information flow and the blossoming of cohesive collaboration, thereby perpetuating the existence of communication silos within the organizational tapestry.

It is essential to leverage technological advancements and robust communication infrastructure to bridge geographical divides and facilitate smoother communication and collaboration across regions (Powell et al., 1996). Initiatives focused on cultural sensitivity and training programs can help foster mutual understanding and mitigate the impact of cultural differences on communication within regional contexts (Stahl et al., 2010). These strategies aim to alleviate the obstacles posed by regional communication silos, enabling more effective collaboration and information exchange among diverse geographical and cultural landscapes. Communication silos, prevalent within organizational boundaries, between distinct entities, and across regional landscapes, stand as formidable barriers impeding collaborative endeavors and operational efficiency. Within interorganizational and regional frameworks alike, targeted measures such as strategic networking initiatives, leveraging advanced technological tools, and fostering programs aimed at cultivating cultural appreciation and a collaborative spirit emerge as promising strategies to address and surmount these communication barriers (Ansell & Gash, 2008; Chesbrough, 2003). In the current landscape of a progressively interconnected global business environment, adeptness in navigating and dismantling these communication silos assumes paramount importance, directly influencing the capacity of organizations to achieve success and foster innovation in a rapidly evolving landscape.

Organizational structure plays a pivotal role in shaping the dynamics of communication and collaboration within a workplace. Traditional organizational structures frequently rely on departmentalization, segregating employees into distinct functional units to streamline operations and enhance efficiency. However, this compartmentalization can inadvertently foster isolated working environments, hindering cross-departmental collaboration and information sharing. Moreover, hierarchical barriers prevalent in such structures perpetuate vertical information flow within departments while impeding horizontal communication across different units, consequently nurturing the formation of communication silos. These hierarchical arrangements often create constraints in the dissemination of knowledge and insights, limiting the organization's ability to harness collective expertise and impeding innovation and adaptability within the broader organizational landscape.

The gradual shift toward distributed work arrangements has introduced formidable communication challenges for organizations. Physical separation among remote and globally dispersed colleagues inevitably disrupts casual interactions and spontaneity, both of which are crucial for sparking innovation and efficiently solving urgent issues. Moreover, international operations face exacerbated barriers to synchronous communication due to disparate time zones, hampering real-time collaboration across teams. As Gray highlighted in 1989, siloed information flow within interorganizational alliances can impede the free exchange of ideas and collective understanding, stifling innovation. However, Huxham and Vangen proposed that consciously cultivating cross-boundary networks and strategic alliances could help surmount such divides by facilitating seamless knowledge sharing to enhance collaborative efforts.

Furthermore, incompatible technological infrastructure emerges as a significant impediment, with the prevalence of non-integrated systems across divisions obstructing seamless data transmission. The lack of adequate collaborative tools to bridge such divides serves only to perpetuate silos of isolated work, further compounding communication challenges. Mintzberg and Schein rightly asserted that management styles significantly impact communication dynamics within an organization. A top-down approach, where information only flows downward, can unintentionally cultivate silos between departments, as cross-functional collaboration is neither promoted nor prioritized by leadership. This scenario underscores that proactive support from senior executives is paramount to breaking down barriers and incentivizing cooperative relationships across diverse teams.

By visibly championing interdepartmental initiatives and knowledge-sharing activities, leadership can leverage the unique skills and perspectives within each division for the benefit of the entire organization.

Resistance to change is a well-documented phenomenon within organizational studies, reflecting the natural human tendency to prefer stability and predictability over the uncertainty associated with change (Kotter, 1995). This resistance can manifest at various levels within an organization, from individual employees to entire departments, and is often cited as a major impediment to organizational transformation and innovation (Oreg, 2006). The literature identifies several underlying causes of resistance to change, including fear of the unknown, perceived loss of control, and the disruption of established routines and social networks (Ford et al., 2008).

Moreover, organizational cultures that are deeply entrenched in traditional practices and hierarchical structures are particularly prone to exhibiting high levels of resistance to change (Schein, 2010). This resistance not only hampers the implementation of new processes and technologies but also reinforces communication silos by maintaining rigid departmental boundaries and inhibiting cross-functional collaboration.

To address resistance to change, scholars advocate for comprehensive change management strategies that involve clear communication, participation, and engagement of all stakeholders in the change process (Kotter, 1995; Armenakis & Harris, 2009). Creating a shared vision for change, providing adequate support and resources for transition, and recognizing and rewarding adaptability and innovation are critical steps in mitigating resistance and fostering a culture of continuous improvement and openness to change (Hiatt, 2006).

Resource limitations, encompassing financial constraints and shortages in human capital and intellectual resources, pose significant obstacles to effective communication and teamwork within and between organizations. This can lead to competition for scarce resources, even within the same departments, prioritizing objectives other than those at the organizational top level and further reinforcing the silo mentality. Often, financial constraints result in underinvestment in necessary technology and infrastructure for smooth communication and teamwork. Similarly, human resource constraints burden workers, diminishing their power and inclination to engage in functions or projects crossing departmental boundaries (Barney, 1991).

Division is also fueled by financial constraints and budgets. Competition for limited funds often leads to hoarding information for individual gain rather than benefiting the organization as a whole. Divisions persist when money is allocated solely to specific work streams rather than shared cooperatively. Overcoming these challenges requires top-level strategic thinking to reshape budgeting policies and distribute scarce resources to reward cooperation over departmentalism. By fostering cooperation across silos, top managers and leaders can normalize cross-functional relationships and resource sharing.

The management literature emphasizes the importance of addressing this perspective. Resource-based views are considered crucial in strategic management studies. It is argued that firms can achieve a competitive advantage by managing their distinctive resources and capabilities effectively (Barney, 1991; Wernerfelt, 1984). To tackle communication silos, strategic management research advocates for a resource-based view: allocating scarce resources to initiatives encouraging people to work together across organizational boundaries.

Combining the technical and social platforms of integrated communication systems, fostering a culture of knowledge sharing centered around information, and developing employees' skills for mutual cooperation are indispensable methods for overcoming resource limitations, including those related to human resources (Nonaka & Takeuchi, 1995). Furthermore, collaborative networks and partnerships can provide a mechanism for pooling and sharing resources, enabling organizations to overcome individual resource constraints and achieve collective goals (Powell et al., 1996). These networks not only facilitate access to additional resources but also promote the exchange of knowledge and expertise, contributing to dismantling communication silos and enhancing organizational innovation and adaptability.

To address these challenges, it is imperative to develop customized strategies that ensure equal opportunities and level the playing field across the region (Powell et al., 1996). Moreover, the diverse cultural and linguistic backgrounds within the region pose a significant hurdle to effective communication. Therefore, it is essential to implement strategies that embrace and accommodate this cultural diversity (Stahl et al., 2010). Additionally, managing technological diversity within the region is crucial to ensure uniform access to communication tools and platforms (Hargadon & Sutton, 1997).

Navigating the varied regulatory frameworks across different jurisdictions within the region presents another significant obstacle. Understanding and adhering to these regulations are vital for formulating communication strategies that comply with legal standards (Ansell & Gash, 2008). Furthermore, it is essential to recognize and proactively address resource limitations, including financial and human resources, to develop sustainable and effective communication strategies within the regional context (Tsai & Ghoshal, 1998).

Addressing these identified barriers requires comprehensive approaches that acknowledge the varied and intricate nature of regional dynamics. The goal should be to foster an inclusive and supportive environment for effective communication and collaboration.

Defined effective mechanism

In the domain of innovation ecosystems, establishing a comprehensive framework to facilitate open and transparent communication is both complex and crucial. This endeavor requires a strategic and multifaceted approach, fundamental in cultivating an environment where transparency, trust, and unified objectives are paramount. At the core of this initiative lies the development of a structured roadmap, delineating a series of methodical steps to address the intricacies of communication within such ecosystems.

The first step in this process involves conducting a diagnostic analysis to identify and understand current communication silos. This analysis entails a detailed exploration of the root causes and effects of these silos, which primarily stem from entrenched departmental boundaries, geographical dispersion, conflicting stakeholder goals, or the lack of standard communication channels. Engaging a wide range of stakeholders representing various sectors, institutions, and organizational levels in extensive dialogues and interviews is essential. This approach helps provide an in-depth understanding of stakeholder perspectives, communication challenges, and expectations regarding collaboration and information-sharing. Qualitative methodology plays a vital role in this phase, laying the groundwork for developing targeted strategies to break down the defined barriers, especially communication silos.

The subsequent stage involves a detailed mapping and analysis of communication flow patterns within the innovation ecosystem. Using visualization tools and mapping techniques, this phase aims to outline the existing communication pathways among stakeholders. This process includes charting the channels used for information dissemination, examining the frequency of interactions, and identifying nodes that either facilitate or hinder information flow. Analyzing these communication maps enables the identification of bottlenecks, congestion points, or gaps in information exchange, thereby informing targeted intervention strategies.

Moving forward, the framework calls for the creation of collaborative structures designed to foster cohesion and shared objectives among stakeholders. Establishing forums or workshops that align stakeholder interests and develop shared goals is crucial in promoting a unified vision for collaborative initiatives. Concurrently, developing standardized communication protocols or platforms that transcend organizational boundaries is imperative. These mechanisms should facilitate seamless and transparent information exchange, catering to the diverse communication preferences of stakeholders.

The following steps involve implementing measures to enhance cross-sectoral collaboration and cultivate an open culture within the ecosystem. Initiating collaborative projects across different sectors and creating environments that encourage interdisciplinary exchanges and knowledge-sharing platforms are key to stimulating cross-collaboration. This structured and inclusive approach strategically addresses communication silos within the innovation ecosystem, thereby fostering robust collaboration and nurturing an environment conducive to sustained innovation and growth.

To effectively implement these measures, it is essential to identify and engage key stakeholders from various sectors, ensuring their active participation in collaborative projects. This can be achieved through the establishment of joint task forces or working groups that focus on specific areas of mutual interest. These groups should be designed to foster a sense of shared purpose and collective responsibility among participants, thereby enhancing the likelihood of successful outcomes.

Furthermore, the development of knowledge-sharing platforms, such as digital forums or collaborative databases, can play a crucial role in facilitating the exchange of ideas and information. These platforms should be accessible to all stakeholders within the ecosystem and designed to encourage open dialogue and the sharing of best practices. Leveraging advanced communication technologies can further enhance the effectiveness of these platforms, enabling real-time collaboration and the rapid dissemination of information.

The final steps in this framework include developing a unified vision and goals, fostering open communication cultures, implementing collaborative tools, encouraging cross-functional interactions, establishing transparent processes and policies, creating incentives for collaboration, monitoring effectiveness, building trust and relationships, and adapting strategies based on continuous assessments and stakeholder feedback. This holistic approach to enhancing communication and collaboration within an innovation ecosystem represents an ongoing process that requires commitment at all ecosystem levels to foster integrated and successful collaboration.

The defined effective mechanism represents a multifaceted approach to establishing and maintaining effective collaborative ecosystems. This concept

Figure 4.3 The components and the process of a defined and effective mechanism in a collaborative ecosystem.

Source: own development

is integral to orchestrating successful collaborative efforts, particularly in environments where diverse stakeholders and complex dynamics are involved. The mechanism encompasses several key elements: defined roles, strategic activities, and a well-structured process, each contributing to the overall efficacy of the collaborative ecosystem.

The concept begins with a clear delineation of roles among various stakeholders. These roles encompass ecosystem facilitators, industry leaders, technology providers, educational institutions, and community representatives. In Chapter 2, a comprehensive framework was established, delineating the distinct roles and responsibilities of various stakeholders within the ecosystem. The mechanism involves a series of strategic activities designed to foster engagement, innovation, and development within the ecosystem. These activities include community engagement and feedback, ensuring that the ecosystem remains responsive and aligned with the community's needs and goals. Innovation challenges, hackathons, and other events serve as platforms for stimulating creativity and problem-solving, while skill-sharing and mentorship programs facilitate knowledge transfer and capacity building among participants. The inclusion of a sustainability and social impact tracker reflects a commitment to responsible and ethical practices, ensuring that the ecosystem's activities contribute positively to societal and environmental well-being.

The process component of the mechanism is structured into distinct phases: planning, design and development, and implementation. In the planning phase, clear objectives are defined, and a thorough stakeholder analysis is conducted. Resource assessment is also carried out to ensure that the ecosystem has the necessary assets to achieve its goals. Establishing a communication infrastructure during this phase is critical for maintaining transparency and engagement.

In the design phase, the ecosystem's strategies and initiatives are pilot-tested in a controlled environment. This allows for the identification and mitigation of potential issues before full-scale implementation. Performance tracking during this phase provides valuable insights into the efficacy of the approach and informs necessary adjustments.

The implementation phase marks the deployment of the mechanism across the entire ecosystem. It involves continuous improvement based on feedback gathering, transparency maintenance, and risk assessment. Feedback is crucial at this stage, enabling stakeholders to voice their opinions and contribute to the refinement of the ecosystem's activities. The acquisition of resources and leveraging of networks are also critical for the successful implementation of the mechanism.

A key aspect of the mechanism is the monitoring and evaluation component, which ensures continuous improvement and adaptability. Performance tracking, feedback gathering, and stakeholder engagement are ongoing processes, providing real-time insights into the effectiveness of the ecosystem's activities. This continuous assessment allows for timely adjustments and enhancements, ensuring that the ecosystem remains dynamic, responsive, and aligned with its intended objectives.

A novel approach to enhancing communication mechanisms within innovation ecosystems involves a reevaluation of traditional methods and the introduction of new strategies aligned with emerging trends in the economy and society. When implementing an effective communication concept for innovation ecosystems, synthesized insights from research and literature yield a comprehensive framework with three essential pillars.

Transparency, the first pillar, establishes an open and accessible information-sharing environment, thereby fostering trust and inclusivity. Within the context of innovation ecosystems, transparency serves as a catalyst for fostering inclusivity, breaking down barriers, and ensuring equitable dissemination of information among all stakeholders. The deliberate cultivation of an environment where information is readily available instills a sense of shared ownership and empowerment among participants. Transparency not only engenders trust but also promotes a collaborative ethos, as stakeholders are afforded equal access to information, facilitating informed decision-making processes.

Diversity and integration, the second pillar, advocate for embracing diverse perspectives and expertise to enrich discussions. This cardinal pillar encapsulates a commitment to recognizing, valuing, and actively seeking out a multiplicity of viewpoints, skills, and experiences. The advocacy for diversity transcends mere acknowledgment of differences; it embodies a proactive and intentional effort to create an inclusive environment that harnesses the full spectrum of human talents and capabilities.

Within the intricate dynamics of innovation ecosystems, diversity serves as a catalyst for fostering a vibrant intellectual milieu. By embracing diverse perspectives, organizations cultivate an atmosphere where varied insights converge, leading to more robust and comprehensive discussions. This pillar is not confined to demographic attributes alone; it encompasses a broad spectrum of cognitive, disciplinary, and cultural diversity. By fostering an environment where individuals from varied backgrounds contribute their unique viewpoints, diversity becomes instrumental in stimulating creativity, enhancing problem-solving approaches, and fostering a culture of innovation.

The inclusion of diverse expertise ensures a well-rounded understanding of multifaceted issues, offering nuanced solutions that reflect a comprehensive range of considerations. This pillar goes beyond the notion of diversity as a symbolic gesture; it actively positions diverse perspectives as indispensable contributors to the innovation process, recognizing that innovation thrives in environments where a multitude of voices are not only heard but also valued and integrated into the collaborative fabric of the ecosystem. The third pillar, technological infrastructure, emphasizes leveraging AI-driven platforms to overcome barriers and enhance collaboration. This forward-looking approach incorporates cutting-edge technologies to revolutionize communication dynamics within innovation ecosystems. Artificial intelligence (AI) plays a key role in facilitating tailored communication by analyzing user preferences, behavioral patterns, and contextual information, thereby delivering personalized and relevant messages to diverse stakeholders. Real-time feedback channels are instituted to facilitate immediate responses and adjustments, making communication more adaptive and responsive.

The incorporation of interactive tools, such as live polling, instant feedback apps, and sentiment analysis software within communication platforms, ensures that stakeholders can actively participate and contribute to ongoing dialogues. Furthermore, predictive analytics is harnessed to anticipate and proactively address communication needs. By leveraging data analytics, patterns and trends in communication are identified, enabling the prediction of future challenges and needs. This foresight allows for preemptive action, ensuring that the communication strategy remains agile and aligned with evolving requirements.

The new communication paradigm advocates a departure from traditional top-down models to a decentralized network. Establishing effective communication within an innovation ecosystem requires a comprehensive strategy fostering transparency, trust, and unified objectives among stakeholders. This involves a structured roadmap to identify, analyze, and mitigate communication silos while promoting collaboration.

Understanding existing communication barriers through diagnostic analysis and engaging stakeholders is the initial phase. Mapping and analyzing communication flow patterns follow, identifying bottlenecks hindering collaborative initiatives. The subsequent phases involve developing collaborative frameworks, implementing remedial measures, fostering a culture of openness, and integrating a bottom-up leadership approach.

By adopting these innovative approaches, ecosystems can foster more effective, dynamic, and inclusive communication, driving collaboration and innovation. While this framework presents conceptual ideas, practical implementation would require careful planning, resource allocation, and continuous refinement based on feedback and evolving technological capabilities.

Bibliography

Adner, R. (2017). Ecosystem as structure: An actionable construct for strategy. *Journal of Management*, *43*(1), 39–58.

Ansell, C., & Gash, A. (2008). Collaborative governance in theory and practice. *Journal of Public Administration Research and Theory*, *18*(4), 543–571.

Aral, S., & Weill, P. (2007). IT assets, organizational capabilities, and firm performance: How resource allocations and organizational differences explain performance variation. *Organization Science*, *18*(5), 763–780.

Armenakis, A. A., & Harris, S. G. (2009). Crafting a change message to create transformational readiness. *Journal of Organizational Change Management*, *15*(2), 169–183.

Bagherzadeh, M., Tavakoli, A., & Dolatabadi, H. R. (2019). A conceptual framework of knowledge management in innovation ecosystems. *Journal of Knowledge Management*, *23*(5), 859–880.

Barney, J. (1991). Firm resources and sustained competitive advantage. *Journal of Management*, *17*(1), 99–120.

Bason, C. (2010). *Leading public sector innovation: Co-creating for a better society.* Policy Press.

Belderbos, R., Carree, M., & Lokshin, B. (2004). Cooperative R&D and firm performance. *Research Policy, 33*(10), 1477–1492.

Borrás, S., & Edquist, C. (2013). The choice of innovation policy instruments. *Technological Forecasting and Social Change, 80*(8), 1513–1522.

Bosch-Sijtsema, P. M., van den Ende, D. C., & Vartiainen, M. (2014). The contribution of multi-stakeholder collaboration to innovation: The case of a European Living Lab. *Creativity and Innovation Management, 23*(4), 426–439.

Brown, S. L., & Eisenhardt, K. M. (1997). The art of continuous change: Linking complexity theory and time-paced evolution in relentlessly shifting organizations. *Administrative Science Quarterly, 42*(1), 1–34.

Carayannis, E. G., & Campbell, D. F. J. (2012). *Mode 3 knowledge production in quadruple helix innovation systems: 21st-century democracy, innovation, and entrepreneurship for development.* Springer.

Carayannis, E. G., & Rakhmatullin, R. (2014). The quadruple/quintuple innovation helixes and smart specialisation strategies for sustainable and inclusive growth in Europe and beyond. *Journal of the Knowledge Economy, 5*(2), 212–239.

Chesbrough, H. (2003). *Open innovation: The new imperative for creating and profiting from technology.* Harvard Business Press.

Chesbrough, H. W., Vanhaverbeke, W., & West, J. (Eds.). (2006). *Open innovation: Researching a new paradigm.* Oxford University Press.

Cohen, W. M., & Levinthal, D. A. (1990). Absorptive capacity: A new perspective on learning and innovation. *Administrative Science Quarterly, 35*(1), 128–152.

Constantiou, I. D., & Kallinikos, J. (2015). New games, new rules: Big data and the changing context of strategy. *Journal of Information Technology, 30*(1), 44–57.

Dahan, N. M., Doh, J. P., Oetzel, J., & Yaziji, M. (2010). Corporate-NGO collaboration: Co-creating new business models for developing markets. *Long Range Planning, 43*(2–3), 326–342.

Dahlander, L., & Gann, D. M. (2010). How open is innovation? *Research Policy, 39*(6), 699–709.

Edmondson, A. (1999). Psychological safety and learning behavior in work teams. *Administrative Science Quarterly, 44*(2), 350–383.

Etzkowitz, H., & Leydesdorff, L. (2000). The dynamics of innovation: From national systems and "mode 2" to a triple helix of university-industry-government relations. *Research Policy, 29*(2), 109–123.

Folke, C., Hahn, T., Olsson, P., & Norberg, J. (2005). Adaptive governance of social-ecological systems. *Annual Review of Environment and Resources, 30*, 441–473.

Ford, J. D., Ford, L. W., & D'Amelio, A. (2008). Resistance to change: The rest of the story. *Academy of Management Review, 33*(2), 362–377.

Freeman, R. E. (1984). *Strategic management: A stakeholder approach.* Pitman.

Garud, R., Gehman, J., & Giuliani, A. P. (2016). Technological, organizational, and institutional change: Emergent and enacted effects. *Organization Science, 27*(2), 319–334.

Gray, B. (1989). Collaborating: Finding Common Ground for Multiparty Problems, San Francisco: Jossey-Bass.

Hagedoorn, J. (2002). Inter-firm R&D partnerships: An overview of major trends and patterns since 1960. *Research Policy, 31*(4), 477–492.

Hargadon, A., & Sutton, R. I. (1997). Technology brokering and innovation in a product development firm. *Administrative Science Quarterly, 42*(4), 716–749.

Hiatt, J. (2006). *ADKAR: A model for change in business, government and our community.* Prosci Learning Center Publications.

Hofstede, G. (1984). *Culture's consequences: International differences in work-related values.* Sage Publications.

Huxham, C., & Vangen, S. (2005). *Managing to collaborate: The theory and practice of collaborative advantage*. Routledge.
Jackson, T. A., Meyer, J. P., & Wang, X.-H. (2012). Leadership, commitment, and culture. *Journal of Leadership & Organizational Studies*, *20*(1), 84–106.
Kaplan, R. S., & Norton, D. P. (1996). *The balanced scorecard: Translating strategy into action*. Harvard Business School Press.
Katz, D., & Kahn, R. L. (1978). *The social psychology of organizations* (2nd ed.). Wiley.
Katzenbach, J. R., & Smith, D. K. (1993). *The wisdom of teams: Creating the high-performance organization*. Harvard Business School Press.
Kemp, R., & Pearson, P. (2007). *Final report of the MEI project measuring eco-innovation*. UM Merit.
Kogut, B., & Zander, U. (1992). Knowledge of the firm, combinative capabilities, and the replication of technology. *Organization Science*, *3*(3), 383–397.
Koschmann, M. A. (2012). The communicative constitution of collective identity in interorganizational collaboration. *Management Communication Quarterly*, *27*(1), 61–89.
Kotter, J. P. (1995). Leading change: Why transformation efforts fail. *Harvard Business Review*, *73*(2), 59–67.
Leonard-Barton, D. (1995). *Wellsprings of knowledge: Building and sustaining the sources of innovation*. Harvard Business School Press.
Leonardi, P. M., & Barley, S. R. (2010). What's under construction here? Social action, materiality, and power in constructivist studies of technology and organizing. *The Academy of Management Annals*, *4*(1), 1–51.
Lorenz, D., Fischer, M., & Lins, D. (2015). Interconnected networks: Measuring extreme risk connectedness between financial institutions. *Journal of Financial Stability*, *20*, 1–15.
Mayer, R. C., Davis, J. H., & Schoorman, F. D. (1995). An integrative model of organizational trust. *Academy of Management Review*, *20*(3), 709–734.
Murray, R., Caulier-Grice, J., & Mulgan, G. (2010). *The open book of social innovation*. NESTA.
Neill, M. S., & Jiang, H. (2017). Functional silos, integration & encroachment in internal communication. *Public Relations Review*, *43*(4), 850–862.
Nonaka, I., & Takeuchi, H. (1995). *The knowledge-creating company: How Japanese companies create the dynamics of innovation*. Oxford University Press.
Oreg, S. (2006). Personality, context, and resistance to organizational change. *European Journal of Work and Organizational Psychology*, *15*(1), 73–101.
Osterloh, M., & Frey, B. S. (2000). Motivation, knowledge transfer, and organizational forms. *Organization Science*, *11*(5), 538–550.
Owen-Smith, J., & Powell, W. W. (2004). Knowledge networks as channels and conduits: The effects of spillovers in the Boston biotechnology community. *Organization Science*, *15*(1), 5–21.
Pfeffer, J., & Salancik, G. R. (1978). *The external control of organizations: A resource dependence perspective*. Harper & Row.
Powell, W. W., Koput, K. W., & Smith-Doerr, L. (1996). Interorganizational collaboration and the locus of innovation: Networks of learning in biotechnology. *Administrative Science Quarterly*, *50*(1), 1–31.
Prahalad, C. K., & Ramaswamy, V. (2004). *The future of competition: Co-creating unique value with customers*. Harvard Business School Press.
Rogers, E. M. (2003). *Diffusion of innovations* (5th ed.). Free Press.
Schein, E. H. (2010). *Organizational culture and leadership* (4th ed.). Jossey-Bass.
Senge, P. M. (1990). *The fifth discipline: The art & practice of the learning organization*. Doubleday.

Stahl, G. K., Maznevski, M. L., Voigt, A., & Jonsen, K. (2010). Unraveling the effects of cultural diversity in teams: A meta-analysis of research on multicultural work groups. *Journal of International Business Studies*, *41*(4), 690–709.
Tsai, W., & Ghoshal, S. (1998). Social capital and value creation: The role of intrafirm networks. *Academy of Management Journal*, *41*(4), 464–476.
Tushman, M. L., & O'Reilly, C. A. (1996). Ambidextrous organizations: Managing evolutionary and revolutionary change. *California Management Review*, *38*(4), 8–30.
Tushman, M. L., & Scanlan, T. J. (1981). Boundary spanning individuals: Their role in information transfer and their antecedents. *Academy of Management Journal*, *24*(2), 289–305.
Van den Ende, J., de Reuver, M., & Schoenmakers, W. (2014). Successful diffusion of telemedicine innovations: Key factors and lessons learned from a longitudinal case study. *Journal of the American Medical Informatics Association*, *21*(5), 832–841.
Wernerfelt, B. (1984). A resource-based view of the firm. *Strategic Management Journal*, *5*(2), 171–180.
West, J., & Bogers, M. (2014). Leveraging external sources of innovation: A review of research on open innovation. *Journal of Product Innovation Management*, *31*(4), 814–831.
Westley, F., Olsson, P., Folke, C., Homer-Dixon, T., Vredenburg, H., Loorbach, D., Thompson, J., Nilsson, M., Lambin, E., Sendzimir, J., Banerjee, B., Galaz, V., & Van Der Leeuw, S. (2007a). Tipping toward sustainability: Emerging pathways of transformation. *Ambio*, *36*(4), 344–354.
Westley, F., Zimmerman, B., & Patton, M. Q. (2007b). *Getting to maybe: How the world is changed*. Random House Canada.
Zhu, H., Liu, Z., Du, S., Li, B., Qian, H., & Yu, S. (2020). Communication-efficient edge AI: Algorithms and systems. *IEEE Access*, *8*, 132677–132688.

5 Practical solutions and recommendations for shaping the future of increasingly interconnected innovation ecosystems

Introduction

This chapter examines various types of innovation ecosystems and delves into practical solutions and strategic recommendations necessary for their successful adaptation to the future. It explores the multifaceted nature of innovation ecosystems, dissecting the crucial factors influencing their development and the mechanisms that can optimize them to foster greater interconnectedness and sustainable outcomes. Drawing upon an extensive literature review and diverse case studies, we emphasize the significance of transparency, openness, and stakeholder engagement in cultivating environments conducive to innovation.

The chapter underscores the dynamic interplay among different aspects of innovation ecosystems, including the integration of environmental sustainability considerations, the importance of data transparency, and finding a balance between bottom-up and top-down engagement strategies. Additionally, it addresses the challenges and opportunities presented by digital transformation, stressing the need for adaptive governance, strategic management, and effective communication in mobile work environments. The chapter also explores the role of government policies in shaping innovation ecosystems and the significance of attracting, nurturing, and retaining talent to ensure their vitality and competitiveness.

The integration of artificial intelligence (AI) into innovation ecosystems signifies a transformative shift, offering unprecedented opportunities for enhancing efficiency, fostering creativity, and driving technological advancements. AI's role within these ecosystems is multifaceted, encompassing aspects such as data analysis, decision-making, personalized solutions, and expediting research and development processes.

Through a series of case studies, the authors illustrate successful initiatives that have harnessed interconnectedness to achieve remarkable advancements in technology, economic development, and environmental conservation. Many of these examples serve as a testament to the potential of innovation ecosystems in tackling global challenges and pushing the boundaries of knowledge.

DOI: 10.4324/9781032697802-6

In conclusion, this chapter provides a comprehensive overview of the strategies and practices essential for shaping the future of increasingly interconnected innovation ecosystems. By prioritizing transparency, openness, stakeholder engagement, and the integration of sustainable practices, we can cultivate innovation networks that are not only efficient and productive but also inclusive and responsive to the evolving needs of society. The insights and recommendations presented herein aim to guide policymakers, industry leaders, and stakeholders in navigating the complexities of innovation ecosystems, thereby contributing to a more sustainable, equitable, and innovative future.

Fostering greater interconnectivity and sustainable development

In order to achieve sustainable results and establish durable innovation networks, transparency and openness must be integrated across different sectors. Through a review of literature and analysis of case studies, the authors highlight the mechanisms through which interconnectedness can drive sustainable innovation and development. The dynamic interplay between these aspects forms the cornerstone of effective innovation ecosystems, facilitating the exchange of ideas and fostering a culture of collaboration (Chesbrough, 2003; West & Bogers, 2014). Fostering interconnectedness is not merely a goal but a constant process. Only by continuously reassessing strategies can they remain viable and effective. Environmental sustainability and climate change require the attention of innovation projects and partnerships. Interconnected innovation ecosystems can stimulate economic growth, technological innovation, and environmental conservation efforts. In addition to these aspects, the emphasis is on the roles of interconnecting factors in envisioning an environment conducive to innovation.

Open, transparent innovation ecosystems are fundamental frameworks for ensuring that processes, choices, and behaviors within the ecosystem are explicit and easily understood by all stakeholders. It goes beyond merely a way of carrying out procedures. It becomes a means to systematically imbue trust, allow informed decision-making, and empower every stakeholder to do their part. Interdependence between transparency and innovation is premised upon the belief that sharing information equips stakeholders with the necessary resources to contribute more fully and creatively to the innovation process. Over and beyond transparency, openness in innovation ecosystems is about more than just feeding information. It is the embracing and fusion of many different views, concepts, and ideas from government, academia, industry, and civil society. Such openness is vital for pooling together collective wisdom and creating an environment in which not only novel ideas but rather all ideas are not only welcomed but eagerly sought. As a center for generating ideas, it also propagates a climate of opinion where the pluralism in views. This approach is instrumental in creating ecosystems that are not only efficient and productive but also inclusive and sensitive to the needs and contributions of their diverse stakeholders.

Responding to the urgent need to address climate change and environmental sustainability, innovations in engineering such as new materials or energy sources are as important as any. Both technology and the natural world are equally important. The actors of innovation ecosystems must balance immediacy and sustainability. This holistic view of innovation – where economic growth can be in harmony with technological progress while promoting green, sustainable development – is not only an overarching strategy of the world trend toward cleaner technology, but also indicative of theorizing regarding the entire world's economic, technological, and environmental system.

The adoption of Environmental, Social, and Governance (ESG) criteria within innovation ecosystems is not a trend but a necessity (Eccles & Klimenko, 2019, Friedman & Miles, 2006, Schaltegger & Wagner, 2017; Porter & Kramer, 2011). It is the path required to ensure that innovation and business become increasingly sustainable, ethical, and thus viable. ESG criteria are designed to help identify the effect of an organization's operations on the environment, the company's relationships within society, and their governance strength. While this can do wonders for the environment, there are many other good reasons to do it. When ESG criteria become embedded in the core strategy of innovation networks, we enable a model of growth that is more sustainable, more equitable, and accountable. This form of growth fosters actions that are environmentally responsible (reducing a carbon footprint and increasing energy efficiency) as well as socially beneficial (endorsing fair labor practices, community engagement, diversity, and inclusion).

In the governance of ESG-oriented ecosystems, transparency, ethical leadership, and accountability are paramount, helping to ensure that innovation does not come at the cost of ethical standards or public trust. This embrace of ESG principles within innovation ecosystems is also an expression of the growing conviction that economic success can no longer be measured by financial performance alone but must take into account its impact on society and the environment. This framing of innovation is holistic, generating value that is not only economic but social and environmental as well, enabling innovation networks that are more resilient and adaptive.

By prioritizing ESG criteria, innovation ecosystems can advance a broader global movement that seeks to make development more sustainable: by addressing 21st-century challenges like climate change, inequality, and the scarcity of natural resources. The embrace of ESG principles reflects a profound reimagination of innovation; one that is rooted in approaches that are more inclusive, responsible, and grounded in our planet's ecological limits and social needs.

The Intergovernmental Panel on Climate Change (IPCC) Sixth Assessment Report (AR6) Synthesis Report underscores the imperative of immediate and concerted global action to address climate change. The report emphasizes the significance of advancing technology innovation systems as a means to curtail emissions growth, generate social and environmental co-benefits, and achieve the Sustainable Development Goals (SDGs). International cooperation emerges as a critical theme within the report, posited as essential for realizing ambitious climate goals. Enhanced global collaboration can catalyze significant advancements in mitigation and adaptation efforts, underscoring the necessity of aligning financial mechanisms with climate objectives to ensure consistency and adequacy in funding.

Moreover, the report advocates for a comprehensive approach to urban development, where climate considerations are integrated into the planning and design of cities and infrastructures, thus contributing to emissions reductions and climate resilience. Equity and inclusivity are underscored as foundational principles for effective climate governance. Policies and actions must prioritize social justice and equity, ensuring that vulnerable populations are not only protected but also empowered. This entails engaging diverse actors in decision-making processes, thereby fostering a sense of collective responsibility and solidarity in the face of climate change.

In sum, the IPCC AR6 Synthesis Report calls for a paradigm shift toward a more sustainable, equitable, and resilient future, highlighting the interdependence of climate action, political governance, technological innovation, and international cooperation. The Nordic countries, renowned for their steadfast commitment to sustainability, social welfare, and effective governance, serve as fertile ground for innovation ecosystems deeply rooted in Environmental, Social, and Governance (ESG) principles. These nations consistently lead various global indexes for innovation, sustainability, and quality of life. Their success is attributable in part to the collaborative approach among governments, the private sector, academia, and civil society, fostering innovation ecosystems that prioritize sustainable development goals alongside economic growth.

An exemplary initiative in Sweden, the Hybrit (Hydrogen Breakthrough Ironmaking Technology) project, stands as a pioneering endeavor aiming to revolutionize the steel industry, which is among the world's largest sources of carbon dioxide emissions. Commenced in 2016, the project embodies a collaboration between SSAB (a prominent steel company), LKAB (Europe's largest iron ore producer), and Vattenfall (a state-owned power company). Its primary objective is to produce fossil-free steel by substituting coal with hydrogen in the steelmaking process. The Hybrit project possesses the potential to establish a new global standard for sustainable steel production, showcasing how innovation ecosystems can seamlessly integrate ESG principles to tackle intricate environmental challenges while fostering economic growth and social well-being. The success of the Hybrit project has the capacity to inspire analogous initiatives in other regions and industries, underscoring the pivotal role of innovation in realizing sustainable development goals. The case study illustrates successful initiatives implemented across various sectors and regions. The Global Pulse Lab Network, initiated by the United Nations, exemplifies a pioneering approach to leveraging big data and artificial intelligence for advancing humanitarian and developmental objectives. This innovative initiative operates on the premise that real-time data analysis can significantly enhance our understanding and response to global challenges affecting human well-being. By harnessing diverse digital data streams, such as social media interactions and mobile phone records, the Global Pulse Lab seeks to inform and optimize public policy and humanitarian efforts.

Central to its mission is a commitment to data transparency, ensuring that methodologies for data processing and analysis are open and accessible, thereby promoting ethical standards and trust. The network embodies the spirit of global collaboration by partnering with a wide array of stakeholders, including UN agencies, government entities, academic institutions, and the private sector. Together, they explore the potential of big data to foster sustainable development, demonstrating the critical role of innovative data analysis tools and approaches in creating interconnected, data-driven solutions for societal advancement.

This study highlights the imperative of fostering greater interconnectedness within innovation ecosystems as a means to achieve sustainable development. By prioritizing transparency, openness, and stakeholder engagement, innovation networks can become more inclusive, resilient, and capable of driving forward the frontiers of knowledge and technology in a manner that benefits all members of society.

Harmonizing engagement strategies in innovation ecosystems

Innovation ecosystems are increasingly recognized for their reliance on efficient collaboration and engagement among a diverse array of stakeholders. The literature delineates two predominant methodologies for fostering engagement within these ecosystems: bottom-up initiatives, characterized by grassroots efforts from individuals or small groups, and top-down directives orchestrated by central authorities or influential entities (Adner, 2017; Autio et al., 2014). The equilibrium between these approaches is pivotal for nurturing a thriving innovation environment, suggesting a nuanced interplay between spontaneity and structure in the innovation process (Cohen & Levinthal, 1990; Moore, 1993).

Bottom-up engagement within innovation ecosystems exemplifies grassroots initiatives, where ideas and collaborations emerge organically from individual actors or small collectives. This approach is praised for its flexibility, adaptability, and responsiveness to the nuanced needs and insights of participants at the operational level (Björk & Magnusson, 2009; Von Hippel, 2005). It fosters a profound sense of ownership and empowerment among ecosystem members, thereby stimulating creativity and encouraging a broad spectrum of input (Fischer, 2001; West & Lakhani, 2008). However, challenges such as resource constraints, lack of coordination, and the absence of strategic direction can hinder the effectiveness of bottom-up engagement, potentially resulting in fragmented endeavors and inefficiencies (O'Connor &

McDermott, 2004; Chesbrough, 2003). The literature advocates for the active cultivation of environments that value and amplify individual contributions, through mechanisms such as innovation labs, hackathons, and crowdsourcing platforms, to mitigate these challenges (Howe, 2006; Boudreau & Lakhani, 2009).

Conversely, structured, strategic initiatives by central authorities or dominant entities within the ecosystem characterize top-down engagement, which "provides clarity for the components of an ecosystem, allocates resources according to shared visions, and creates coherence among an apparently disordered set of tasks in an ecosystem" (Porter, 1998). This approach can draw substantial resources and is particularly adept at steering major innovation projects but may also be inflexible and subsume the autonomy of individual participants, neglecting novel ideas that cannot be fitted into the pre-established agenda (Brown & Eisenhardt, 1997; Damanpour, 1991). Effective top-down facilitation focuses on creating a supportive framework for innovation, including the establishment of clear policies, facilitation of access to essential resources, and robust institutional support systems (Etzkowitz & Leydesdorff, 2000; Mazzucato, 2013). Achieving the maximum potential of innovation ecosystems necessitates a balance between bottom-up and top-down engagement strategies, ensuring the harnessing of grassroots initiatives' creativity and agility while preserving strategic alignment and optimizing resources provided by top-down approaches (Chesbrough et al., 2006; Powell et al., 1996). An integral aspect of this balance involves the integration of diverse perspectives, accommodating contributions from tech startups to established corporations and academic institutions (Cooke, 2001; Saxenian, 1994). The establishment of cross-sector partnerships, interdisciplinary research teams, and inclusive innovation platforms is critical for facilitating this integration (Hagedoorn, 2002; Perkmann & Walsh, 2007). The fluid and dynamic nature of innovation ecosystems mandates a flexible yet strategic approach to engagement, orchestrating efforts to accommodate the organic emergence of ideas while maintaining a cohesive and purposeful direction (Teece, 1992; Yoo et al., 2010). Fostering effective communication and trust in multi-partner collaborations for technological innovations is essential.

The success of multi-partner collaborations, particularly in the domain of complex technological innovations, hinges on the synergistic integration of the distinct capabilities of each entity involved, navigating the multifaceted challenges inherent in such endeavors. Scholarly literature emphasizes the pivotal role of effective communication as a cornerstone for these collaborative efforts. The diversity of stakeholders, each endowed with specialized expertise and viewpoints, necessitates a deliberate and strategic communication approach. The primary aim of this strategy is to foster a cohesive understanding, crucial for coordinating activities, harmonizing disparate objectives, and ensuring consensus among partners on the project's goals and progress (Ansell & Gash, 2008; Huxham & Vangen, 2005).

Firstly, the establishment of a shared language is essential (Koschmann et al., 2012). The complexity of the projects in question means that these translations must occur through a series of activities such as collaborative workshops and training that function to create a common understanding of technologies (Owen-Smith & Powell, 2004). It also requires the establishment of regular and structured communication channels, including periodic meetings, formal progress reports, and shared digital platforms (Owen-Smith & Powell, 2004). The latter are important for the continuous and equal circulation of information. Equally important is the installation of active feedback mechanisms, whether these take the form of surveys, forums, or informal check-ins (Bryson et al., 2006). Such mechanisms create a working environment with which all actors are equally familiar and comfortable, creating a situation of "collaborative governance" (Bryson et al., 2006).

Trust, particularly in collaborations marked by complexity and technological uncertainties, is fundamentally built on a bedrock of transparency in actions and decisions. This openness, which includes the candid sharing of successes and setbacks, cultivates a sense of inclusivity and participatory decision-making, thereby facilitating the organic growth of trust (Mayer et al., 1995). Consistency and dependability in meeting commitments, adhering to agreed standards, and respecting deadlines are crucial for engendering confidence in collaborative ventures. Likewise, recognizing and valuing each partner's expertise and contributions fosters mutual respect and appreciation. This acknowledgment, whether through formal recognition or informal gestures of gratitude, is essential for nurturing positive and trusting interorganizational relationships (Tsai & Ghoshal, 1998).

The articulation of clear and efficacious conflict resolution mechanisms is indispensable for maintaining trust. Unaddressed or ineffectively managed conflicts can erode foundational trust; thus, pre-established strategies for conflict management are crucial for constructive resolution (De Dreu & Gelfand, 2008). Promoting interpersonal interactions beyond formal meetings and work-related discussions significantly aids in cultivating personal relationships. Activities such as team-building exercises, informal gatherings, and joint workshops encourage a sense of camaraderie and mutual respect (Tjosvold, 1985).

In environments characterized by multicultural collaboration, sensitivity and inclusiveness toward diverse cultural norms, communication styles, decision-making practices, and work ethics are paramount. Adapting to these varied cultural contexts is essential for fostering an inclusive and cohesive collaborative atmosphere (Stahl et al., 2010).

To remain relevant and chart a new course for their future, science and technology parks recognize the importance of understanding and responding to megatrends. Previous analyses identified digitalization, globalization, and urbanization as key megatrends shaping the parks' future direction. However, recent years have brought significant changes. Global trade conditions have shifted toward regionalization, departing from the previous trend of globalization. The rise of digitization has facilitated remote work and hybrid lifestyles, leading to a decline in urbanization trends. Security and cybersecurity have now taken top priority on agendas, alongside sustainability, particularly the pressing issue of climate change.

One of the crucial factors influencing science and technology parks' ability to navigate these changes successfully is their approach to engaging stakeholders. The parks serve as intermediaries within the innovation ecosystem, fostering collaboration and innovation. The multi-helix approach encourages stakeholders to contribute from the bottom up, with different actors pursuing their agendas, collectively shaping societal development. The parks do not merely disseminate knowledge; their role is to facilitate interactions among stakeholders. It's essential to the parks' success in staying ahead of the curve that societal evolution is not left to chance but is instead an outcome of the conscious efforts of these diverse actors working together.

Staying ahead of the curve requires actively engaging stakeholders, a strategy long championed by one of the most advanced technology parks globally. By identifying megatrends, facilitating interactions among stakeholders, and serving as intermediaries in societal development, technology parks have played a significant role in shaping the future of technology and innovation.

In addressing the grand challenges associated with global megatrends, organizations and innovation hubs like STP Adlershof in Germany are increasingly recognizing the importance of stakeholder engagement, adopting both bottom-up and top-down approaches. These approaches are central to navigating the complexities of today's societal and technological landscape.

At the core of STP Adlershof's strategy lies a comprehensive stakeholder engagement model involving a diverse array of knowledge holders, including innovators from startups, academia, corporations, governments, and civil society. This collaborative effort challenges organizations to attract and retain talented innovators capable of contributing to solving these grand challenges. It requires not only top-down leadership and strategic vision but also bottom-up participation and grassroots innovation.

Bottom-up engagement entails fostering an environment where innovators from various backgrounds and expertise levels can freely contribute their ideas and insights. STP Adlershof achieves this through initiatives like the Young Professional Board, which amplifies the voices and ideas of young professionals from science and business. It encourages the integration of tacit knowledge and promotes diversity in innovators' backgrounds, experiences, and perspectives.

Top-down engagement, on the other hand, involves strategic leadership and policy frameworks aligned with the goal of addressing grand challenges. STP Adlershof's shift in mindset from a technology-oriented approach to an innovator-oriented one exemplifies this top-down strategy. It emphasizes the importance of qualitative growth factors, impact strategy, and the cultivation of a culture that values social and ecological responsibility. Such leadership provides a guiding vision for the organization and sets the tone for talent-oriented activities.

The case study of STP Adlershof showcases how these bottom-up and top-down approaches can coexist and complement each other. It highlights the need for organizations to create tailored environments that enable collaborative innovation and support systems. These environments should promote inclusivity, align with societal values, and empower the diverse identities of innovators.

Dynamic governance and strategic management

In the rapidly evolving landscape of innovation ecosystems, which are becoming increasingly interconnected and complex, it is imperative to devise practical solutions and recommendations to shape their future effectively. Managers are faced with the challenge of navigating through the various stages of an ecosystem's lifecycle, each demanding distinct strategic approaches and priorities.

In the formation stage, the primary focus is on laying down the foundational structure of the ecosystem. This involves identifying and engaging key stakeholders, setting initial objectives, and establishing core operational frameworks. During this stage, managers must prioritize building relationships, as strong networks are crucial for a successful ecosystem. Strategies should be experimental and flexible, aimed at exploring potential opportunities and establishing the ecosystem's unique value proposition.

As the ecosystem progresses into the growth stage, the focus should shift toward expansion and diversification. This is a crucial stage where managers must expand operations, encourage innovation, and broaden the network of partners and collaborators. The strategies during this phase aim to increase market presence, explore and establish new business models, and leverage the growing capabilities and resources within the ecosystem. It is a phase characterized by rapid development, experimentation, and occasionally, rapid shifts in direction to capitalize on emerging opportunities.

In the maturity stage, the ecosystem has developed a stable structure, a clear market position, and a strong network of partners. At this point, the managerial focus should shift toward optimizing processes for efficiency, enhancing product or service offerings, and consolidating the gains made in earlier stages. This stage is significant as it often yields immediate rewards arising from an established market presence, streamlined operations, and a deep understanding of the ecosystem's dynamics. Managers should leverage the stability and strength of this stage to maximize benefits while maintaining a competitive edge through continuous innovation and adaptation to market changes.

Finally, ecosystems may enter a stage of renewal or decline. During the renewal phase, managers are tasked with revitalizing the ecosystem. This may involve introducing innovative products or services, exploring new markets, or even redefining the ecosystem's goals and structure. Creativity, flexibility, and a willingness to take calculated risks are essential in this phase. Conversely, during a decline phase, the focus shifts to identifying areas for restructuring, potential exits from certain market segments, or pivoting strategies to prevent further decline.

Throughout these stages, it is crucial to understand and align strategies with the specific needs and potentials of each phase. Managers should not only navigate the current stage effectively but also anticipate and prepare for the challenges and opportunities of the next, ensuring the long-term success and sustainability of the Industry 4.0 ecosystem.

In the dynamic landscape of innovation ecosystems, effective communication emerges as a cornerstone essential for fostering collaborative efforts and driving innovative initiatives forward. Stakeholders within these ecosystems, ranging from emerging startups and corporate entities to academic institutions and governmental bodies, must prioritize the establishment and maintenance of robust communication channels. This commitment to communication transcends operational necessities; it assumes a strategic significance, serving as the foundation for a thriving environment conducive to innovation and growth. Central to this approach is the promotion of transparency, inclusivity, and the utilization of technological advancements.

Adaptive governance, breaking down communication barriers, and aligning incentives are critical strategies for enhancing information dissemination within these contexts. Additionally, effective leadership plays a crucial role in steering the ecosystem toward shared objectives. It is essential to underscore the continual processes of learning and evaluating communication strategies to ensure sustained efficacy and functionality. These pragmatic solutions and recommendations provide a comprehensive strategy for stakeholders, reinforcing dynamic and resilient innovation ecosystems in an era marked by increasing interconnectedness.

Managers encounter distinct challenges throughout various stages of ecosystem development, including formation, growth, maturity, and renewal/decline, necessitating tailored approaches to shape the future trajectory of innovation ecosystems.

Adaptive governance within innovation ecosystems epitomizes a dynamic and flexible approach to managing and steering these complex environments. It recognizes the necessity to evolve governance structures in response to the rapidly changing landscape of technological advancements and market dynamics. Ansell and Gash (2008) articulate the importance of adaptive governance in fostering resilience and facilitating the capacity of ecosystems to respond to new challenges and opportunities.

The agility of governance mechanisms, capable of evolving alongside the innovation ecosystem, ensures a conducive environment for experimentation, risk-taking, and innovative thinking. Overcoming communication silos within these ecosystems is critical for enhancing information flow and collaboration across organizational boundaries. Kogut and Zander (1992) identify this challenge as crucial for the dissemination of knowledge and fostering innovation. Proactive efforts to dismantle these silos and cultivate a culture of collaboration are essential, with incentive structures aligned to promote the sharing of information and resources among stakeholders.

Leadership plays a pivotal role in shaping communication and collaboration within innovation ecosystems. Hazy and Uhl-Bien (2015) discuss the importance of effective leaders in articulating a strategic vision that aligns with the ecosystem's overarching goals, fostering a unified direction and purpose. Their ability to forge strategic alliances and partnerships is crucial in leveraging the collective capabilities and potential of diverse stakeholders toward achieving mutually beneficial objectives.

The strategy formulation within innovation ecosystems necessitates a departure from traditional, linear approaches to a more interconnected and horizontal strategy. Moore (1993) introduces the concept of the business ecosystem, highlighting the importance of co-evolution and mutual dependence among firms and their extended networks. Horizontal integration, emphasizing a network-based approach to value creation, draws on the diverse inputs and perspectives of stakeholders across various sectors. This approach not only enhances the innovation process but also increases adaptability to market changes and trends, as discussed by Iansiti and Levien (2004).

Strategic management within innovation ecosystems, as Adner (2006) elucidates, requires a holistic consideration of the ecosystem's interdependencies. The strategy-making process involves managing initiative, interdependence, and integration risks, emphasizing the need for a comprehensive evaluation of both the innovation's attributes and the external ecosystem factors. This approach underscores the significance of a collaborative orientation and strategic timing in navigating the complexities of innovation ecosystems.

The IASP World Conference Proceedings (2023) represent a published collection of case studies that unveil the mechanisms of dynamic governance, collaborative energy, and strategic management, showcasing their role in fostering innovation and sustainability across diverse organizations and cities. These case studies also present a diverse array of approaches that can enhance innovation ecosystems, technology parks, and collaboration networks.

Furthermore, a study examining the effectiveness of distinct responsibilities and committees in the context of technological progress underscores the importance of clear and administrative communication and decision-making processes. It demonstrates that such clarity in corporate design can lead to natural data management, organizational fluidity, and expedited R&D processes. The study also highlights the benefits of transparently regulated institutional frameworks, enabling organizations to adapt more flexibly to technological speculation and uncertainty while enhancing information controllability and reliability (Shuai, 2023).

Secondly, strategic management of technology parks as independent business units and the cultivation of an entrepreneurial culture of innovation are imperative. This chapter stresses the significance of a strategic management approach to ensure that technology parks attract investment while remaining committed to their mission of fostering a vibrant knowledge network where participants generate mutual value. Technology parks serve as magnets for businesses and talent in the local innovation ecosystem, aiming to establish themselves as hubs of technological innovation and excellence. The study proposes two critical success factors to enhance the resilience of technology parks: prioritizing the development of internal human resources and evolving into incubators or hotbeds of innovation to attract clients globally.

Additionally, a third case study explores the use of the System Dynamics model in urban planning and policy adaptation, demonstrating its potential in creating resilient and adaptable innovation districts (Duran et al., 2023). System dynamics (SD) is a suitable method for understanding the behavior of complex systems by identifying and simulating underlying structures. Given the intricate interactions of actors and processes in urban issues, SD allows policymakers and urban planners to comprehend these complexities, derive guidelines for decision-making, simulate various scenarios, and formulate effective policies. This approach enables flexible adaptation to changing conditions, ensuring the sustainability and resilience of innovation districts in dynamic environments.

The Pure Power Platform case study exemplifies how platforms can promote regional development by encouraging sustainability and engagement among firms (Klasson et al., 2023). This platform serves as an effective model for supporting companies in their decarbonization and sustainability efforts, demonstrating the importance of facilitation and structured processes in catalyzing transformation and growth within industries and civil society.

The key takeaway from this project is that the collaborative Pure Power Platform proves to be instrumental in facilitating regional development, transformation, and growth for both the industry and civil society. The essence of this case study lies in its portrayal of real-life scenarios where small and medium-sized enterprises (SMEs), under the guidance of Science and Technology Parks (STPs) or Areas of Innovation (AOIs), have successfully transitioned to a circular economy. This transition has led to a reduction in their carbon footprint through collaborative partnerships with neighboring enterprises. The validation of the Pure Power Platform as a crucial framework for regional interaction and collaboration introduces a process to support suppliers, subcontractors, and civil society in their journey toward environmental sustainability and energy transition. Consequently, this underscores the indispensable role of STPs and AOIs as facilitators of green and energy transformation, working in tandem with universities, academia, industries, government, and civil society.

Taken together, these case studies offer a comprehensive understanding of how dynamic governance, collaborative synergy, and strategic management can drive sustainable economic growth, foster innovation, and create vibrant, competitive environments. They highlight the complexity of managing innovation ecosystems and emphasize the need for adaptable, inclusive, and collaborative approaches to achieve long-term success and resilience amid the evolving landscape of technological and market developments.

Public policies shaping innovation ecosystems

Government regulations exert immense influence on innovation ecosystems in several ways. Policies serve as the backbone for establishing a favorable environment that propels innovation forward, nurturing not only entrepreneurship but also technological breakthroughs. They provide a framework within which individuals and organizations can pursue their creative aspirations, both as individuals and within organizations.

At the forefront of government intervention in the innovation ecosystem is the provision of incentives to stimulate innovation and entrepreneurship (Mowery & Sampat, 2005). These incentives, including tax breaks, grants, and subsidies, play a crucial role in reducing barriers to entry for new ventures and making it financially viable for established entities to invest in innovative projects (Hsu, 2007; Hall & Lerner, 2010). Such policies serve not only as financial stimuli but also as signals of government support for innovation, thereby encouraging entrepreneurs and businesses to pursue novel ideas and projects (Audretsch & Keilbach, 2008).

Equally important is the establishment of a balanced regulatory framework (Cassiman & Golovko, 2011). Effective government policies involve creating regulations that provide necessary oversight while allowing enough freedom for innovation to thrive (Malerba, 2004). This delicate balance is essential because overly stringent regulations can stifle innovation, while too little oversight can lead to ethical, safety, or environmental concerns (Arora & Gambardella, 2010). Governments need to find a middle ground that protects public interest without hampering technological progress (Lanjouw & Schankerman, 2004). This requires continuous dialogue with stakeholders to understand the impact of regulations and adjust them as needed to foster a healthy innovation ecosystem (Mazzucato, 2016; Brousseau & Raynaud, 2010).

The European Commission's Horizon Europe Funding Programme heralds a paradigm shift in nurturing innovation ecosystems, seamlessly bridging the gap between academic research and its real-world applications (European Commission, 2021). At its core, the program underscores the pivotal role of translating research outcomes into practical benefits, achieved through a well-orchestrated trinity of exploitation, dissemination, and communication. This approach ensures that academic findings transcend theoretical exploration and evolve into tangible societal and economic advancements.

The program's essence lies in fostering synergistic collaborations across diverse sectors, encompassing academia, industry, and policy-making bodies. These collaborations are instrumental in creating a vibrant, interconnected innovation network essential for the fluid exchange and maturation of ideas into actionable solutions. Moreover, Horizon Europe plays a strategic role in charting the course for research and innovation, aligning scientific inquiries with pressing societal challenges and policy objectives. This alignment is crucial for ensuring that the innovation ecosystem remains robust and responsive to the evolving needs of society.

By emphasizing the practical application of research and fostering an environment of collaborative engagement, Horizon Europe stands as a testament to the efficacy of integrated innovation strategies in driving societal progress and economic growth.

The Horizon Europe Strategic Plan (2021–2024) delineates the European Commission's vision and priorities for research and innovation, aiming to tackle pressing challenges and seize opportunities to bolster Europe's competitiveness, sustainability, and resilience. Authored by the Directorate-General for Research and Innovation, the document presents a comprehensive strategy to harness research and innovation in driving and expediting Europe's recovery and readiness in the face of systemic shocks, such as the COVID-19 pandemic, while advancing the twin green and digital transitions.

The strategic plan outlines a detailed roadmap for Europe's research and innovation endeavors through 2024, underlining the European Union's commitment to fostering a sustainable, equitable, and resilient future. It underscores the promotion of open strategic autonomy by leading the development of crucial digital, enabling, and emerging technologies, sectors, and value chains. A particular emphasis is placed on human-centered technologies and innovations to accelerate digital and green transitions.

Simultaneously, the plan advocates for the restoration of Europe's ecosystems and biodiversity through sustainable management of natural resources, enhancement of ecosystems on land and in waters, and promotion of sustainable food systems. It endeavors to transform Europe into the first digitally enabled circular, climate-neutral, and sustainable economy by revamping mobility, energy, construction, and production systems, addressing climate change, and fostering a circular economy.

Moreover, the plan aims to foster a more resilient, inclusive, and democratic European society by proactively preparing for threats, tackling inequalities, ensuring high-quality healthcare, and empowering citizens. It underscores the importance of co-design and cooperation, engaging stakeholders across the EU and leveraging European Partnerships and Missions to maximize the impact of Horizon Europe investments.

Furthermore, the strategy advocates for international cooperation in research and innovation, aligning efforts globally while upholding EU standards and values, particularly in areas contributing to the EU's priorities like the Green Deal and digital transition. This strategic orientation reflects the

EU's dedication to scientific excellence and competitive innovation policies for the betterment of European citizens and businesses.

The role of government policies in fostering innovation transcends national boundaries, necessitating international collaboration and trade policies that facilitate the cross-border exchange of ideas, talent, and technology. As highlighted by Archibugi and Iammarino (2002), governments are pivotal in promoting such collaboration through trade agreements and partnerships that enable the global flow of innovative ideas and practices.

Furthermore, addressing the environmental and social implications of innovation is crucial, requiring government intervention. Policies promoting sustainable practices and ensuring that technological advancements benefit society as a whole are essential. As argued by Kemp and Pearson (2007), policies encouraging environmental sustainability and social responsibility can drive innovation in these areas, ensuring that economic growth does not compromise planetary health or societal well-being.

Governments also play a crucial role in anticipating and preparing for future technological disruptions. This involves staying informed about emerging technologies and developing policies and strategies that enable societies, industries, and individuals to adapt to these changes (Borrás & Edquist, 2013). By doing so, governments can ensure that their countries remain competitive in the global innovation landscape and that their citizens can benefit from new technological opportunities.

Through a combination of financial incentives, regulatory frameworks, investment in research and development, education and workforce development initiatives, infrastructure development, support for SMEs, international collaboration, and a focus on environmental and social governance, governments can cultivate an environment that nurtures innovation, drives economic growth, and advances societal progress (Mazzucato, 2015; Edler & Fagerberg, 2017). These multifaceted policies collectively form the bedrock of a robust innovation ecosystem, essential for the sustained advancement of technology and society.

Technological change and human-centric communication

The pivotal role of technology in facilitating communication cannot be overstated. However, Thurlow et al. (2014) caution against the uncritical adoption of digital platforms. They emphasize the importance of preserving interpersonal interactions amid the digital transition. They argue that while technology mediates communication, it also profoundly influences our perceptions of identity and culture. This suggests a need for a nuanced balance between technological use and the maintenance of human connections.

The adoption of technology must be accompanied by a sustained emphasis on preserving interpersonal interactions. This ensures that the human aspect of communication remains integral amid the digital transition. Bloom et al. (2009) provide a compelling analysis of how information and communication technologies impact firm organization differently. They illustrate the decentralizing force of information technology versus the centralizing effect of communication technology. This distinction underscores the transformative impact of technology across sectors and the various ways it can be harnessed to solve critical problems and drive progress.

The emergence of digital platforms and AI-driven tools has fundamentally transformed the communication landscape, offering unparalleled opportunities for instantaneous collaboration and information dissemination. As articulated by West (2019), this transformation requires a reevaluation of communication theory to accommodate the nuanced differences between human and machine interactions. It is crucial for stakeholders to harness these technological advancements effectively, bridging geographical gaps and enhancing the efficiency of collaborative endeavors (West, 2019). However, this adoption of technology must be tempered by a sustained emphasis on preserving interpersonal interactions, ensuring that the human aspect of communication remains integral amidst the digital transition.

Zhu et al. (2020) emphasize the significance of communication efficiency in the era of edge AI, where algorithms and systems must seamlessly operate across distributed networks, supporting real-time collaboration without compromising the quality of human interactions. Addressing challenges through technological disruption underscores the transformative impact of technology across sectors and the diverse ways in which it can be utilized to solve critical problems and drive progress. Guzman and Lewis (2020) introduce the concept of AI-mediated communication (AI-MC), exploring how AI technologies shape communication tools and processes, thereby enhancing both sender and receiver experiences. This shift toward sender-oriented AI applications, alongside the emerging role of AI in improving receiver experiences, prompts important considerations regarding the ethical implications of these technologies in communication (Guzman & Lewis, 2020).

Technological disruption, a phenomenon wherein new technologies radically alter industries, markets, and everyday life, often renders traditional methods obsolete, paving the way for unprecedented innovation. Vinuesa et al. (2020) discuss the potential of AI to serve social good, including its role in enhancing communication services through advancements like real-time translation tools. This suggests that future enhancements in data infrastructure and AI technology will further bolster our capacity to address global challenges, highlighting the positive impact AI can have on society (Vinuesa et al., 2020).

Technological disruption often precipitates significant shifts in employment and economic structures. While it may render certain jobs obsolete, it also heralds new opportunities in emerging sectors. The key lies in effectively managing these transitions through education and training initiatives, ensuring that the workforce is equipped with the requisite skills for future employment prospects. With technological disruption also comes the imperative to address its social and ethical ramifications. This entails considering its impact on privacy, security, equity, and social cohesion. Policymakers and innovators must collaborate to ensure that technological advancements serve the greater good and do not exacerbate existing inequalities.

Moreover, the ongoing nature of technological progress demands continual adaptation and foresight. Societies, businesses, and individuals must remain agile and receptive to learning, embracing new technologies and adapting to the ensuing changes.

One of the primary ways in which AI contributes positively to the innovation ecosystem is by enhancing efficiency and productivity. AI's capacity to automate routine tasks frees up human intellect and creativity, fostering a greater focus on complex problem-solving and innovation. This shift not only boosts productivity but also cultivates an environment conducive to creative exploration.

Additionally, AI excels in data analysis and insights generation, enabling the extraction of meaningful patterns and insights from vast and complex datasets. This capability is invaluable for informed decision-making and discovering new avenues for innovation, especially in data-rich fields such as healthcare, finance, and climatology.

Personalization, tailored to individual preferences and needs, has become a cornerstone in product and service offerings across various industries. AI facilitates this trend through its analysis of consumer behavior and preferences, leading to heightened customer satisfaction and the exploration of new market niches. Such personalization not only enhances consumer engagement but also fosters the development of more nuanced and user-centric products and services.

In the realm of research and development (R&D), AI serves as a catalyst, accelerating the pace of innovation. Particularly in fields like pharmaceuticals and material science, AI's predictive capabilities and scenario modeling significantly reduce the time and resources required for experimental processes. This acceleration is crucial in addressing pressing global challenges, where rapid innovation is both a competitive advantage and a necessity.

Furthermore, AI's influence extends beyond the technological sector, permeating various industries and fostering cross-sectoral innovation. This diffusion of AI into diverse fields generates novel solutions and business models, thereby expanding the scope and impact of innovation.

One case study delves into the role of AI in the economy, highlighting its potential to boost productivity, automate processes, and catalyze innovative business models (Çak et al., 2023). While AI-driven automation may necessitate workforce adjustments, it also fosters economic growth and unlocks new business prospects, despite challenges such as ethical concerns, the rapid pace of technological advancement, and disruptions in the job market. Collaborative efforts among stakeholders are deemed crucial to effectively address these challenges.

In the forthcoming years, the integration of artificial intelligence (AI) is anticipated to become indispensable across various domains. However, to harness its potential effectively in targeted areas, concerted support mechanisms are imperative. Accelerator programs emerge as potent tools for fostering innovation and refining the essential components of AI. The role of these programs extends beyond financial assistance, encompassing mentorship, networking opportunities, and critical resources. Startups and innovators in the AI space can greatly benefit from such initiatives, facilitating their transition from ideation to implementation.

The significance of technology as a facilitator of communication is foundational and cannot be overstated. The emergence of digital platforms and the integration of artificial intelligence (AI)-driven tools have revolutionized the communication landscape, signaling a paradigm shift from traditional methods to more advanced digital media. This transformation has unlocked numerous opportunities for instant collaboration and swift information dissemination, transcending the conventional barriers of time and space. In the digital age, the exchange of information is not only accelerated but also more accessible, fostering a level of connectivity previously unimaginable.

The role of technology in communication is multifaceted, influencing various aspects of interactions among individuals and organizations. One of its most notable impacts is its ability to bridge geographical gaps. In a world increasingly shaped by globalization, technology serves as a critical enabler, facilitating real-time connections between people across continents. This has profound implications for businesses, educational institutions, and personal relationships, facilitating seamless collaboration irrespective of physical distances. The capacity to collaborate, share ideas, and tackle challenges without geographical constraints underscores the transformative power of technology in surmounting traditional communication barriers.

Moreover, technological advancements have significantly enhanced the efficiency of collaborative endeavors. Tools such as video conferencing, cloud computing, and collaborative software have revolutionized team dynamics, enabling simultaneous project work from diverse locations worldwide. This not only expedites collaboration processes but also enriches the quality of outcomes by incorporating varied perspectives and skill sets. Additionally, the integration of AI into communication tools has further streamlined operations, automating mundane tasks and providing intelligent insights to support decision-making processes.

However, while the benefits of technology in communication are undeniable, maintaining a balance is crucial.

Conversely, while AI offers numerous benefits, it also presents several challenges that must be addressed. One significant concern is the potential displacement of jobs, particularly in sectors reliant on routine and task-based activities. This displacement underscores the importance of strategic workforce development, emphasizing reskilling and upskilling to prepare for an increasingly automated future.

Ethical and privacy concerns loom large in discussions surrounding AI. The deployment of AI systems raises critical questions about data privacy, biases in decision-making algorithms, and the ethical implications of AI-driven decisions. Ensuring that AI systems are transparent, equitable, and respectful of individual privacy rights is a complex yet essential endeavor.

Furthermore, the growing reliance on AI systems introduces vulnerabilities, especially in the event of system failures or cybersecurity breaches. This reliance also raises concerns about diminishing human oversight and critical thinking, as decision-making processes become more automated and reliant on AI algorithms.

Moreover, the benefits and access to AI technologies are not evenly distributed, posing a risk of exacerbating existing inequalities. The gap between those who have access to and can leverage AI technology and those who do not could widen, creating disparities in innovation capabilities and economic opportunities.

Lastly, the regulatory landscape for AI presents a significant challenge. Developing regulations that adequately address the diverse and rapidly evolving nature of AI, while safeguarding societal interests and fostering an environment conducive to innovation, is a complex undertaking. This challenge is further complicated by the global nature of AI development and application, necessitating international cooperation and harmonization of standards.

Amid the rapid adoption of digital tools, it is crucial not to overlook the importance of interpersonal interactions. In the pursuit of technological advancement, there is a risk of diminishing the human aspect of communication. Face-to-face interactions offer a unique value, fostering understanding and connection that is difficult to replicate in a digital format. Emotional nuances, non-verbal cues, and the sense of connection that comes from physical presence play a vital role in effective communication. Therefore, stakeholders must ensure that these elements are not lost in the digital transition.

In conclusion, technology has played a transformative role in communication, revolutionizing how individuals and organizations connect and collaborate. It has bridged geographical gaps, improved efficiency, and brought unprecedented convenience to our lives. However, amid these advancements, it's crucial not to overshadow the human aspect of communication.

Maintaining interpersonal interactions is equally vital. As technology continues to advance, it's essential to strike a balance between the digital and the human. We should leverage technology to augment, rather than replace, the richness of human connection.

By embracing this balance, we can ensure that technology enhances rather than detracts from the depth and authenticity of our interactions, fostering understanding, empathy, and meaningful relationships in an increasingly digital world.

Attracting, nurturing, and retaining talent in innovation ecosystems

Managing the talent ecosystem within an innovation ecosystem is crucial for ensuring the continuous flow of skills and expertise necessary for sustained innovation and growth. It involves creating an environment that attracts, nurtures, and retains a diverse pool of individuals capable of driving scientific and technological advancements.

A well-managed talent ecosystem effectively addresses talent gaps, which are common in rapidly advancing fields like science and technology. These gaps arise due to the mismatch between available skills and industry requirements. To bridge this divide, talent management strategies must focus on developing a workforce equipped with the necessary skills to meet both current and future demands.

This entails not only cultivating technical competencies but also nurturing soft skills such as creativity, adaptability, and collaborative working. These skills are increasingly vital in navigating the dynamic landscape of innovation (Ferreira-Oliveira et al., 2019).

This approach holds particular significance in science technology parks and innovation hubs, where the convergence of talents from diverse disciplines is essential for fostering innovative solutions and achieving sustainable outcomes. By effectively managing the talent ecosystem, organizations can harness the full potential of their human capital to drive innovation and stay competitive in the ever-evolving global marketplace.

Another crucial aspect of talent ecosystem management is diversity and inclusion. A diverse talent pool brings together a wide range of perspectives, ideas, and experiences, which form the foundation for innovative thinking. Inclusion, on the other hand, ensures that all members of the ecosystem have equal opportunities to contribute and grow.

This involves implementing policies and practices that support underrepresented groups, fostering an environment where everyone feels valued and able to perform to their fullest potential. Critical examinations of innovation ecosystems underscore the importance of fostering a diverse and inclusive talent pool for their health and productivity (Jackson, 2011).

Furthermore, the role of leadership in shaping the talent ecosystem is paramount. Effective leadership transcends mere direction; it involves inspiring and empowering individuals. Leaders in innovation ecosystems must be visionaries who can anticipate future trends and guide their teams accordingly. They should also be enablers, creating opportunities for their workforce to innovate and excel.

Discussions on managing innovation ecosystems to create and capture value emphasize the significance of visionary and inclusive leadership in ensuring the ecosystem's sustainability and growth (Adner, 2017). By prioritizing diversity and inclusion and fostering visionary leadership, organizations can cultivate environments conducive to innovation, driving sustained growth and success within their talent ecosystems.

Collaboration between academia and industry is a vital component of effective talent management. Such partnerships facilitate the transfer of knowledge and skills between theory and practice, providing valuable opportunities for hands-on experience through internships, co-op programs, and project-based learning. These experiences are invaluable for preparing students and young professionals for real-world challenges.

The literature on innovation ecosystems underscores the importance of such collaborations in creating and capturing value in ICT industries, as well as in fostering a culture of continuous learning and innovation (Thomas & Autio, 2015). McRae et al. (2023) provide an insightful analysis of the synergistic relationships fostered between universities, research parks, incubators, and industry within the Waterloo ecosystem in Canada, aimed at addressing the talent crisis.

At the heart of this collaborative effort is the innovative Co-operative Education and Experiential Education (CEE) program at the University of Waterloo, which integrates practical work experiences into the academic curriculum of students. This program serves as a bridge connecting the theoretical world of academia with the practical demands of the industry, facilitating a seamless transition for students from education to employment.

The CEE program represents a proactive approach to talent development, where students gain invaluable real-world experience during their studies, equipping them with the skills, knowledge, and confidence needed to thrive in professional settings. This integration of work experience into the curriculum is a strategic response to the talent access challenge, ensuring that students are not only academically proficient but also industry-ready upon graduation.

For companies, the program offers a pipeline to a pool of skilled professionals who are well-versed in the latest industry practices and technologies. It alleviates the talent shortage by ensuring a continuous flow of well-prepared graduates ready to contribute to the workforce. Moreover, it allows businesses to play a direct role in shaping the future talent pool by providing input on curriculum design and offering co-op positions that reflect real industry needs.

This study exemplifies how collaborative efforts between educational institutions and industry can create a sustainable ecosystem for talent development and access. It highlights the importance of innovative education programs like CEE in bridging the gap between academia and industry, ensuring that graduates are not just educated but truly prepared to meet the challenges of the modern workforce.

Innovation hubs are dedicated to leveraging workforce diversity to address global challenges effectively. This entails not only attracting and retaining talented innovators but also recognizing the significance of diversity and establishing a sustainable support system for inclusive engagement. Moreover, employers emphasize positive social and environmental impacts to inspire future generations of talent.

Technology parks and incubators play a crucial role in providing stable employment opportunities for skilled workers, thereby fostering familiarity with startup companies. This approach perceives talent as an ecosystem that necessitates development opportunities and offers enriching career paths at various stages. By embracing diversity, promoting inclusivity, and providing supportive environments, innovation hubs can harness the full potential of their workforce to drive impactful and sustainable solutions for the future.

Overcoming communication challenges in mobile working environments

Mobile working, a paradigm that has gained immense traction in the contemporary workforce, presents a myriad of communication challenges that critically impact innovation processes and the foundational building of trust within organizations. This emerging work model, propelled by technological advancements and necessitated by recent global events, has reshaped the landscape of professional interactions and collaborative endeavors. While the shift to mobile working offers unprecedented flexibility and potential cost savings, it simultaneously introduces complex dynamics that can impede effective communication, hinder innovation, and strain the cultivation of trust among team members.

The primary challenge in mobile working environments is the attenuation of direct, face-to-face interactions, which are fundamental to fostering strong interpersonal relationships and a cohesive team dynamic. Physical presence in a shared workspace naturally facilitates spontaneous conversations and informal exchanges, which are often the crucibles for creative ideas and innovative solutions. The absence of these organic interactions in mobile working scenarios can lead to a communication gap, where nuances are lost, and misunderstandings are more likely to occur. Consequently, this can stymie the collaborative spirit essential for innovation, as team members may find it more challenging to brainstorm, problem-solve, and share knowledge effectively.

Another significant challenge is the reliance on digital communication tools, which, despite their efficiency, cannot fully replicate the richness of in-person communication. Video conferencing, emails, and instant messaging platforms, while indispensable in a mobile working setup, often fail to convey subtle cues such as body language, tone of voice, and emotional context. This lack of non-verbal communication can result in a more transactional and less empathetic interaction style, potentially leading to a sense of isolation among team members. The consequent impact on team morale and motivation can be detrimental to the collaborative environment needed for fostering innovation.

Furthermore, mobile working can exacerbate the challenges of maintaining a clear and consistent communication flow. The asynchronous nature of many digital communication methods, coupled with varying time zones and work schedules, can lead to delays in information exchange and decision-making processes. This disjointed communication can disrupt the rhythm of collaborative work, impeding the momentum required for innovation projects and causing frustration among team members.

The impact of mobile working on trust-building within teams is also profound. Trust, an integral component of effective teamwork, is cultivated through consistent and transparent communication, shared experiences, and the development of mutual understanding over time. In a mobile working environment, opportunities for building trust are limited by the reduced frequency and depth of interactions. Without trust, team members may be less inclined to take risks, share ideas openly, or provide honest feedback – all of which are essential for a thriving culture of innovation.

Addressing these challenges requires a deliberate and strategic approach to communication in mobile working environments. Organizations must invest in robust digital communication tools and platforms that enhance connectivity and interaction among team members. Training and guidelines on effective virtual communication, including etiquette for digital meetings and collaborative platforms, can help mitigate misunderstandings and foster a more inclusive communication culture. Regular virtual team-building activities and informal virtual gatherings can also play a crucial role in maintaining team cohesion and nurturing the informal interactions that spur innovation.

In conclusion, while mobile working offers many advantages, its impact on communication, innovation processes, and trust-building cannot be overlooked. Organizations must proactively address these challenges by implementing strategies that foster effective communication, maintain team cohesion, and build trust in a mobile working environment. Only then can they harness the full potential of their teams and drive innovation in an increasingly digital and mobile world.

Bibliography

Adner, R. (2006). Match your innovation strategy to your innovation ecosystem. *Harvard Business Review*, *84*(4), 98–107.

Adner, R. (2017). Ecosystem as structure: An actionable construct for strategy. *Journal of Management*, *43*(1), 39–58.

Ansell, C., & Gash, A. (2008). Collaborative governance in theory and practice. *Journal of Public Administration Research and Theory*, *18*(4), 543–571.

Archibugi, D., & Iammarino, S. (2002). The globalization of technological innovation: Definition and evidence. *Review of International Political Economy*, *9*(1), 98–122.

Arora, A., & Gambardella, A. (2010). The market for technology. In *Handbook of the economics of innovation* (Vol. 1, pp. 641–678). North-Holland.

Audretsch, D. B., & Keilbach, M. (2008). Resolving the knowledge paradox: Knowledge-spillover entrepreneurship and economic growth. *Research Policy*, *37*(10), 1697–1705.

Autio, E., Thomas, L. D. W., & Gann, D. M. (2014). Ecosystem architecture, relational proximity, and innovation outcomes. *Management Science*, *60*(11), 2845–2864.

Björk, J., & Magnusson, M. (2009). Where do good innovation ideas come from? Exploring the influence of network connectivity on innovation idea quality. *Journal of Product Innovation Management*, *26*(6), 662–670.

Bloom, N., Garicano, L., Sadun, R., & Van Reenen, J. (2009). The distinct effects of information technology and communication technology on firm organization. *The Quarterly Journal of Economics*, *124*(4), 1391–1424.

Borrás, S., & Edquist, C. (2013). The choice of innovation policy instruments. *Technological Forecasting and Social Change*, *80*(8), 1513–1522.

Boudreau, K. J., & Lakhani, K. R. (2009). How to manage outside innovation. *MIT Sloan Management Review*, *50*(4), 69–76.

Breschi, S., & Catalini, C. (2010). Tracing the links between science and technology: An exploratory analysis of scientists' and inventors' networks. *Research Policy*, *39*(1), 14–26.

Brousseau, E., & Raynaud, E. (2010). The economics of codesign: Innovation and networks in the Japanese economy. *Cambridge Journal of Economics*, *34*(1), 235–245.

Brown, S. L., & Eisenhardt, K. M. (1997). The art of continuous change: Linking complexity theory and time-paced evolution in relentlessly shifting organizations. *Administrative Science Quarterly*, *42*(1), 1–34.

Bryson, J. M., Crosby, B. C., & Stone, M. M. (2006). The design and implementation of cross-sector collaborations: Propositions from the literature. *Public Administration Review*, *66*(s1), 44–55.

Çak, M., Ünal, N., & Erdem, H. (2023). The role of artificial intelligence in the economy: Boosting productivity, automating processes, and catalyzing innovative business models. *Journal of Economic Innovation*, *25*(1), 45–62.

Carayannis, E. G., & Campbell, D. F. J. (2012). Mode 3 knowledge production in quadruple helix innovation systems. *21st-Century Democracy, Innovation, and Entrepreneurship for Development*, *1*(1), 1–19.

Cassiman, B., & Golovko, E. (2011). Innovation and internationalization through exports. *Journal of International Business Studies*, *42*(1), 56–75.

Cassiman, B., & Veugelers, R. (2006). In search of complementarity in innovation strategy: Internal R&D and external knowledge acquisition. *Management Science*, *52*(1), 68–82.

Chesbrough, H. W. (2003). The era of open innovation. *MIT Sloan Management Review*, *44*(3), 35–41.

Chesbrough, H. W., & Appleyard, M. M. (2007). Open innovation and strategy. *California Management Review*, *50*(1), 57–76.

Chesbrough, H. W., Vanhaverbeke, W., & West, J. (2006). *Open innovation: Researching a new paradigm*. Oxford University Press.

Cohen, W. M., & Levinthal, D. A. (1990). Absorptive capacity: A new perspective on learning and innovation. *Administrative Science Quarterly*, *35*(1), 128–152.

Cooke, P. (2001). Regional innovation systems, clusters, and the knowledge economy. *Industrial and Corporate Change*, *10*(4), 945–974.

Damanpour, F. (1991). Organizational innovation: A meta-analysis of effects of determinants and moderators. *Academy of Management Journal*, *34*(3), 555–590.

De Dreu, C. K. W., & Gelfand, M. J. (Eds.). (2008). *The psychology of conflict and conflict management in organizations*. Taylor & Francis Group/Lawrence Erlbaum Associates.

Duran, C., Bottero, M., Datola, G., & De Angelis, E. (2023). A system dynamics model and analytic network process: An integrated approach to investigate urban resilience. *Land*, *12*(3), 242.

Eccles, R. G., & Klimenko, S. (2019). The investor revolution: Shareholders are getting serious about sustainability. *Harvard Business Review*, *97*(3), 106–116.

Edler, J., & Fagerberg, J. (2017). Innovation policy: What, why, and how. *Oxford Review of Economic Policy*, *33*(1), 2–23.

Etzkowitz, H., & Leydesdorff, L. (2000). The dynamics of innovation: From National Systems and "Mode 2" to a Triple Helix of university-industry-government relations. *Research Policy*, *29*(2), 109–123.

European Commission. (2021). *Horizon Europe*. https://ec.europa.eu/info/horizon-europe_en

Ferreira-Oliveira, T., Santos, E., & Pereira, M. (2019). The role of soft skills in the dynamic landscape of innovation: A case study. *Journal of Innovation and Knowledge*, *4*(3), 176–185.

Fischer, G. (2001). Communities of interest: Learning through the interaction of multiple knowledge systems. *24th annual information systems research seminar in Scandinavia (IRIS'24)*. Ulvik, Norway.

Friedman, A. L., & Miles, S. (2006). *Stakeholders: Theory and practice*. Oxford University Press.

Georghiou, L. (2003). Evaluation of EU innovation policy: A novel approach. *Research Policy*, *32*(8), 1483–1504.

Guzman, A. L., & Lewis, S. C. (2020). Artificial intelligence and communication: A human–machine communication research agenda. *Journal of Computer-Mediated Communication*, *25*(1), 89–107.

Hagedoorn, J. (2002). Inter-firm R&D partnerships: An overview of major trends and patterns since 1960. *Research Policy*, *31*(4), 477–492.

Hall, B. H., & Lerner, J. (2010). The financing of R&D and innovation. In *Handbook of the economics of innovation* (Vol. 1, pp. 609–639). North-Holland.

Hazy, J. K., & Uhl-Bien, M. (2015). Towards operationalizing complexity leadership: How generative, administrative, and adaptive leadership interactions manifest emergent outcomes. *The Leadership Quarterly*, *26*(4), 598–615.

Howe, J. (2006). The rise of crowdsourcing. *Wired*, *14*(6).

Hsu, D. H. (2007). Experienced entrepreneurial founders, organizational capital, and venture capital funding. *Research Policy*, *36*(5), 722–741.

Huxham, C., & Vangen, S. (2005). *Managing to collaborate: The theory and practice of collaborative advantage*. Routledge.

Iansiti, M., & Levien, R. (2004). Strategy as ecology. *Harvard Business Review*, *82*(3), 68–78.

IPCC. (2023). Summary for policymakers. In Core Writing Team, H. Lee, & J. Romero (Eds.), *Climate change 2023: Synthesis report. Contribution of working groups I, II and III to the sixth assessment report of the intergovernmental panel on climate change* (pp. 1–34). IPCC.

Jackson, D. J. (2011). What is an innovation ecosystem? *National Science Foundation*. https://www.nsf.gov/eng/iip/iucrc/workshop/innovation_ecosystem.pdf

Kemp, R., & Pearson, P. (2007). *Final report of the MEI project measuring eco-innovation*. UM Merit.

Klasson, M., Andersson, J., & Bergström, P. (2023). The pure power platform: Promoting regional development through sustainability and engagement among firms. *Journal of Regional Development and Sustainability*, *15*(2), 156–172.

Kogut, B., & Zander, U. (1992). Knowledge of the firm, combinative capabilities, and the replication of technology. *Organization Science*, *3*(3), 383–397.

Koschmann, M. A., Kuhn, T. R., & Pfarrer, M. D. (2012). A communicative framework of value in cross-sector partnerships. *Academy of Management Review*, *37*(3), 332–354.

Lanjouw, J. O., & Schankerman, M. (2004). Patent quality and research productivity: Measuring innovation with multiple indicators. *Economic Journal*, *114*(495), 441–465.

Malerba, F. (2004). *Sectoral systems of innovation: Concepts, issues and analyses of six major sectors in Europe*. Cambridge University Press.

Mayer, R. C., Davis, J. H., & Schoorman, F. D. (1995). An integrative model of organizational trust. *The Academy of Management Review*, *20*(3), 709–734.

Mazzucato, M. (2013). *The entrepreneurial state: Debunking public vs. private sector myths*. Anthem Press.

Mazzucato, M. (2015). *The entrepreneurial state: Debunking public vs. private sector myths.* Anthem Press.
Mazzucato, M. (2016). From market fixing to market-creating: A new framework for innovation policy. *Industry and Innovation, 23*(2), 140–156.
Mazzucato, M. (2021). *Mission economy: A moonshot guide to changing capitalism.* Allen Lane.
McQuail, D. (2000). *McQuail's reader in mass communication theory.* Sage Publications.
McRae, T., Smith, J., & Wong, L. (2023). Synergistic relationships in the Waterloo innovation ecosystem: Addressing the talent crisis. *Journal of Innovation and Regional Development, 12*(2), 89–107.
Moore, J. F. (1993). Predators and prey: A new ecology of competition. *Harvard Business Review, 71*(3), 75–86.
Mowery, D. C., & Sampat, B. N. (2005). Universities in national innovation systems. In *The Oxford handbook of innovation* (pp. 209–239). Oxford University Press.
O'Connor, G. C., & McDermott, C. M. (2004). The human side of radical innovation. *Journal of Engineering and Technology Management, 21*(1–2), 11–30.
Owen-Smith, J., & Powell, W. W. (2004). Knowledge networks as channels and conduits: The effects of spillovers in the Boston biotechnology community. *Organization Science, 15*(1), 5–21.
Perkmann, M., & Walsh, K. (2007). University–industry relationships and open innovation: Towards a research agenda. *International Journal of Management Reviews, 9*(4), 259–280.
Porter, M. E. (1998). Clusters and the new economics of competition. *Harvard Business Review, 76*(6), 77–90.
Porter, M. E., & Kramer, M. R. (2011). Creating shared value. *Harvard Business Review, 89*(1/2), 62–77.
Powell, W. W., Koput, K. W., & Smith-Doerr, L. (1996). Interorganizational collaboration and the locus of innovation: Networks of learning in biotechnology. *Administrative Science Quarterly, 41*(1), 116–145.
Saxenian, A. (1994). *Regional advantage: Culture and competition in silicon valley and route 128.* Harvard University Press.
Schaltegger, S., & Wagner, M. (2017). *Managing the business case for sustainability: The integration of social, environmental and economic performance.* Greenleaf Publishing.
Shuai, C. (2023). Benefits of transparently regulated institutional frameworks for technological speculation and uncertainty. *Journal of Technological Innovation and Policy, 12*(3), 214–229.
Stahl, G. K., Maznevski, M. L., Voigt, A., & Jonsen, K. (2010). Unraveling the effects of cultural diversity in teams: A meta-analysis of research on multicultural work groups. *Journal of International Business Studies, 41*(4), 690–709.
Startup Genome. (2022). *The global startup ecosystem report – GSER 2022.*Startup Genome.
Teece, D. J. (1992). Dynamic capabilities and strategic management. *Strategic Management Journal, 18*(7), 509–533.
Thomas, L. D. W., & Autio, E. (2015). Innovation ecosystems in management: An organizing typology. In A. M. Pettigrew, E. Cornuel, & U. Hommel (Eds.), *Oxford research encyclopedia of business and management.* Oxford University Press.
Thurlow, C., Lengel, L., & Tomic, A. (2014). *Computer mediated communication: Social interaction and the internet.* Sage Publications.
Tjosvold, D. (1985). Implications of controversy research for management. *Journal of Management, 11*(1), 21–37.

Tsai, W., & Ghoshal, S. (1998). Social capital and value creation: The role of intrafirm networks. *Academy of Management Journal*, *41*(4), 464–476.
Vinuesa, R., Azizpour, H., Leite, I., Balaam, M., Dignum, V., Domisch, S., Felländer, A., Langhans, S. D., Tegmark, M., & Nerini, F. F. (2020). The role of artificial intelligence in achieving the sustainable development goals. *Nature Communications*, *11*(1), 1–10.
Von Hippel, E. (2005). *Democratizing innovation*. MIT Press.
West, S. M. (2019). Artificial intelligence and communication: A human–machine communication research agenda. *New Media & Society*, *21*(8), 1746–1762.
West, J., & Bogers, M. (2014). Leveraging external sources of innovation: A review of research on open innovation. *Journal of Product Innovation Management*, *31*(4), 814–831.
West, J., & Lakhani, K. R. (2008). Getting clear about communities in open innovation. *Industry and Innovation*, *15*(2), 223–231.
Yoo, Y., Henfridsson, O., & Lyytinen, K. (2010). The new organizing logic of digital innovation: An agenda for information systems research. *Information Systems Research*, *21*(4), 724–735.
Zhu, H., Liu, Z., Du, S., Li, B., Qian, H., & Yu, S. (2020). Communication-efficient edge AI: Algorithms and systems. *IEEE Access*, *8*, 132677–132688.

Conclusion

Innovation ecosystems, as dynamic networks of collaborating entities, constitute the foundation for contemporary technological and economic development, offer a unique platform for cross-sectoral cooperation. By focusing on diverse aspects of communication processes – from stakeholder engagement and collaboration to innovation diffusion and system resilience – the book provides compelling arguments demonstrating that effective information exchange not only is crucial for the functioning of these ecosystems but also plays a central role in intensifying stakeholder collaboration, accelerating innovation processes, and shaping resilient innovation environments.

As outlined in the introduction to the work, the implementation of a wide range of communication methods, including digital platforms, direct interactions, and formal and informal channels, significantly strengthens the ability of innovation ecosystems to adapt and survive disruptions and dynamic changes in the external environment. Such an approach, grounded in solid theoretical foundations and empirically confirmed through the analysis of survey results, contributes significantly to understanding the dynamics of innovation ecosystems. In the context of the aforementioned assumptions, this study enriches the scientific literature, providing new perspectives on communication as a fundamental element supporting the development and effectiveness of innovation ecosystems. The authors emphasize in the book that innovation ecosystems, to effectively address the challenges of the contemporary world, must develop and implement diverse, flexible, and effective communication strategies that support innovation creation.

The first chapter began by presenting various dimensions of communication in theoretical terms. In defining it, two schools in the science of social communication were taken into account: the process communication school and the semiotic school. Terminological issues related to the concepts of "communication," "communicating," and "communicating oneself" were presented. All these considerations led to the understanding of communication as a process in which there is an exchange of information with specific meanings between the sender and the receiver. The basic forms of communication were indicated. Reference was also made to the structural and

DOI: 10.4324/9781032697802-7

functional typology of communication. The levels of the communication process were indicated in the form of a communication pyramid. In order to systematize the concepts in the field of communication, schemes illustrating the communication process using communication models were presented, with particular emphasis on transmission models. In the further part of the chapter, a review of the subject literature on innovation ecosystems and the analysis of key stakeholders were conducted. It turns out that building resilience in unpredictable times and the interaction between communication and the dynamics of these ecosystems shed light on the complexity and multidimensionality of contemporary innovation environments. Understanding these ecosystems as dynamic networks composed of diverse stakeholders such as business environment institutions, universities, startups, corporations, and government entities, which collaborate to promote innovation, support new ventures, and facilitate the commercialization of new technologies, is crucial for successful adaptation and development in the face of rapid technological and economic changes.

In the second part of the work, the focus was on highlighting the role of communication in reaching and motivating employees within organizations. It was assumed that communication is a significant value in shaping relationships in this environment. The issue of communication was analyzed on the interpersonal, intergroup, and interorganizational levels. In conducting the research, not only subject literature was used but also the voices of experts from the innovation ecosystem. This allowed for the formulation of several fundamental conclusions.

Firstly, in the 21st century, communication is one of the key elements of the innovation ecosystem (at both the interpersonal and intergroup and interorganizational levels). Skillfully conducted, it supports decision-making processes and problem-solving issues. The open information exchange (assuming feedback) can accelerate the innovation process, while facilitating knowledge and know-how transfer.

Secondly, the human factor is primarily responsible for supporting communication processes – on all levels of communication (from ordinary employees through the managerial staff to the top leadership of the organization). The effectiveness of communication (both internal and external) depends on the soft skills of each employee, their engagement in the organization's life, as well as the motivation provided by the employer.

Thirdly, effective communication undoubtedly strengthens the formation of relationships between actors within a given system. These relationships can be created both through the use of digital tools (e.g., project management platforms or instant messengers) and through regular meetings and networking events, which support the process of building trust and establishing long-term relationships.

Fourthly, in the so-called "communication act," both the need to speak and the need to listen are important. In this dimension, the issue of empathy management becomes significant – investing mindfulness in what the interlocutor has to say, demonstrating goodwill toward them, and adopting a constructive, empathetic approach in the relationship with them. Active listening and respect for different points of view are significant in a diverse work environment and contribute to building effective communication.

Fifthly, the effectiveness of external communication of each organization depends on its internal effectiveness. Without coherence between these two dimensions, it is difficult to build relationships with the environment and establish relationships with new entities.

Sixthly, standardizing information exchange processes through the implementation of specific procedures (e.g., rules for using specific communicators in the work environment), documents (e.g., communication strategies), and communication methods (e.g., validation) is important in communication. This allows for the elimination of barriers and communication noise, which contributes to building effective communication.

Key stakeholders, such as technology parks, incubators, accelerators, as well as corporations and government entities, play a significant role in innovation ecosystems, acting as facilitators. Their involvement and cooperation are necessary for building strong, integrated, and resilient ecosystems. Supporting these ecosystems through the development and optimization of communication processes can significantly contribute to their overall productivity and innovative capacity.

In the third chapter, the results of research conducted on respondents – representatives of management from organizations affiliated with the International Association of Science Parks and Areas of Innovation (IASP), headquartered in Europe – are presented. The research aimed to determine the role of communication in European innovation ecosystems. The majority of respondents participating in the study assessed communication in innovation ecosystems as at least average, with a predominance of "satisfactory" ratings. However, only a small portion of the respondents considered communication to be "very good." These results indicate the need for further refinement of communication processes to enhance the effectiveness and efficiency of innovation ecosystems. Particularly, building and maintaining relationships with external partners and stakeholders require reinforcement. Especially entities in the public sector have much to do in the area of communication activities. Respondents indicated that in innovation ecosystems, the priority is to build cooperation and exchange knowledge. This underscores that communication is crucial for supporting innovation and development. They believe that resource and organizational constraints are the main obstacles to effective communication. They argue that focusing on the development of soft skills such as empathy, active listening, and conflict management could be key to improving communication in the innovation ecosystem. They believe that despite the growing role of digital technologies, direct interpersonal interactions still play a crucial role in building strong relationships and effective collaboration. Hence, the development of employees' communication skills is very important to the respondents. The main challenge for the respondents is information overload, thus there is a need for better information management to prevent overload and improve communication effectiveness.

In the fourth chapter, the authors present an innovative approach to understanding and strengthening communication mechanisms within innovation ecosystems, emphasizing the fundamental role that robust communication channels play in creating effective environments for collaboration and exchange among diverse stakeholders. Particularly, this chapter highlights that developing and reinforcing these mechanisms is crucial for supporting dynamic and integrated innovation ecosystems. Through a thorough analysis, the authors present integrated theoretical-empirical frameworks that combine an understanding of necessary conditions with existing barriers to innovation, providing readers with a clear picture of how to transform communication challenges into effective collaboration strategies.

Furthermore, the chapter defines an effective communication mechanism in innovation ecosystems, emphasizing that a comprehensive approach is key to supporting open and transparent communication while eliminating communication silos. Achieving this goal requires a strategic and multifaceted approach that addresses the complexity of ecosystems by identifying and overcoming communication barriers. This process involves diagnosing current communication challenges, conducting a detailed analysis of information flows, and engaging a wide range of stakeholders in dialogue to create an environment conducive to the effective exchange and collaboration that are essential for the dynamic development of innovation ecosystems.

In light of the rapid development of communication technologies, the authors emphasize that innovation ecosystems are faced with a unique opportunity to strengthen collaboration and idea exchange on an unprecedented scale, which can significantly contribute to increasing their productivity and innovative capabilities. Consequently, the conclusions drawn from this chapter depict communication as essential, serving as a bridge that connects diverse stakeholder groups in pursuit of common goals, thereby stimulating technological and socio-economic progress on a broad scale.

In the final chapter, which addresses practical solutions and recommendations for the future of innovation ecosystems, significant attention has been drawn to the particular role that artificial intelligence (AI) plays in transforming these ecosystems. The integration of AI not only enhances efficiency, supports creativity, and drives technological progress, but also introduces new possibilities for data analysis, decision-making, providing personalized solutions, and accelerating research and development processes. This multifunctional application of AI underscores its fundamental importance in shaping the future of innovation ecosystems, offering not only optimization of existing processes but also opening new directions for development and exploration.

Another key aspect emphasized in this chapter is the importance of transparency, openness, and stakeholder engagement. These elements are recognized as critical in building environments that foster innovation, highlighting the need to create a platform where diverse participants can collaborate and shape the future together. Involving various stakeholder groups not only facilitates knowledge and experience exchange but also supports innovative processes at various stages – from conception to commercialization.

An important theme addressed in this part of the book is also the role of government innovation policies and how they can shape innovation ecosystems by attracting, developing, and retaining talent. These policies can significantly impact an ecosystem's ability to innovate and its competitiveness in the global market, underscoring the importance of a strategic approach to talent management and creating favorable conditions for their development.

This chapter also demonstrates how innovation ecosystems can address global challenges such as climate change through the integration of sustainable practices. Case study examples illustrate how initiatives based on cross-sectoral partnerships can contribute to technological, economic, and environmental development, highlighting the potential for innovation ecosystems to transcend knowledge boundaries and address the complex challenges of the modern world.

In conclusion, practical solutions and recommendations presented in this chapter demonstrate that the future of innovation ecosystems depends on their ability to adapt, integrate new technologies such as AI, and engage diverse stakeholder groups in the innovation process. By prioritizing transparency, openness, and sustainable development, these ecosystems can not only meet current needs but also shape future directions of technological and social development.

Given the presented arguments and considering the challenging geopolitical situation and the climate crisis, further research is recommended to develop and optimize communication processes in innovation ecosystems, which could further increase their ability to generate breakthrough innovations and resilience to changing external conditions. Additionally, interdisciplinary research is warranted to better understand how different aspects of communication influence various elements of innovation ecosystems, which could contribute to the development of more integrated and efficient innovative environments. There is also a need for research focusing on how innovation ecosystems can contribute to achieving sustainable development goals. This includes analyzing practices of ecosystems that effectively combine innovation with environmental protection and social responsibility. The authors also recommend further research on the role that public policy and regulations play in shaping and supporting innovation ecosystems, including the analysis of best practices and policy strategies that effectively support innovation.

Index

Note: Page numbers in *italic* indicate a figure, and page numbers in **bold** indicate a table on the corresponding page.

FSC
www.fsc.org
MIX
Papier | Fördert
gute Waldnutzung
FSC® C083411

Kolibri 360 GmbH
Ferdinand-Jühlke-Straße 7
99095 Erfurt, Deutschland
produktsicherheit@kolibri360.de